Angler's Mail

GUIDE TO
FISHING

Angler's Mail

GUIDE TO
FISHING

GENERAL EDITOR • ROY WESTWOOD

WHSMITH
EXCLUSIVE
· BOOKS ·

Acknowledgments
All photographs by Roy Westwood
Line artwork by Oxford Illustrators

Some of the material published here has appeared in
previous publications.

**This edition produced exclusively for
W H Smith**

Published by
The Hamlyn Publishing Group Limited
a division of The Octopus Publishing Group,
Michelin House, 81 Fulham Road, London SW3 6RB

Produced by Mandarin Offset
Printed in Hong Kong

CONTENTS

INTRODUCTION

I have yet to meet the angling genius who can write with total authority and conviction on coarse, sea and trout fishing. Many have tried but their contributions are shallow compared with the specialists who dedicate themselves to a single department of the sport.

That's why we have taken a team approach to this comprehensive book of angling instruction by hand-picking contributors with a lifetime's experience of the three disciplines.

It still represents an ambitious undertaking because of the sheer breadth of the subject matter – but I believe the fundamentals have been covered in masterly fashion.

Each author is a respected expert in his field with an outstanding record of achievement. Their collective advice can be relied upon as the very best obtainable.

ROY WESTWOOD
Editor, Angler's Mail

COARSE FISHING

It's amazing how many anglers make the mistake of concentrating on a single species before mastering the fundamentals of coarse angling. But if you absorb the basic float and leger lessons contained in this opening section you will be well on the way to achieving lasting success in the sport.

Which leads onto the two major specialist coarse fishing areas also covered in this section – carp and pike. Carp is the number one obsession in coarse angling and it demands specialist tackle and baits, while fishing for pike has made enormous advances, in both tackle and techniques.

BASIC PRINCIPLES

Understanding how to go about locating fish then finding the best possible means of presenting the bait is the cornerstone of successful coarse fishing.

LICENCES

Your first move must be to obtain a water authority rod licence. Check with your local tackle shop which authority licence is required. They can be bought to cover you for a full year, six months or a shorter term if required. There are usually concessionary rates for juniors, disabled anglers and pensioners.

It's important to appreciate that a rod licence confers no rights to actually fish. If you want to use more than one rod then additional licences must be obtained.

CHANGING SEASONS

A 4lb tench – the class of fish that's comfortably within reach of all anglers once the fundamentals have been mastered.

The traditional coarse fishing season runs from June 16 to March 14 inclusive but this has gradually been eroded, in certain regions. Some authorities have scrapped

the Close Season completely while others allow landlocked waters to remain open all year round and limit the restrictions to rivers.

DAY TICKET WATERS

There are two types of day ticket fishery: on some waters the bailiff issues tickets on the bank, while on others the permit must be purchased in advance, normally from a tackle shop. Day tickets can work out expensive if you fish the same venue regularly. It may be cheaper to take out a season ticket.

CLUB WATERS

If a club leases or owns waters then membership automatically gains you a permit for these at inexpensive rates. Generally, club waters tend to be well stocked and managed. Joining normally simply involves writing to the secretary enclosing the required fee.

ASSOCIATION WATERS

The large angling associations with affiliated clubs boast extensive fishing rights. You can either join through a club which tends to be cheaper or as an individual. The membership book will give details of all the association's fisheries including maps and type of fish you can expect.

PRIVATE WATERS

These are often described as syndicate fisheries as they are frequently run by a group of individuals sharing the same interests who secure a lease on the fishing for their own private use. Payment of the lease is normally divided equally between the syndicate.

Personal contact is the key of the door to syndicates and if you're fortunate enough to gain a place it's normally the result of somebody dropping out.

THE COMPLETE OUTFIT

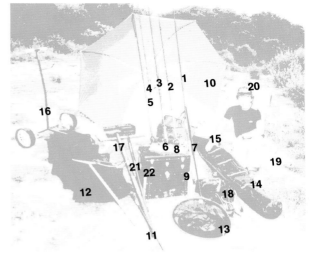

Here's the stockpile of tackle that Dave Coster has settled on for most of his fishing. It allows him to compete at the highest level in match-fishing or get maximum enjoyment from a pleasure session on a big fish water.

1 13ft Daiwa carbon/ kevlar match rod. Traditional three-piece with cork handle, hardened Dynaflo rings and finely tapering tip to take a range of different breaking strain lines. Generally used for long range waggler work and stick float fishing.

2 12ft Normark Microlite carbon match rod. Three-piece with cork handle but much softer through-action than the Daiwa 13-footer. Fitted with lightweight Fuji ceramic rings and used for light waggler and stick float fishing with fine lines and small hooks.

3 11ft 3in custom made, heavy duty swimfeeder rod. Carbon with ceramic rings and cork handle. It is made from a stiff actioned blank for punching out a feeder or big leger bomb a long way. There's a quivertip built-in which is made from solid carbon.

4 10ft custom-made, general purpose leger rod. Two-piece carbon with optional top sections: one takes three different actioned quivertips the other is for swingtipping.

5 7ft custom made, fibre glass wand. A short, soft through-actioned quivertip rod for delicate legering work at close range.

6 Ryobi Master match fixed spool reel. Light-weight carbon body with automatic bale arm for quick release of line. Good, general-purpose reel but mainly used for all forms of waggler fishing.

7 Mitchell Match fixed spool reel. Heavier and more robust than the Ryobi but with the same automatic, one touch bale arm. Now used by the author chiefly for swim feeder and leger fishing.

8 Daiwa Harrier closed-face reel. Wide diameter spool and made from graphite with a finger-dab line-release on the face. Mainly used for stick float fishing but also good for waggler work in windy conditions as this reel is almost tangle proof.

9 Continental style tackle seatbox. The base has lightweight aluminium sides which form a large compartment for carrying reels, groundbait and other bulky accessories. Adjustable legs are fitted to the base of the box so a comfortable sitting position can be maintained on awkward banks. The top half of the box is made from wood in four sections, comprising two pull-out tackle drawers and two lift-up trays.

10 Umbrella with tilt mechanism, nylon coated, 100 percent waterproof Steadefast design. Essential part of the angler's equipment. The tilt comes in handy when the brolly is needed as a windbreak.

11 Assortment of bank sticks, some of which are extending types. Among the rod-rest heads note the distinctive Drennan quivertip design that allows the rod to be lined up at exactly the right angle.

12 Micromesh, knot-less 10ft keepnet. Built-in mechanism for easy positioning. Keepnets have either round or square rings but many anglers are switching to the square variety because they offer more room for the fish when the net is staked in shallow margins.

13 Three-piece, fibreglass telescopic landing net handle with pan type landing net head. The pan shape is favoured by match anglers because its shallow design makes fish removal and unhooking a great deal more easy and faster.

14 Rod carryall manufactured by Kevin Nash. This de-luxe matchman's model has two side pockets for umbrella and banksticks. Note the vertical zips for easy access. The main compartment holds up to eight rods and poles.

15 General purpose carryall. Originally designed for wet keepnets and landing nets. Now its chief use is to house various bait containers, flask, catapults and other bulky accessories as well as those wet nets to a side pocket.

16 Many anglers now use a trolley to help carry their tackle to the waterside if the terrain is suitable.

17 Bait waiter and bait boxes. This waiter is made from aluminium and takes several bait boxes or a groundbait mixing bowl. It can be positioned so the bait is easy to hand from a sitting or standing position.

18 Groundbait mixing bowl. Folds flat for easy storage.

19 Green, thigh length waders.

20 A cap with a substantial peak or an anti-glare visor takes the strain out of studying a float or bite indicator for many long hours.

21 Olympic Champion pole, 13.5 metres, made from high modulus carbon in take-apart sections. Very light, slim diameter model. There's a choice of three top sections which are fitted out with different grades of internal elastic shock absorber. It is used for all pole fishing beyond six metres and the different tips will deal with fish ranging from a few ounces to several pounds. Depending on the choice of tip section, lines from a delicate 5oz breaking strain up to 3lb can be used.

22 Kevin Ashurst carbon whip, 6 metres in length. Part telescopic and the rest take-apart sections. Bottom three sections have been modified to break down for shallow canal swims. Another light pole with an extremely fine flicktip to compensate for light breaking strain lines. No shock absorber system is fitted to this model. Often used as a backup to the Olympic when a secondary shorter line is being fished under match conditions. Basically for small fish when speed fishing to hand at distances up to seven or eight metres.

ODDS AND SODS DRAWER

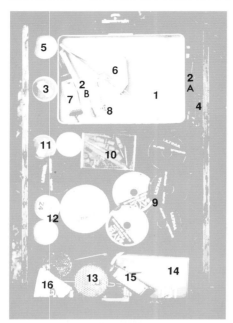

1 Breadpunch board.

2 Breadpunches with multi-heads for different hook sizes.

3 Small diameter float silicone.

4 Disgorgers.

5 Small eyed specimen hooks in sizes 14, 16 and 18. Used for tench fishing when small baits are needed.

6 Styl pinchers.

7 Red Mystic paste. Synthetic bait which imitates bloodworm.

8 Packet of size 26 silver Gamakatsu hooks for fishing squatts on hard canal venues.

9 Selection of hook-length lines, Bayer Ultima fine diameter nylon and standard Bayer

ranging from 1.1lb to 4.6lb.

10 Cut lengths of Sandvik tungsten-tube for locking big wagglers in SSG and AAA sizes.

11 Large diameter float silicone for top attachment on stick floats.

12 Various hookpots.

13 Bait droppers. Mainly used with pole.

14 Wallet of licences.

15 Black Mystic paste to imitate hemp on the hook.

16 Mini Starlights for night fishing. Several uses for floats, quivertips and bobbins.

FLOATS

This is the comprehensive range of floats carried by Dave Coster to cover every eventuality. How and when they are used is covered in chapters three and four.

Wagglers

1 Large bodied wagglers for distance fishing up to 40 metres on lakes, gravel pits or reservoirs. Also, bodied, bottom-end sliders for deep stillwaters.

2 These are not wagglers but nobody's box is perfect! They're big top and bottom attached balsas for fast, turbulent water and top and bottom sliders for deep, sluggish rivers.

3 Short bottom-end, bodied wagglers called Trent Trotters which are intended for very shallow, fastish river swims. Plus an assortment of very short balsa floats for shallow streams.

4 Light wagglers with extra fine inserts for delicate canal presentation. These floats are up to 3BB loading only and will be used up

to a maximum range of 15 metres.

5 Even lighter, custom-made wagglers with longish, fine inserts for surface fishing or close-in presentation on-the-drop style.

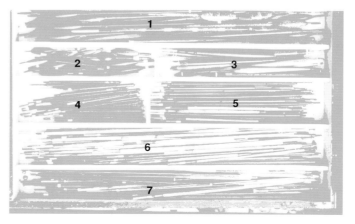

6 Home-made, dyed sarkandas reed, insert wagglers from 3BB to 5BB. Chiefly for fishing tight up to the far bank of canals or small rivers. The large selection means a float carrying exactly the weight for spot-on, accurate casting can be selected.

7 Insert and straight Crystals for clear, shallow waters where a dark float could throw a shadow on the bottom and scare wary fish. The longer inserts carry up to 5AA and will help combat surface drift problems on stillwaters. Straights have more buoyant tips and are used for fishing the bait on the bottom when drift would drag under an Insert model.

Sticks

1 Wire stem stick floats with different types of top. Shown here are the pointed and the more traditional taper. The actual choice of float depends on the bait presentation required. Shot loadings range from just three No.8 dust-shot, up to eight No.4s. Generally this type of stick float is used on pacey rivers in depths ranging from 60cm to 2.5metres (2 to 8ft).

2 Conventional stick-floats with cane and lignum or straight plastic stems for medium paced river fishing. Again, there's a mixture of tip shapes.

3 Smaller sticks and all-balsas for mid-water work or small stream fishing.

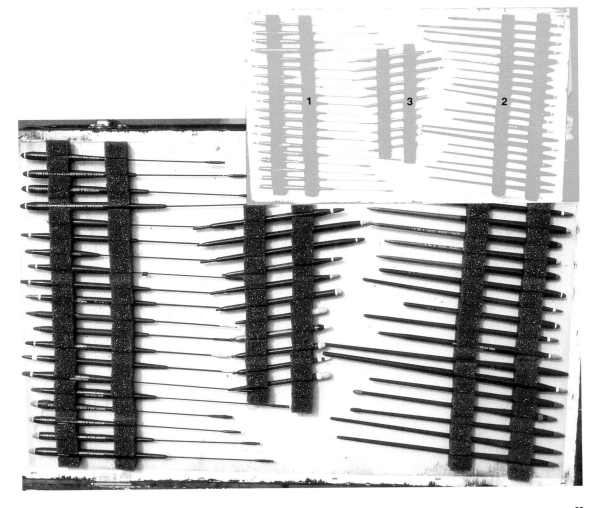

WHAT THE TACKLE BOX CONTAINS

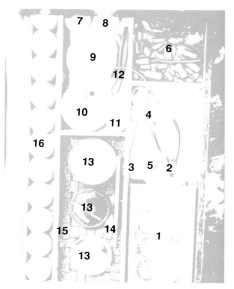

1 Sliding-top container of mixed non-toxic shot·in sizes from SSG down to No. 8s.

2 Shot pliers made from soft plastic.

3 Forceps. Useful for un-hooking fish, also for fine tackle adjustments like snipping the barb off hooks.

4 Scissors. Make sure they are small and sharp.

5 Non-toxic Arlesey-bomb.

6 Selection of non-toxic Screwbombs and Snapshot Arlesey bombs. Also silicone tubing in uncut lengths used for making bomb and feeder links.

7 Swivels and swivel links. (See page 26.)

8 Silicone quick-change float adaptors.

9 Container of Styl leads in legal sizes from No.7-12.

10 Container of micro-shot from No.8-12 for fine hooklengths.

11 Dinsmore No.8 shot.

12 Feeder links, some fitted with Power-gum.

13 Sylcast, Ultima and Bayer hooklength lines in strengths from 12oz to 1.7lb.

14 Disgorger.

15 Plummets.

16 Pots of hooks ranging from No.6s down to 26s. Patterns include fine wire, forged, spade-end and eyed. These types of hooks are used for fishing a variety of baits including hemp, tares, maggots, blood-worm and bread.

NON-TOXIC WEIGHTS

BALANCING THE TACKLE

Coarse fishing can be split into two distinct categories: floatfishing and legering. Both methods rely on some form of weighting to cast the bait out and to balance it in a way that attracts the fish to bite.

FLOATFISHING

The term floatfishing applies to any rig which uses a buoyant surface indicator to show up bites. There are purpose-designed floats for canals, rivers, lakes and gravel pits. Floats for fishing close-in and at distance. And specialist floats for deep water and shallows. But there is not as yet a universal float to meet all these demands. A floatfished bait can be presented anywhere from the surface through midwater to the bottom. It can also be given varying rates of descent to try and catch the fish's attention by looking either natural or just plain odd. Weights called split-shot balance the float and provide casting weight.

SPLIT-SHOT SIZES

Split-shot have been an integral part of floatfishing for many generations. Originally these weights were a by-product from the manufacture of shotgun cartridges. When cut centrally in their lead form, they proved ideal as fishing weights. The larger sizes were known as SSG, AAA and BB and the smaller shot numbered 1 to 8. The higher the number, the smaller the size and weight of split-shot. This somewhat confus-

ing classification has persisted through the change-over period to non-toxic replacements for lead. The modern substitutes are almost all graded in the same way as lead.

The biggest weights like SSGs and AAAs are often described as **locking shot** when used to fix a bottom-end float, or waggler, on the line. The middle sizes known as No.1s, 3s, 4s and 5s have a wealth of different applications. When any of these sizes are grouped together, they are popularly labelled as **bulk-shot**. Small shot from No.6 to 8 are commonly used on the hooklength for very fine adjustments. The No.8s have become known as **dust-shot** because of their small size. In more recent times, **micro-shot** have filtered into fishing — chiefly as a result of the explosion of interest in pole fishing which utilises a fixed line and extremely delicate rigs.

THE LEGER

It would be fair to say legering is less complicated and certainly less frantic than floatfishing. The float is discarded for a single weight, usually an **Arlesey bomb**, which even in its smallest size is much larger and heavier than a split-shot. The bomb is attached to the line by a swivel and anchors the bait firmly on the bottom.

Bites are registered by fitting various indicators to the rod like swingtips, quivertips, bobbins or electronic alarms. The leger is a good method when the float is found wanting because of bad weather, very fast currents or the fish being beyond the range of float tackle.

NON-TOXIC WEIGHTS

It is surely a credit to the ingenuity of anglers that we now have a whole range of replacement, non-toxic weights on the market in different sizes and materials. After intensive evaluation, certain brands have inevitably emerged as the market leaders. The following are among the best.

Metryk Supa Shot

A secret mixture of non-toxic alloys with a fingernail recess for easy reopening. The bright finish is dulled with a black coating which is reasonably permanent. They are reusable and very robust. A shade larger, size-for-size, than lead shot but they look

*Dinsmore Safe Shot –
tin based with
permament black
finish.*

line. Approximately 80 percent weight equivalent when compared with lead of same size. Sizes are SSG, AAA, BB, No.1, 3, 4, 5, 6 and 8.

Aiken Super Shot

This is another alloy based material with a very uniform shape and easy-to-open fingernail recess. Almost identical to Metryk Supa Shot and works in similar fashion. It is reusable with a silvery finish which eventually dulls down. Sizes comprise SSG, AAA, BB, No, 1, 3, 4, 5, 6 and 8.

Thamesly Sure Shot

These are probably the toughest substitute weights on the market. They'll open and close repeatedly with no sign of weakening. They are a good, spherical shape darkened down with graphite. Because of their uniformity, Thamesly weights have become popular with match anglers who demand highly accurate shotting. They're made from a hard mixture of alloys and a silicone buffer is recommended to cushion the larger sizes on the line. It's possible to carefully trim off pieces from larger SSG, AAA and BB sizes with scissors.

remarkably similar. Metryk are available in sizes SSG, AAA, BB, No, 1, 4, 6 and 8.

Dinsmore Safe Shot

Tin based with an excellent semi-permanent black finish. Larger sizes are very uniform. For example, 2BB equals 1AA precisely. The smaller shot are not quite as well formed but the cut is less severe than other substitutes and they hang far better on the

*Right: Thamesly Sure
Shot, alloy based and
uniform shape.*

CARRY A MIXTURE

Obviously it is impractical to carry all the substitute shot mentioned here, but a mixture is recommended because certain brands perform better for some functions than others. Remember that the objective always is to try and achieve the best possible presentation of the hookbait.

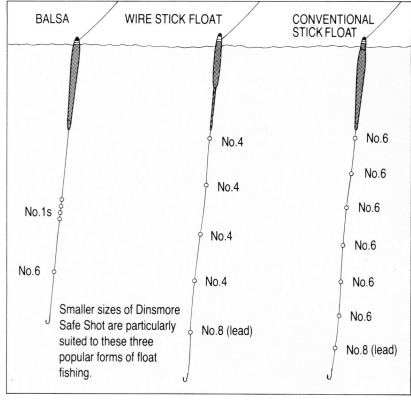

BALSA — WIRE STICK FLOAT — CONVENTIONAL STICK FLOAT

No.1s

No.6

No.4
No.4
No.4
No.4
No.8 (lead)

No.6
No.6
No.6
No.6
No.6
No.8 (lead)

Smaller sizes of Dinsmore Safe Shot are particularly suited to these three popular forms of float fishing.

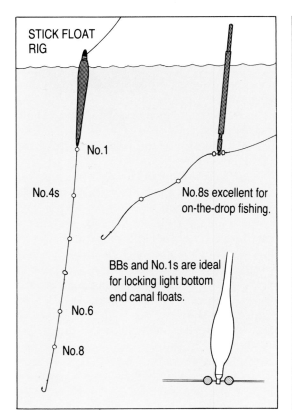

STICK FLOAT
RIG

No.1

No.4s

No.8s excellent for
on-the-drop fishing.

BBs and No.1s are ideal
for locking light bottom
end canal floats.

No.6

No.8

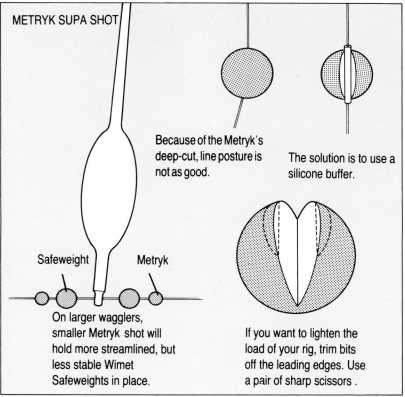

METRYK SUPA SHOT

Because of the Metryk's
deep-cut, line posture is
not as good.

The solution is to use a
silicone buffer.

Safeweight   Metryk

On larger wagglers,
smaller Metryk shot will
hold more streamlined, but
less stable Wimet
Safeweights in place.

If you want to lighten the
load of your rig, trim bits
off the leading edges. Use
a pair of sharp scissors .

NON-TOXIC LEGER WEIGHTS

Screwbomb

The first non-toxic Arlesey bomb to reach the market was the Screwbomb made from blackened brass. As the name suggests, it has a screw-on top fitting which incorporates a swivel head. Once the swivel section is attached to the line, any of this range of weights running from one eighth of an ounce up to one ounce can be fitted in seconds. That means you don't have to break down the rig to change up or down in weight size if conditions dictate a modification to your set-up. When any of the base units are fitted to the swivel attachment, the finished Screwbomb vaguely resembles the profile of a conventional Arlesey made from lead. In fact, it works better in flowing water because there is a slightly more pronounced step from the body to the swivel section and this results in the Screwbomb gripping the bottom more securely in strongish currents. For uncluttered legering rigs this is the best form of weighting because the quick-change facility eliminates the need to rely on any other type of swivel or link for attachment to the line.

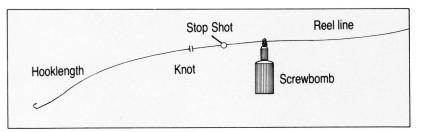

Stop Shot   Reel line

Hooklength   Knot   Screwbomb

More conventionally shaped Arleseys moulded from non-toxic materials are marketed by several companies but some are decidedly lighter than others, size for size.

Apart from sometimes finding a need to change leger weight size, it is also common to switch between a swimfeeder and Arlesey bomb several times during a session. The swimfeeder deposits loose offerings in the vicinity of the hookbait but can frighten the fish once they are drawn into the swim. So if an Arlesey is to be used in these circumstances it is best to make the tackle up with an American swivel-link running on the line. This has a conventional swivel at one end and a quick-release attachment at the other which can be unclipped to take any leger weight or swimfeeder.

The simplest, most uncluttered form of legering using a Screw bomb.

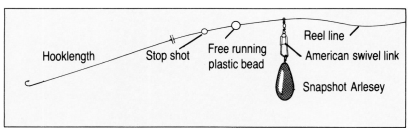

Hooklength — Stop shot — Free running plastic bead — Reel line — American swivel link — Snapshot Arlesey

Top: *Non-toxic leger bombs come in all shapes and sizes.*

Above: *Legering rig with a swivel-link for quick change.*

Olivette with internal silicone buffer (approx X3).

THE POLE

Pole fishing has recently grown into something of a cult among both matchmen and pleasure anglers. The method had its origins on the Continent where countries like France and Italy developed this form of fishing without reels to the point where they began to dominate the world matchfishing arena.

The chief benefit of the pole is improved tackle presentation. Today we have lightweight carbon poles as long as 13 metres. Using a pole of that length you can fish incredibly light and sensitive rigs at distances that could never be reached using a traditional 13ft rod and running line. The pole tip can be positioned directly over the float so as to lift into the slightest indication of a bite.

Because the pole tip is usually only a couple of feet from the float, the tackle can be manipulated in many ways. For example, on rivers the bait can be held back against the current much further out than with a shorter rod and reel and on stillwaters it's possible to induce all kinds of bait movement to provoke bites.

NON-TOXIC POLE WEIGHTS

There are four recognised ways of weighting pole tackle. The first is with normal shot which have been covered earlier in this chapter. Then there are specialist Olivettes, Styl leads and micro-shot. The last two are still legal in lead because they are so small and don't present any problems for wildlife. But some fisheries ban the use of any size of lead.

Styl Leads

These are tiny elongated weights, shaped much like celery with a groove running down one side into which the line is inserted. They are fixed on the line with special pincers.

The biggest legal size is a No.12 weighing less than 0.06 of a gram and they run through several sizes down to a No.7 scaling 0.010 of a gram. Their main benefit is that they give a much slower rate of descent to the end tackle than shot.

Micro-shot

These run from No.9s down to 15s which are so small you really need a magnifying glass to clip them on the line! But there's no real need to go that tiny. The No.10s and 11s are the most popular sizes for use on the hooklength when pole fishing. Like Styls, these weights fall slowly through the water and offer very delicate presentation. The fish almost seem oblivious to them because they're so small.

Olivettes

These are used when a bulk weight is needed for swinging a tackle out on the pole or when there's a need to get the hookbait down to the fish quickly in deeper water. It's also the first choice to hold the tackle stable in fast currents. This streamlined weight offers little resistance against flow and by concentrating the loading in one area helps keep the rig simple and tangle-free.

FLOATS

When everything is brought together float-fishing can be the most satisfying method of catching fish. If you can present the right bait at the right depth and make it behave in the right manner, learn efficient loose feeding or groundbaiting then all other things being equal you should catch fish – or at least tempt bites.

The basic principles of floatfishing are really simple, but remember the float has to be utilised to its maximum sensitivity. It needs to be weighed down with correctly positioned split-shot on the line until only the pointed sight tip remains visible. This is a fundamental technique known as **dotting the float**. The shot needs to be positioned carefully, particularly near the hook, to avoid spooking the fish.

LINE STRENGTH FACTORS

Lines are very important. Use too heavy a breaking strain for the float or hook and it will adversely influence the way the tackle performs. As a general guide, a light float requires a lightish line otherwise it won't cast very well and the line will drag it out of position. When you graduate into more specialist forms of fishing this particular rule can be broken but start out by making life easy for yourself!

For normal floatfishing requirements, reel lines of 2lb to 3lb are satisfactory if matched with slightly lighter hooklengths. Today's advanced rods and reels are designed to cope with even finer lines without fear of breakages.

Fish are naturally inquisitive creatures but can become extremely wary, particularly on the more heavily fished waters. To overcome their natural caution you will need to fish delicate rigs.

CHOOSING THE RIGHT FLOAT

When selecting a float, try running through the following questions:

- Will it carry sufficient shot to reach the spot where you want to cast the hookbait?

- On flowing waters, will it take enough weight down the line to get the hookbait down to the fish?

- Has the tip got the right amount of sensitivity or buoyancy for the conditions.

- Is the float long enough to combat surface drift? And is it short enough so as not to spook feeding fish in shallow water?

Basically, there are three chief categories of float – sticks, wagglers and balsas.

Stick floats

These are designed exclusively for flowing water and are strapped to the line with two short lengths of silicone tubing fixed at the top and bottom of the float. There are three popular stick designs: the conventional model with a wooden stem, modern plastic

Mission accomplished on light float tackle and a big fish hits the net.

stem types and wire stems. Float manufacturers sometimes switch to plastics to find the right balance when suitably heavy wood is in short supply. We'll concentrate on the two main varieties, conventional wood stem and wire stem.

Wood stems

Most conventional sticks rely on a stem made from a heavy wood like lignum for their stability. This also aids casting and prevents the float from lifting out of the water excessively when the line is straightened to maintain tight control when trotting – letting the tackle travel in a controlled manner with the current. The action of straightening the line in this manner is known as **mending the line**.

Tips
A heavier base material also helps to cock the float quickly. Clearly, you don't want the float to have travelled halfway down the swim before it begins working correctly and registering bites. A balanced conventional stick is usually trotted through at the speed of the current. But it can be adapted for on-the-drop work, shallow or deep fishing and also slowed down, if you wish, to a complete stop.

- There is one very important point to grasp with all stick float fishing and that's the shotting method. The fewer shot you use to **dot down** a stick to its correct weighting, the less versatile it becomes. The essence of stick float work

is that it is a method for searching out the fish in the swim. The idea is to juggle the shotting pattern to suit the changing whims of the fish as they rise in the water to feed in the upper layers or drop down to the bottom.

- Use a minimum of half-a-dozen similar sized medium or small shot instead of two or three big ones. Then you'll have the flexibility to string out the shot when you feel you might get better results by presenting the hookbait on-the-drop. Or you can begin to bulk the weights together when the fish congregate near the bottom. You could, of course, start off with two or three large bulk shot but you can't string them out sufficiently for a balanced, on-the-drop rig without completely taking the whole set-up to pieces which is time consuming.

Wire stems

The reason wire is used to replace a wooden stem is to give the float even greater stability, either in awkward blustery conditions or for faster, more turbulent currents.

The wire stem stick gives tighter control over the tackle thanks to the increased weight of the stem. This semi-cocks the float before the shotting has any effect. Wire stems are simple to fish and are recommended for novices. They're much easier to use on pacey rivers with a faster top layer of water. You can slow them down without flattening them out on the surface.

Tip shapes

The tips of stick float designs can vary from dome-shaped to gradually tapered or sharply pointed. These are not just cosmetic – they serve a purpose.

Domed top sticks are dotted down so they form just a dimple in the surface film. They work better on faster waters and are popular on powerful rivers like the Trent. Slightly tapered tips are more visible when the surface is choppy. Switch to a pointed tip when the fish become finicky as it presents less resistance to the bite. These types work best on slower moving waters for species like dace and roach.

A very basic highly effective stick float shotting pattern. Start the session by trotting with the current using groups of bulk shot, later modify to a strung out (shirt button) on-the-drop rig. The change only takes a matter of seconds.

TROTTING RIG

ON-THE-DROP RIG

No.4

No.4

No.4

No.4

4 No.4s Bulk

No.8

No.8 Drop shot

No.10

No.10 Drop shot

WAGGLERS

The waggler family fall into three divisions – inserts, straights and bodied.

Insert wagglers

These sport a finer sight-tip for added sensitivity. They're the best float for taking quality fish on the far bank of canals and small rivers. And they are also superb stillwater floats, particularly for on-the-drop fishing.

Straight wagglers

These have no insert thus giving increased buoyancy at the tip making the float more visible in rough conditions. You can use the buoyant tip to its full advantage when fishing well overdepth on slow moving rivers, flowing canal venues and big lakes with strong surface drift. These floats can be anchored or at least slowed down on the-trot, to present a hookbait more naturally when normal floats would shoot through the water too quickly.

Bodied wagglers

These take over when you are unable to cast the two previous designs the required distance because of high wind or other problems. The body gives extra weight carrying capacity and the longer stem helps to beat bad drift.

Because of their size, bodied floats are more stable in flowing water or drift. Under these conditions they'll slow down a hookbait's movement more effectively than a conventional waggler.

All wagglers are attached to the line by the base of the float and never with float rubbers or silicone tubing. Usually, a quick-change float adaptor is slipped over the bottom eye. The base of the float simply plugs in the adaptor. That makes it easy to change the size of float without having to break down the end tackle.

Wagglers are locked on the line with shot which should be evenly balanced on either side of the quick-change adaptor. For close-in work you can use small shot and bulk the main weight loading down the line. But for distance fishing very little weight is generally used down the rig. The majority is bulked around the float to assist effortless

Above: Insert and straight wagglers.

Above left: Pointed and domed top sticks. The choice depends on the pace of the water.

Left: A brace of wire-stemmed sticks and traditional lignum patterns.

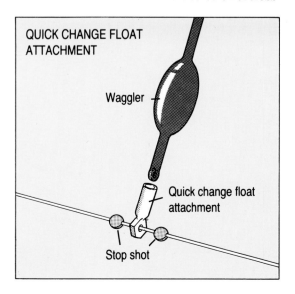

QUICK CHANGE FLOAT ATTACHMENT

Waggler

Quick change float attachment

Stop shot

casting. Never try to even out the weight distribution between float and drop shot – you'll find the rig impossible to cast. At the very most, use only up to a third of a waggler's capacity down the line, the rest goes around the base of the float.

BALSAS

There'll be a time when the stick float can't cope with the current, depth or distance you want to fish. This is when to switch to a larger float such as an Avon or all-balsa pattern.

The Avon

This is best described as a cross between a stick float and a balsa. It has a bulbous balsa body and stabilising cane or wire stem.

All-balsas

Above: Bodied wagglers for fishing at distance.

Right: Balsa (left) and Chubber floats take over when the going gets too turbulent for the stick.

There are two main designs of all-balsa floats: the conventional slimmer balsa tapers into a slight step at the sight tip for improved sensitivity; and the more awkward looking cigar-shaped balsas for carrying big baits in fast water, sometimes at long range.

These **Chubber type** floats, as they are known, are mainly meant for fishing with large pieces of breadflake, cubes of luncheon meat or lobworms. Their extra buoyancy and weighting capacity will cope with most of the rough water you're likely to come across. The normal all-balsa is really a scaled down version for use with smaller baits like casters and maggots. Conventional balsas work well in boiling slacks on flooded rivers and in areas where you can find a steadier pace on coloured, fast venues. Both designs respond best to bulk shotting and just one or two dropper shot.

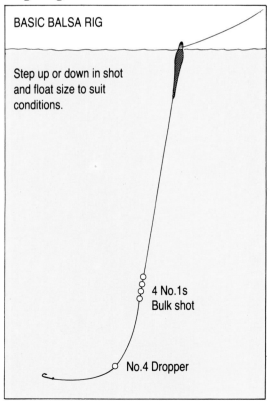

BASIC BALSA RIG

Step up or down in shot and float size to suit conditions.

4 No.1s
Bulk shot

No.4 Dropper

THE RIGHT ROD

How do you define the right rod for float-fishing when there are so many lengths, actions and materials to consider?

Do you want a rod designed for a specialist form of floatfishing or will an allrounder fit the bill? Frankly, what you settle for in the end all boils down to personal preference.

The material from which the rod blank is formed dictates the price tag. Fibreglass is cheap and if you are seeking a really low-cost entry into the sport then it's worth considering. But lightweight carbon is much more responsive and pleasing to handle. Prices in real terms have reduced over the years and there are now composite rods made from carbon and glass which represent good value for money.

There is a trend for the actual carbon content of a rod to be specified in percentages. It goes without saying that the rods with a higher percentage of carbon fibres cost more. But they are also thinner in diameter and much lighter. For example, a 12ft match rod can weigh as little as 4oz.

Top class float rods will deal with most, if not all, floatfishing demands. It is also at the top end where materials like boron and Kevlar have been introduced to reinforce the performance qualities of these ultra-thin rods. Boron tends to mellow a rod's action while Kevlar tightens up on casting accuracy and the overall strength of a blank.

Actions and length

If you've got around £100 to spend you might find a rod made from a high modulous carbon or carbon and Kevlar combination which will, in theory, meet all your float-fishing needs.

Lower down the price range a little more attention to rod action needs to be taken into account. Most anglers prefer a tip-actioned rod for stick float or balsa fishing, sometimes with a fine spliced tip if light lines are being used.

For waggler work, more of a through-action blank is used. This will punch out a float surprisingly well and with great accuracy.

Forget about test curves when choosing a float or match rod, the classification is in mere ounces, anyway. It is as well to go by feel when judging whether a rod is suitable for light line fishing.

The length of the rod is far more important. Don't make the mistake of selecting too short a rod because you will incur a loss of control over your tackle. Rods of 12 and 13ft will pick up the line on the strike far more effectively than 10 or 11ft models. As a guide, 12ft is a good length for canal fishing while 13ft is acceptable for most floatfishing needs including stick float and wagglers.

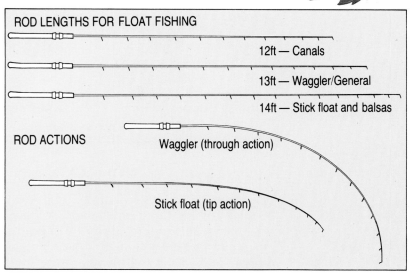

ROD LENGTHS FOR FLOAT FISHING

12ft — Canals

13ft — Waggler/General

14ft — Stick float and balsas

ROD ACTIONS

Waggler (through action)

Stick float (tip action)

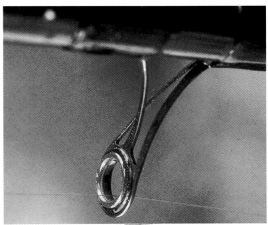

Left: *Rings with diamond-tough inserts improve the line flow on any float rod.*

Rods of 14ft or longer may have a control advantage when fishing the stick or any other top and bottom attached float but they become unwieldy for other forms of fishing.

RING TYPES

Plain chrome rings are fitted to some float rods but you'll get more mileage out of those which have steel, ceramic or silicone carbide linings.

Chrome rings in their original blackened state are the most basic design and they remain surprisingly popular. The line runs through them sweetly enough but they soon start showing signs of wear and will need replacing regularly. With heavy use, chrome rings last about a year.

Lightweight ceramic or steel lined rings are fitted to nearly all the top rod designs and are very smooth running. Their life expectancy is several years.

The latest development is silicone carbide

guides. These are very hard wearing and outlast all other designs but cost a small fortune. You will only find these installed on the most expensive rods.

A float rod should have a minimum of one intermediate ring every 12in of rod, although the rings are not spaced equal distances apart. They should gradually get closer together towards the tip.

REEL SEATS AND HANDLES

Chrome reel fittings seem to be on the way out but it's doubtful if cork handles will ever disappear. In the future there will be undoubtedly more rods with black duplon grips and other synthetic, waterproof handles.

Some manufacturers make sure you position the reel correctly to achieve the right balance on the rod by restricting the manoeuvrability of sliding type collar fittings to the top of the handle. The number of

Below: The clean lines of a Browning fixed-spool reel.

Bottom: Deep spool (left) for heavier lines and match spool.

anglers who insist on fishing with the reel down towards the butt clearly makes this a worthwhile innovation.

THE RIGHT REEL

Fixed spool reels are the leading models for floatfishing. They may be called open-faced because the line is visible when loaded compared with closed-face reels where it is hidden by the housing.

Open-faced reels are very versatile. They're ideal for all waggler fishing, especially long range work, as an ultra shallow spool will prevent the line from bedding down and fouling itself during repeated casting and retrieving.

These reels are also suitable for stick and balsa fishing but their downfall comes in a facing wind when the line will tend to blow back over the bale arm. That is when many anglers switch to a closed face model with its internal line spool which is shielded from wind.

Before buying a fixed spool, check that your forefinger can comfortably touch the forward lip of the line spool when the reel is fixed in place on the rod. You'll need to feather line off the reel with this finger of your rod hand while trotting with an open bale arm.

Then confirm that the bale arm closes smoothly when engaged by winding the handle. If it causes a severe jolt then you're likely to lose fish when trotting a float. Ideally, the bale takes the line smoothly off your forefinger after the strike has been made and a fish hooked.

Many fixed spool reels are sold with an ultra shallow spool that is perfectly loaded when 100m of 2-3lb line are wound on. That compares with a deep spool which might swallow at least 300m of the same breaking strain. Apart from being more expensive to load, deep spools tend to cause line bedding.

Clutch, bale and roller

Clutch or drag systems can be pre-set at varying degrees of tension to allow the spool to rotate and release line with the bale arm closed. This is a useful safeguard with light line as the drag can be finely adjusted to give line to a big fish before its powerful boring exerts more pressure than the breaking strain of the nylon can withstand.

It is also a useful cushion if you strike too hard with the anti-reverse on. This is the switch which stops the handle rotating backwards and means you can strike one-handed. Clutch mechanisms are now largely installed at the rear of the reel where they are much easier to operate should adjustment prove necessary during the playing of a fish. They have become known as sterndrags.

The automatic bale arm speeds up casting and your fishing technique as a whole. It is only available at the top end of the reel market on models like the Mitchell Match 440A and Daiwa Autocast. These reels allow the bale arm to be opened with the forefinger of the rod hand by depressing the bale or operating a trigger mechanism.

With normal reels you have to open the bale arm with your free hand first before trapping the line against the spool with the rod hand.

The rate at which reels retrieve line back onto the spool varies between models but this isn't critical.

Finally, purchase a reel which incorporates an efficient line roller on the bale arm. This will virtually eliminate line grooving. The majority of reels possess a roller but if yours doesn't then keep an eye open for

Left: Closed-face helps keep wind tangles at bay.

signs of wear as a groove on the bale arm will rapidly damage the line.

CLOSED-FACE CONFUSION

There's considerable confusion in coarse fishing about the role of the **closed-face** reel.

Generally, closed-face reels are a safe bet for stick float fishing and certain forms of waggler use. They're popular for trotting sticks because of the superb control they give in feeding line at differing rates to let a float push through naturally or to hold it

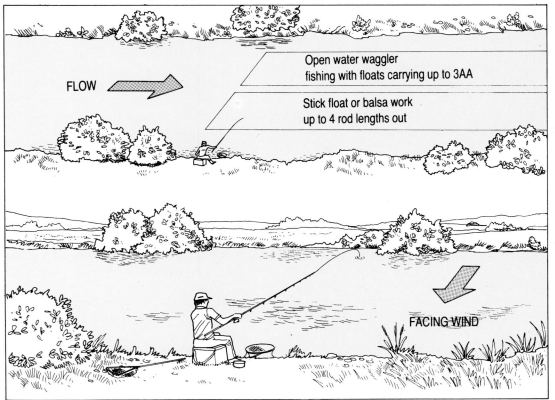

FLOW

Open water waggler fishing with floats carrying up to 3AA

Stick float or balsa work up to 4 rod lengths out

FACING WIND

When to use closed-face reels with float gear. Because a facing wind can defeat more accurate open-faced reels (when fishing tight in to the bank) it may be adviseable to switch to a closed-face model. This eliminates the possibility of bag tangles if the line blows back over the bale arm on the open-faced model. The difference needed to bring back a degree of accuracy would be a slightly larger float, with an additional BB weight loading.

back against the flow. Better still is the smooth pick-up when a fish has been hooked. This compares very favourably with the nasty kick you tend to get with some open-faced reels when the bale arm is engaged following the strike. This jolt can result in fish being bumped off the hook.

As line feeds off the spool from within the housing on the closed-face, there is a certain amount of friction although not sufficient to damage the nylon in any way. But it's enough to restrict the flow of the cast and that's a drawback when trying to achieve spot-on accuracy with the waggler. It would make it difficult to consistently place a waggler within inches of far bank cover.

Open-faced reels are preferred for the bulk of waggler fishing but the closed-face is called up when a facing wind blows line back over the bale arm producing frustrating tangles.

THE RIGHT LINE

Some special hooklength lines are sold in 50m spools but usually lines are packaged in 100m lengths. Providing you have a shallow spool on your reel, this is more than adequate for floatfishing.

A trend you'll have to monitor when choosing modern line is the swing towards low diameter monofilaments. These claim the same breaking strain as standard lines but with a greatly reduced diameter. Obviously, this is a good idea in theory because thinner lines cast better and bring you more bites when used as hooklengths.

But to achieve such a low diameter, the line is pre-stretched and this eliminates a great deal of its ability to absorb shock impact. For the novice, indeed even expert anglers, this loss of elasticity can be disastrous because a hasty strike can result in break-offs – losing a lot of tackle and perhaps leaving a hook in a fish.

Standard lines will catch you plenty of fish anyway. The differences in diameter on light hooklengths are so minimal that good tackle presentation can overcome the slight increase in thickness compared with a pre-stretched nylon.

COLOUR FACTORS

Lines are dyed numerous shades from black to green. On the reel, none of this matters

very much but with hooklengths a little care should be taken. For instance, in bright sunny conditions on a gin-clear water it is inadvisable to use a black dyed line because it will stand out like a sore thumb.

But the same line would probably work very well in coloured, muddy water. If the hooklength is being fished overdepth, a black line on a dark, muddy bottom will blend in well. It's all a matter of simple logic. Just remember to use clear lines for on-the-drop fishing and dark lines for bottom fishing and you won't go far wrong.

As for breaking strains, try and use the lightest you feel happy with because the thinner diameter does make tackle presentation and casting a lot easier. There is no need to go below 2lb – very fine lines wear much too quickly on the reel and can let you down badly at critical moments of stress.

The average angler will more than likely carry a spool of 2.5 or 3lb sinking line for most of his waggler fishing and another spool of the same breaking strain but in a floating line for stick or balsa work. Most matchmen, however, tend to step down to 2lb in both cases.

SINKERS AND FLOATERS

Daiwa Harrier, Drennan Floatfish and standard Bayer Perlon are all good floating lines. Maxima, Racine and Drennan Specimen are excellent sinkers. As a guide, shiny lines float well and matt finished lines sink.

Sometimes new lines will not behave correctly until they have been broken in. This particularly applies to sinking lines which are best soaked in a container of soapy water, preferably the night before a trip.

As for floating lines, you can reel them in occasionally through a pad of **floatant grease** which is marketed in tins for flyfishing or spray them with a Leeda aerosol intended for dry flies. Hooklength lines will be looked at in more detail for river and lake fishing, but it is worth carrying a selection ranging from 1lb breaking strain for when the fishing is hard, through to 1.5 or 1.7lb for normal conditions and 2 or 2.5lb in case big fish are expected on the float.

THE RIGHT HOOK

The most widely used hooks are spade-ends which have a flattened top to the shank. The

line is knotted on the shank and prevented from slipping off the hook by the spade-like, flattened shape.

Eyed hooks are formed by bending the top of the shank into a small circle through which the line is threaded and tied on the shank or directly knotted to the eye itself.

Spade-end patterns are more tricky to tie than eyed hooks but it's worth the effort because they give superior presentation, particularly with small hooks.

As a last resort, ready-tied hooks are available but they're expensive.

How they are numbered

The standard numbering of hook sizes in this country for freshwater use starts at 2, which is the largest, and runs in even numbers up to a tiny 26. On the Continent, odd numbered hooks are also used and some of these have found their way into specialist tackle shops in Britain.

Bigger hooks between 2 and 8 are intended for big baits like luncheon meat, lumps of bread and boilies.

Middle-range hooks from size 10 to 16 can be used with the same baits scaled down in size plus sweetcorn, worms and groupings of smaller offerings like maggots and casters. Small hooks from 18 down are for baits like maggot, caster, hemp, tare, breadpunch and bloodworm.

Size considerations

Selecting a suitable hook size must take into account the type of bait being used and target species. The swim you're fishing could affect the eventual choice as well.

In theory, you want the hook size to perfectly match the bait. The hook needs to be as small and unobtrusive as possible with small baits and as big as you can for better penetration using larger baits.

Shy biting fish like dace and roach will often give unhittable bites if the hook size is too large. They can see the hook so they simply pluck at the bait without taking it down. In this case try and find a hook you can completely hide in a bait like casters – an 18 would be suitable – or scale down to a 20 with offerings like maggots where the hook point must be left exposed for efficient penetration. You'll also find hook size important on gin clear or hard fished

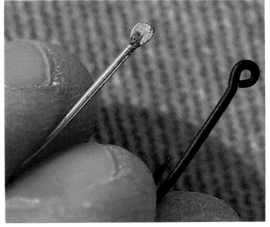

Spade or eyed? It's worth taking the trouble to perfect the spade-end hook tying – the end product gives superior presentation.

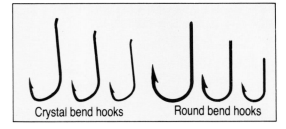

Crystal bend hooks   Round bend hooks

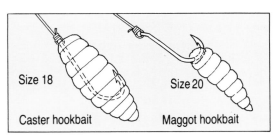

Size 18   Size 20

Caster hookbait   Maggot hookbait

Original barbed hook

De-barbed version
Slight bump keeps lively baits in place

waters. Where you might tempt bites on a size 14 or 16 with maggot on an easy water, a hard venue is more likely to need 18 or 20 hooks for a response.

Another important hook factor is the shape of the pattern you choose and the thickness of the wire.

The most popular freshwater hook patterns are the crystal bend and the round bend. Both are obtainable in a range of wire gauges. Obviously, finer wire is used with smaller, lighter baits so as to give them a more natural fall through the water. If big fish are expected you may have to settle for a thicker, forged hook regardless. Hook shape is normally determined by the bait. Maggots and worms tend to stay on a crystal bend better whereas on a round bend they can fly off on the cast. Casters suit either design but seed baits like hemp, tares and sweetcorn are more effective on round bends as their wider gape gives improved hooking with these harder skinned baits.

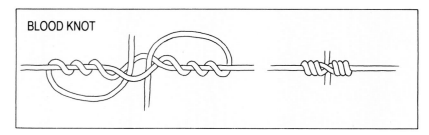

BLOOD KNOT

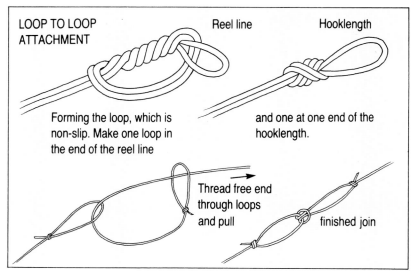

LOOP TO LOOP ATTACHMENT

Reel line   Hooklength

Forming the loop, which is non-slip. Make one loop in the end of the reel line

and one at one end of the hooklength.

Thread free end through loops and pull

finished join

Top: *Blood knot. An alternative method of securing the hooklength to the reel line. This knot is often preferred by match anglers.*

Above: *Loop to loop attachment. The most popular way of attaching a hooklength to the reel line.*

Barbed or barbless?

Some fisheries have banned barbed hooks. This can cause problems as maggots, for example, can fall off barbless hooks on the cast although baits like bread and corn are unaffected.

The solution is to flatten the barb on a barbed hook leaving a slight bump which will keep the bait in place. To all intents and purposes you are now fishing with a barbless pattern and obeying the rules of the fishery.

In fact, if you can use barbless hooks they are much kinder on the fish and penetrate

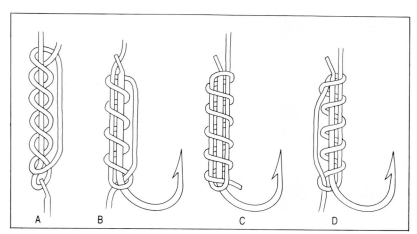

A   B   C   D

more effectively on the strike. You will not lose more fish on them – the only time a barbless design is likely to come adrift is if you give a fish slack line. And that should be avoided with any type of hook.

PUTTING IT ALL TOGETHER

Once you've sorted out all your tackle for a floatfishing session, assembly is straightforward. First, the line is loaded on the reel and to avoid twist it should be wound on in the same direction it leaves the manufacturer's plastic spool.

Fill the reel until the line level is just below the lip of the spool and then it will peel off smoothly. You should never underfill a spool otherwise the line will scrape against the lip causing friction and retarding its flow.

When the reel has been fitted to the rod at the top of the handle, open the bale arm and thread the line through the rod rings making sure they have been lined up in a perfectly straight line on each section of the rod. If it's windy, point the rod away from the direction of the gusts to prevent the line blowing back over the reel's bale-arm and tangling.

Once the line has been fed through all the rings, pull several feet off the reel and you can put the rod down in its rests while the end tackle is sorted out. The float goes on first, either as a double-rubber if it's a top and bottom model or locked by shot if you're fishing the waggler.

Position the float a couple of feet away from the end of the line so it doesn't impede tying on the hooklength. There are two good line-to-line knots for attaching hooklengths – the loop to loop and blood knot.

When the hooklength is attached it is better to shot-up the rig correctly at this stage placing any bulk shot above the joining knot and the tell-tale droppers on the hooklength. You must make sure the hooklength is not too short, 18in (45cm) is about right to retain some of the stretch of this lighter line.

After you've checked the float is cocking satisfactorily, the final job is to tie on the hook. There are many hook knots, those shown are the easiest and most secure.

All that remains is to plumb up the depth and space the tackle out accordingly. We'll be looking at this in the next.

RIGS AND SPECIALS

The starting point in float selection is the type of venue being fished. This largely dictates the pattern of float you use and shotting required. Float attachment falls into the two basic categories: **Double-rubber** – attached to the line at top and bottom; and **Bottom-end only** – attached, naturally enough at the bottom only.

Understanding which to use is the beginning of the decision-making process which leads to expertise in shotting.

Double-rubber or bottom ender?

Double-rubbers are nearly always fished on flowing water because here they give more control than bottom-enders. That is not to say that bottom-end floats are ruled out – they can be just as good if the fish will only bite if the hookbait is presented in a specific way. But remember they are less versatile and consistent on running water.

The reverse applies on stillwaters where bottom-end floats come into their own because they are more stable. They are particularly stable when the line from rod tip to float is submerged beneath the surface. A double-ended float will not work this way since the line has to remain on the surface for a clean strike to be made. Without a current to work against, double-ended floats become very unstable. Wind or surface drift quickly puts them off course.

With a bottom-ender, the only modification you have to make, assuming the line has been sunk to defeat drifting, is to strike sideways instead of upwards in order to set the hook home.

The only time a top and bottom float has an application on stillwaters is when fishing the margins with the float directly under the rod tip, or when the tackle is dropped into a hole among thick weed where it will be prevented from drifting.

Remember we are talking about **running line rigs** here. Later you'll discover that top and bottom attached floats can be used to good effect when pole fishing on stillwaters where the control over the tackle is that much greater.

Shot position

The biggest difference between river and lake rigs, apart from the float, is the position of the shot. On flowing water more weight tends to be used down the line to keep the hookbait near, or on, the bottom. But a leisurely fall of the hookbait can be beneficial on stillwaters where rigs tend to be fished further out and the main shot loading is around the float.

RIVER RIGS AND HOW TO USE THEM

SLUGGISH WATER

Let's assume you want to fish a sluggish river using the on-the-drop style. Select a stick with a light wooden stem to carry just over six No.6 shot. Space out four of the shot at equal distances between the float and hooklength, storing the remaining two directly underneath the float. For the time being, these two shot will balance the light float, making it react in much the same way as a heavy based stick.

The rig is completed by adding a No.8 about a third of the way down the hook-length and a No.10 micro-shot between this and the hook. Now the rig is nicely balanced to allow you to search out the swim with plenty of shot spread down the line which can be shuffled around if need be to change the way the hookbait behaves. With the shot spread out, the float can be held on a tight line as it hits the water and the tackle will fall at a slower rate of descent for on-the-drop bites. Or you can let the float run the second it hits the water and the hookbait and shot will settle a lot quicker.

It's also possible to fish this set-up over-depth by **deepening-off** (lengthening the

*Opposite: **A.** How to tie an eyed-hook knot formed above the hook. **B.** How to tie an eyed-hook with knot formed on the shank. **C.** Conventional spade-end knot. It takes practise to tie this knot without damaging the line. **D.** Reversed spade-end knot. A foolproof knot which will not damage the line because the knot is tightened by pulling the loose end.*

Angler's Mail

Right: Stick floats and how they behave on landing.

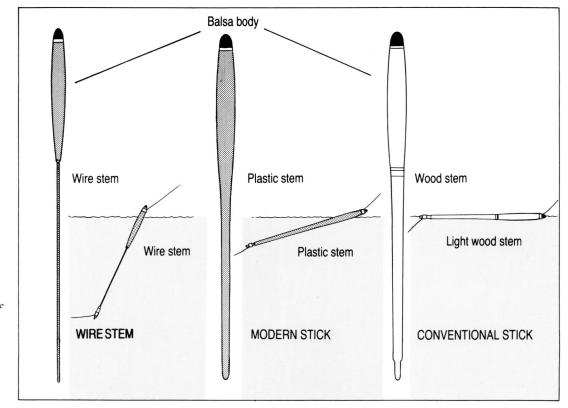

Balsa body

Wire stem

Plastic stem

Wood stem

Wire stem

Plastic stem

Light wood stem

WIRE STEM

MODERN STICK

CONVENTIONAL STICK

Below: Light stick rigs.
Left: *This set-up is the starting point and can satisfy a variety of styles – including on-the-drop and dragging overdepth.*
Right: *When fish are feeding near the bottom the rig is modified to bulk shotting.*

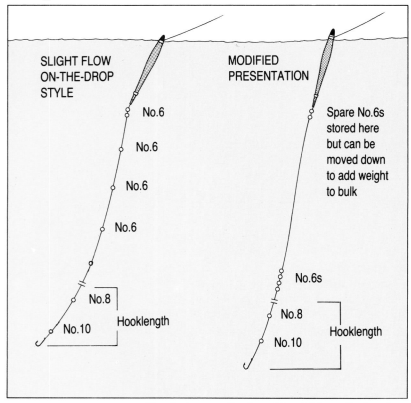

SLIGHT FLOW
ON-THE-DROP
STYLE

MODIFIED
PRESENTATION

No.6

No.6

No.6

No.6

No.8

No.10

Hooklength

Spare No.6s
stored here
but can be
moved down
to add weight
to bulk

No.6s

No.8

No.10

Hooklength

line between float and hook) by a foot or two and holding back hard on the float. The great thing about this rig is its flexibility. If the fish stay deep in the water some or all the No.6 shot are moved down to a point just above the hooklength to form a bulk shotting pattern. This will considerably speed up the fall of the hookbait.

When the fish rise in the water, the two No.6s originally stored under the float are spread out in unison with the other four split-shot to slow the rate at which the float and tackle settles. Often, this ploy brings very savage takes on-the-drop.

MEDIUM-PACED WATER

A plastic or heavier wooden-stemmed stick float is likely to be selected on medium-paced water. The objectives are much the same as with the lighter, wooden-based float. All that changes is the shotting which would normally be slightly heavier – possibly substituting the No.6s with No.4s.

The reason for upping the weight loading is to stabilise the rig against the stronger current otherwise the float would lift up flat on the surface, when held back, or scoot through the swim too fast. The increased loading obviously means a bigger float must also be used.

The starting point for this rig is to evenly

space out between four and eight No.4s down to the hooklength.

As a guide, you'll require one No.4 for each foot of water fished, excluding the hooklength. If the hooklength is the standard 18in, it takes a No.6 followed by a No.8 dust-shot fixed 6-8in from the hook.

FASTER WATER

For faster water where the surface of the river is possibly even boiling slightly, the wire stem stick is very useful. Its extra stem weighting also makes life easier when wind causes presentation problems. Oddly, the same kind of shotting as conventional sticks usually does the trick. The float switch itself is sufficient to establish control on the faster flow rate.

The sign that the stick float has reached its limits of use is when it cannot be held back against the current without riding up too high or flattening out completely on the surface. Another indication that the stick is running through too quickly for a fish to intercept the hookbait is when the float tip leans away from you as it procedes down the swim.

Providing you've fixed the stick or any

other kind of top and bottom float correctly on the line with silicone tubing, it should always lean back slightly towards you as it trots down the swim. If it's upright or leaning away then you're not controlling it properly or the tackle is out of balance.

With lighter stick floats there are a couple of tricks worth trying if the float fails to behave properly because of the conditions. In fast currents, you can overshot the rig so it must be fished on a tight line to keep the float tip visible. Overshot by one, two or three No.4s while attempting this tactic to slow the tackle down.

The other dodge is to **backshot** in awkward downstream winds to try and prevent the line overtaking the float or bowing out and pulling it off course. Depending on the strength of the wind, fix a shot between a No.8 and 4 approximately 1-2ft above the float to help control the line and keep it directly behind the float.

BALSAS AND AVONS

There'll be times when the stick float can't cope with the current, depth or distance you want to fish. That's the moment to call up an Avon or all-balsa design.

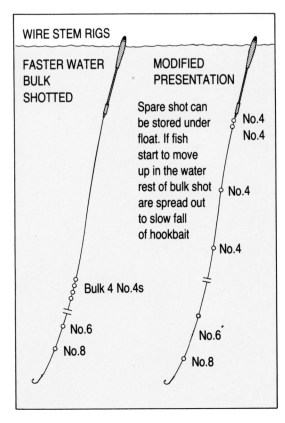

Far left: Conventional stick rigs. This example is recommended for a swim of about 1.2m (4ft) in depth. Add an extra No.4 per extra 25cm (10in) of water and increase the float size to accomodate. *Left:* Wire stem rigs.

Opposite top: Quick-change float adaptors make life a lot easier when you're forced to permutate rigs.

Opposite bottom:
A. Extra-fine insert waggler. A good laying-on float. The extra-long tip shows lift bites well. Add an extra No. 6 or No. 4 at No. 8 position for more positive bites when fishing over depth.
B. Drennan Canal Crystal. An on-the-drop rig for clean shallow lakes.

Below right:
Shotting close-range rigs.

Below left:
A. Conventional balsa.
B. Chubber type balsa.
C. Conventional Avon.
D. Wire-stem Avon.

All-balsas

The conventional all-balsa model has a streamlined body which tapers into a slight step at the sight tip for better sensitivity. The other all-balsa design called the Chubber is cigar-shaped and its role is to carry big baits through fast water, sometimes at long range. It's buoyant at the tip and will take weighty baits like large chunks of breadflake, cubes of luncheon meat or lobworms. The streamlined balsa is really a scaled down version for use with smaller baits like casters and maggots. It's also a good choice for tackling boily swims on a flooded river.

Both these balsa floats need to be bulk shotted with just one or two dropper shot.

They are not suitable for on-the-drop fishing and are certainly less versatile than the stick float.

Avons

Among the jobs for the Avon float is long-trotting on streamy runs where fish like big roach and chub are expected. The slightly prouder sight tip on this float shows up well at long range. Again, bulk shotting with one or two dropper-shot is recommended. It can also carry longer strings of scaled down bulk shot to pick up undertow in deep swims. A traditional technique is to fish the Avon with a free-running centrepin reel which helps slow the hookbait to a more natural speed.

LAKE RIGS

CLOSE-RANGE LAKE RIGS

Several float designs cope equally well with canal or lake fishing although their size is a limiting factor, as far as distance casting is concerned, on the bigger expanses of water.

For close range lake fishing the Drennan Canal Crystal is excellent in shallow, clear swims. This see-through float does not throw a shadow on the bottom and has a very sensitive tip. It performs most effectively carrying up to 3BB locking-shot and a couple of lightish dropper-shot for fishing on-the-drop style or on the bottom. It's a float to use with light line and small baits for small fish.

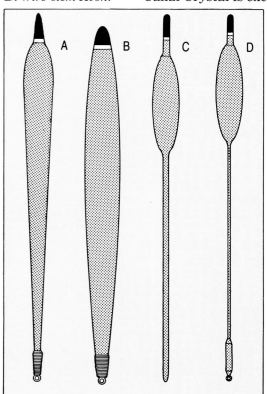

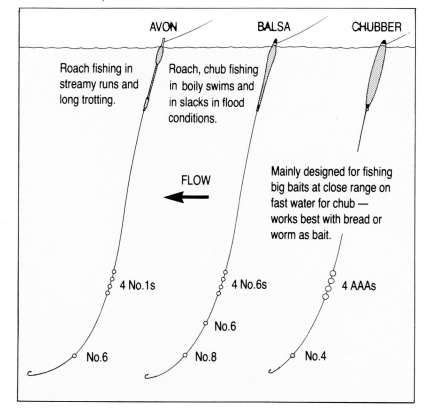

Sarkandas waggler

A slightly different version of this float is the Sarkandas waggler with an extra long, fine nylon sight-tip. It's locked on the line the same way with up to 3BB or 2AA shot. The main application is for fish like skimmer bream and tench which often give tiny indications on a float without actually taking the hookbait positively. If you use a longer, finer tip these bites show up better and you can wait until the float sinks away properly.

To achieve an even more positive indication, fish with an extra No.6 or 4 shot on the bottom positioned several inches below the hookbait. When a fish picks up the bait, the extra weight sinks the float very decisively.

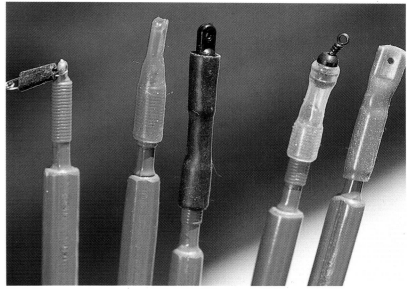

Stillwater Blue

When surface drift makes the Canal Crystal or extra long Insert Sarkandas lose stability, then the Stillwater Blue is a better bet. Its lower slung body and slightly increased weight carrying capacity gives it better holding power in drift. It is fished with similar shotting patterns – perhaps with just a little more weight around the float and an extra No.8 or so down the rig.

MIDDLE DISTANCE AND LONG RANGE

Most middle distance and long range stillwater floatfishing revolves around Insert, straight and bodied wagglers.

Insert wagglers

These were described on page 19 as being the best float for fishing the far bank of small rivers and canals. This is because they'll cast very accurately to within inches of fishy-looking cover which is often found on the far side of these waterways.

The same situation arises on lakes when the fish are lying against rushes on the far side of narrow bays or beneath foliage overhanging from islands. But the Insert waggler has a great deal to offer apart from casting accuracy.

It will carry plenty of weight for casting out fair distances and still retain extraordinary sensitivity by virtue of its fine tip.

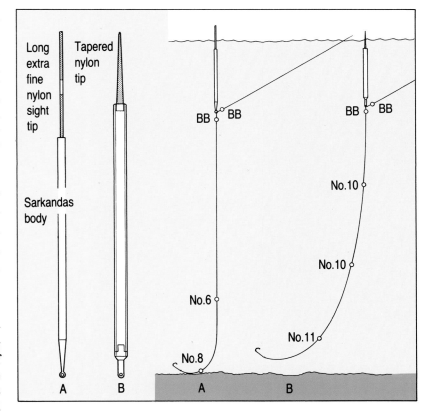

Inserts made from fine plastic, nylon or Sarkandas will sink away under a mere No.8 or 10 shot. Therefore, it's unlikely that fish will feel much resistance when towing them under.

Lake fish have plenty of time to reject a suspicious offering but the Insert gives similar sensitivity to a much smaller float at a greatly increased distance. It usually brings very positive bites. As with most waggler rigs, Inserts work best with the bulk weighting around the float base.

Shotting down the line is determined by the type of swim being fished. If the float needs to be cast tight to far bank or island cover, then very light shot is fixed down the line so it doesn't influence the way the float flies through the air. In shallow water or for mid-depth fishing, a couple of No.8s or 10s or a mixture of the two is usually enough.

In deeper, open water a few more shot may be positioned below the float to stabilise the rig. Several No.8s spread out in stick float fashion is OK. Otherwise, step up to something like a No.4 or 5 just below mid-depth and taper the drop-shot down to a No.7 or 8, then a 10.

Straight wagglers

These take over from the Insert design if drift pulls the finer tipped float under when the hookbait is presented on the bottom – or choppy conditions make it difficult to see the Insert. Several small shot can be dragged around on the bottom by a Straight waggler if required to try and anchor the rig. In these conditions, an Insert would simply sink out of sight.

Straights are bulk-shotted much the same as Inserts but leave just a little bit more weight loading to go down the line. Insert or Straight wagglers will comfortably cope with distances up to five or six rod

Right: Shotting for the Stillwater Blue.

Below: Rig for fishing tight into cover or shallow water up to 1.2m in depth (left). A slightly bigger inset waggler for deeper water – more shot is added down the line (right).

Below centre: A shallow water rig (left) that takes over when the insert float is difficult to see or is dragged under by drift. A deeper straight waggler rig (right). If a single No.8 drag shot fails to steady the rig, try trimming a little weight from the locking shot and putting another No.8 or two down the line, 2.5cm apart, on the hooklength.

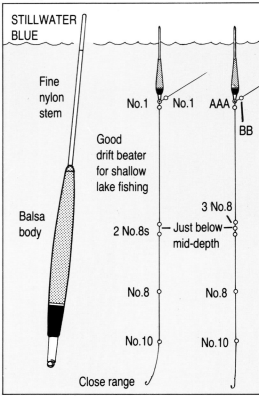

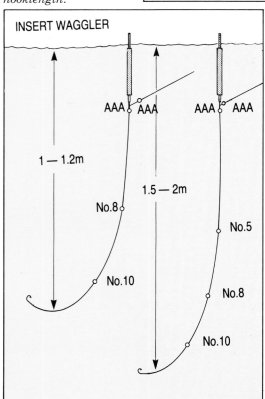

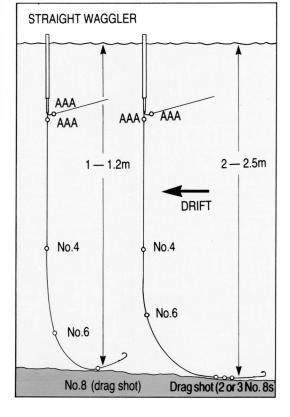

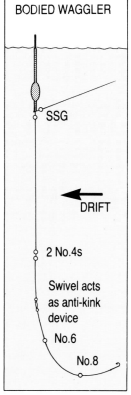

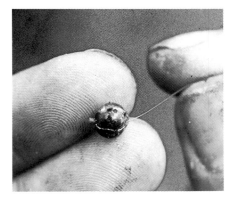
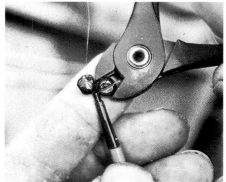
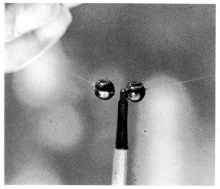

lengths in normal conditions. Beyond that range, or when wind or drift make fishing even shorter distances a struggle, then you should change to a big bodied waggler.

Commercial models take up to three or four swan shot but many anglers construct specials taking a lot more than that.

Bodied wagglers

These are usually fished from five to eight rod lengths out and because big, robust shot are needed to lock them on the line it's recommended that you use hard, non-toxic brands like Thamesly Sure Shot. Remember to close them on a silicone buffer to avoid damaging the line.

Again, when stepping up in float size a little more shot is needed down the line to balance the rig. Two or three No.4 shot fixed a little below half depth are usually adequate, tapering off with a No.6 followed by an 8. It's possible that you'll find the hooklength twisting on the retrieve with these big floats. This tends to happen particularly when using double caster or maggot which set up a spinning action when reeled in very quickly. The answer is to join the hooklength to the main line with a swivel which acts as an anti-kink device.

Apart from being very effective on lakes, bodied wagglers can be used on flowing water. When it is not feasible to fish a top and bottom float they are the next best thing to slow a hookbait down with their extra weighting. A two swan bodied waggler will trot through a lot slower than a 2AAA or 3AAA Straight or Insert waggler.

Fixing a silicone buffer
A. Most large sizes of shot need a silicone buffer when used as lockers on a waggler. Cut a length of silicone to the full width of the shot and gently fix on the line as shown.
B. Once positioned, trap the lockers securely with shot-pliers.
C. Leave some room for movement between the shot so the waggler can collapse with less splash on entering the water.

SPECIAL FLOATS

CANAL GREYS

The Canal Grey float was developed by matchman Billy Makin and has become a classic. It is a brilliant, all-purpose bottom-ender made from balsa, and tapering to a very fine tip. It works very differently to the normal Peacock and Sarkandas wagglers. Stability and super sensitivity are its strengths and it comes into its own in the 2-3BB sizes for fishing two thirds of the way across canals with baits like breadpunch, squatts and pinkies on running line. (See page 35). The Canal Grey is weighted like a waggler with bulk locking-shot and very small drop-shot, normally No.10s or 11s. It can be fished on-the-drop or dragging over-depth. Its streamlined shape casts well but it is quite a dumpy float and will not spook fish in shallow, clear water.

SLIDERS

Sooner or later you will want to fish a swim which is too deep for conventional float tackle. For instance, if your rod is 13ft then depths beyond 12ft are difficult to fish effectively with a fixed float. In swims where there is more than 14ft of water you'd find it impossible.

The solution is to switch to a slider float. There are two designs for deep water – the bottom-end only, waggler style float for stillwaters and the double-eyed balsa for running swims. The waggler slider is normally bodied and may also be semi-weighted in the stem. Usually, these floats are fished with a bulk weight positioned approximately 3-4ft from the hook with a No.4 or 6 dropper-shot midway between bulk and hook. A small shot is also fixed a

Opposite right:
Shotting can be modified for on-the-drop fishing but fish slightly heavier for more positive registration i.e. string out several No.8 shot.

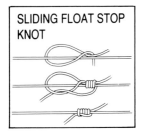

SLIDING FLOAT STOP KNOT

Below: *A bottom-end slider rig for stillwaters.*

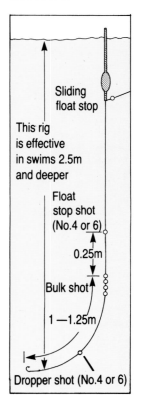

Sliding float stop

This rig is effective in swims 2.5m and deeper

Float stop shot (No.4 or 6)

0.25m

Bulk shot

1—1.25m

Dropper shot (No.4 or 6)

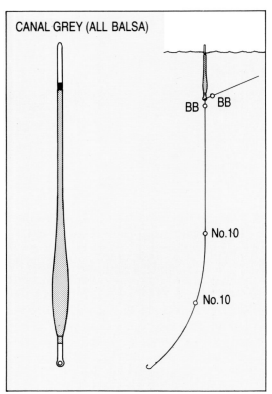

CANAL GREY (ALL BALSA)

BB   BB

No.10

No.10

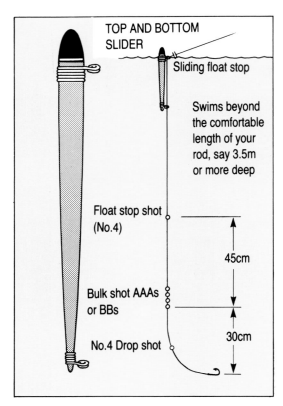

TOP AND BOTTOM SLIDER

Sliding float stop

Swims beyond the comfortable length of your rod, say 3.5m or more deep

Float stop shot (No.4)

45cm

Bulk shot AAAs or BBs

30cm

No.4 Drop shot

foot or so above the bulk weights to prevent the float from sliding down and tangling on the cast. These floats have either a tiny wire eye at the base or a small swivel through which the line is free running. The float is stopped at the required depth you want to fish by a sliding float knot.

Once a bottom-end slider has been set up it can be fished in a similar fashion to a normal waggler and unless conditions are flat calm this again calls for a sinking line.

The top and bottom slider is basically an all-balsa float with an extra side eye added so the reel line slides unhindered until it is braked by a stop knot.

Again, it is used in water too deep for your rod with identical shotting to the bottom-

ender. For close-in work, it is practical to fish this float on stillwaters if the wind or drift isn't too bad. But really this design is meant for flowing water. The only technique you can't try is to hold back hard because the line is pulled back through the rings.

If the float appears to be moving through the swim too fast, change to a heavier model. The extra weight of a bigger float often slows its progress downstream considerably. Another use for top and bottom sliders is in overgrown swims where an overhead or sideways cast is imposible. Even if the water is only several feet deep, you can flick this float out underarm to quite a distance.

ATTRACTORS

THE CHIEF HOOKBAITS

The plain white maggot has always been the freshwater bait in greatest demand but it needs to be in tip-top condition. Fresh bait is easily recognisable by a black feed spot beneath the skin and the maggot should be soft rather than rubbery to the touch.

There is considerable scope for experiment with a range of coloured maggots. Favourites are red, bronze and yellow although green and blue are not unheard of! Dyed baits increase your options at the bankside. A change to a coloured bait frequently produces extra fish on hard fished waters where whites are widely used.

Some species also seem to have definite colour preferences. This is unclear ground, scientifically, because fish are only supposed to see in monochrome. But match anglers wouldn't be without bronze maggots for roach and chub or dark red ones when after tench and perch. Colour is something each angler must experiment with for himself.

MAGGOT TYPES

Shop maggots are not restricted to large whites. **Pinkies** are about half their size and as the name suggests they have a pinkish tinge in their natural state. They're favourites with matchmen and canal anglers for catching small fish on light tackle with small hooks. Like big maggots, pinkies are sold in their natural form or dyed red, bronze and sometimes yellow.

Squatts

Then there are squatts which were once exclusively used by bream anglers in groundbait. The squatt is half the size again of the pinkie and being so small it is less mobile in water and does not bury itself in the bottom-mud out of sight of the fish.

Squatts have now found their way out of the groundbait bowl and on to the hook as a frontline bait. Canal anglers were responsible for its promotion and they rate it very highly as a bait and as loose feed. Scaled down tackle is a must with the squatt.

Most squatts come as whites stored in damp, red-brick sand. Lately, there has been a trend to feed squatts dyed red to simulate the bloodworm on venues where this tiny worm is banned. But nothing can really compare with the potency of the bright red bloodworm itself which is the larvae of midge found in massive quantities in the bottom mud of many fisheries.

Gozzers

The other maggot type is the gozzer which cannot be reared commercially. It must be home-bred by the angler in a medium-sized heart from the butcher's shop. Producing gozzers is a fiddling business but the end result is a much softer skinned maggot than is obtainable commercially and they're excellent for bream.

To turn out your own gozzers, you'll need to start the process ten days before your planned fishing trip. First, make several cuts through the heart without completely separating the sections and place it on a bed

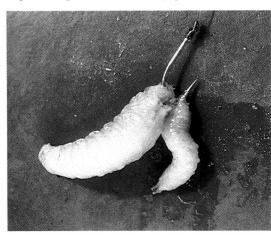

This photograph shows the size difference between a standard white (left) and a pinkie.

Single maggots must be mounted so they wriggle away from the point of the hook.

The correct way to hook a single caster is to bury the hook until it is almost completely hidden.

of clean bran in a large tin or similar sized container with a lid. Leave the lid slightly open or make a hole in it big enough for a fly to enter and lay its eggs in the heart – a process known as the blow. Put the container outside in a shady, dry spot such as under thick bushes in the garden or in a garden shed with an open window. After a couple of days in mild weather there should be several patches of eggs on the cuts in the heart. But you only require two or three clusters of eggs otherwise there will be too many maggots feeding on the meat and the gozzers will be very small. Scrape any surplus blows off the heart with a knife.

Next, wrap the heart quite loosely in newspaper and cover with fresh bran to help prevent smells. After six or seven days the gozzers are ready for riddling off and placing in fresh, slightly dampened bran in a bait box to stop them escaping.

IMPROVING SHOP MAGGOTS

If you haven't got the time or facilities to produce your own special bait, it's still possible to enhance shop-bought bait. A small maggot riddle and some fresh sawdust, even a sprinkling of fine maize meal, can work wonders with indifferent bait.

Maize or bran will make maggots a lot softer to the touch if you store them in a cool spot in a large, open-topped container. Soft maggots bring more positive bites. The only time when tough skinned, older bait should be considered is in very cold water which makes fresh maggots stretch very quickly.

FLAVOURINGS FOR MAGGOTS

There are sound reasons for giving maggots extra appeal with flavouring. If you smoke, it's possible to transfer the taint to the maggot which the fish can detect. And if the bait is warm, an unpleasant smell of ammonia is given off which also repels the fish. If nothing else, the application of a pleasant flavour to the bait masks out any of these negative smells and boosts confidence.

MOUNTING MAGGOTS
ON THE HOOK

The best way to mount a single maggot is through the tiny flap of skin at the tail or blunt end. This doesn't impede the movement of the bait and if anything makes the maggot wriggle even more enticingly. Make certain you don't mask the point of the hook with the maggot otherwise fish will get bumped off on the strike.

Generally, you should use fine wire hooks ranging from 18s to 24s for single maggot. Fish double-maggot when after bigger fish to help deter small fry, possibly with a heavier forged hook down to a 14. A cluster of maggots can be mounted on an even bigger hook to help disguise its size for barbel and carp.

KEEPING CASTERS FRESH

If maggots are kept for several days they eventually turn into chrysalids. At first, these are an attractive light bronze colour but they turn a deeper brown and finally almost black. In their lighter condition, chrysalids sink but as soon as they go dark they float. In their sinking stage they are known as **casters** which are a brilliant big-fish bait.

Better tackle shops sell them ready-packed in airtight plastic bags but they're such a popular bait that they must be ordered several days in advance of your fishing trip. Few shops sell them off the shelf because they turn so quickly. Casters are best stored in a fridge but the bag must be opened to allow fresh air to enter every eight hours. This will prevent them turning grey and dying or getting burn marks from the plastic bag. When replacing the air, leave the bag open for just a couple of minutes and no longer otherwise they'll quickly blacken off and turn into floaters.

The ability to completely hide a hook inside a caster helps considerably in clear water. Quality fish will often seize a caster on days when they won't touch a maggot. It's a bait worth fussing over! Double caster is more effective for fish like chub, barbel, carp, bream and tench and can be fished on a strong, forged hook pattern. Use sizes between 14 and 18 inclusive for double baits with finer wire 16s, 18s or 20s for single caster.

VERSATILE BREAD

Maggots and casters are good standard baits but there are plenty of other possibil-

ities and bread rates as one of the most versatile. It can be fished in crust and flake form on big hooks or as paste and pellets compressed from a punch with tiny hooks.

Crust and flake

Surface fished crust is particularly liked by carp and chub and a slow-sinking piece in weedy swims will rest gently on underwater foliage or muddy bottoms without disappearing out of sight. Depending on its size, a piece of flake can be used on a fair range of larger hooks for a wide cross-section of species. Most fish will take a chunk of bread at some time.

If necessary, it's feasible to step up to as big a hook as a forged size 2 when fishing crust, although a 4, 6 or 8 is normally adequate. The same applies to flake where a 10 or 12 is suitable for roach and bream fishing.

Paste

Paste is presented on all sizes from 2s to 16s but don't go any smaller otherwise it will tend to fall off on the cast. To overcome that limitation, matchmen developed the breadpunch with multi-sized heads for compressing and cutting out tiny pellets of bread from a sliced white loaf. The advantage of this method is that the bait is transferred to the hook without being touched eliminating any possibility of tainting.

Flavouring

While it is unusual to flavour visual baits like floating crust and flake, it is common to spice up paste or breadpunch. Paste is best made from a decrusted, stale white loaf. Slightly dampen the dry interior crumb and squeeze out in a dry cloth. The ball of damp bread is then kneaded into the right texture to stay on the hook.

At this stage you can add some flavouring. Soft cheese is a popular addition and should be kneaded in to slightly harden up the paste. Custard powder is another good firming agent.

With breadpunch it is easier to carry a small bottle of flavouring and to dunk the bait into it after it has been put on the hook. Flavours worth considering include banana, cheese and vanilla.

WORMS

Worms will trick numerous species of fish but this bait is chiefly associated with perch, eels, tench, bream and chub. There are several types you can use ranging from the big lobworm found on grass lawns at night – usually when the weather is damp and mild – to the more easily collectable brandlings and redworms.

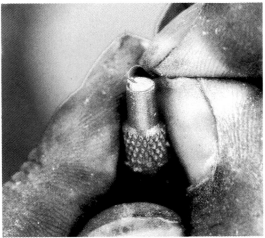

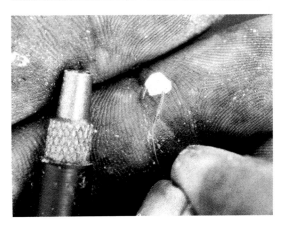

How to work with a breadpunch.
A. Punches make it easy to produce compact pellets of bread for hard fished venues where small hooks are a must. All you'll need for a day's fishing is a few slices of fresh bread and a hard, flat surface on which to work. Select the appropriate size of punch and press down vertically into the bread until you can feel it has penetrated through to your makeshift worksurface.

B. Once the punch is neatly plugged with bread withdraw the pellet on the hook.

C. Make sure the pellet sits on the bend of the hook with the point exposed.

Lobworms

Lobworms are often fished whole on big hooks for chub and tench while the tail end makes a good mouthful on middle-sized hooks for roach, perch and eels.

Brandlings or redworms

If you buy worms from a tackle shop they're likely to be brandlings or redworms. There's something of a stigma attached to brandlings because they ooze a repulsive looking body fluid when impaled on the hook. But take no notice of other anglers' objections. The brandling will catch you plenty of fish and there are occasions in summer droughts when they're the only worm obtainable.

Use brandlings on an 8 or 10 hook if they're on the large side, going down to a pattern between 12 and 18 depending on bait size. They're particularly well liked by tench, perch and bream. Canal anglers sometimes chop up these worms into tiny pieces on hard venues for gudgeon, small perch and ruffe.

Redworms tend to be small and lively which has persuaded many a fine roach to the net. Bream, tench and perch also find them a tasty snack. It's a good worm for chopping up in quantity for introducing into groundbait when you are fishing for tench and bream. A hook size between 10 and 14 is preferred for these species while smaller bream will fall to a redworm lightly hooked in the head on a 16 or 18. Sometimes a cocktail bait of worm tipped off with caster or red maggot works very much better.

SEED BAITS

HEMP AND TARES

There are three popular seed baits associated with summer and to a lesser extent autumn. These are hemp, tares and sweetcorn. But the drawing power of hemp is so powerful that anglers carry on using it as loose feed well into the winter months, normally with maggots or casters. In the summer and autumn, hemp is a superb roach attractor both as loose feed and on the hook. But it must be introduced and fished skilfully to bring results.

Preparing hemp and tares

A pint of cooked hemp is sufficient for a full day's fishing and preparation is simple. Tip a pint of seeds into a large saucepan and cover with water. Then bring to the boil with the lid removed. Once the water reaches boiling point, turn the heat down and let the hemp simmer for 30 minutes with the saucepan lid not quite covering the pan. Check periodically to ensure the water doesn't evaporate completely. If there's not enough water covering the seeds after ten minutes or so, top up the level with an extra cupful.

The bait is ready when small, white shoots emerge on most of the seeds. Rinse off with cold water through a strainer to prevent over cooking. If overdone, hemp splits open too much and is impossible to keep on the hook. Tares are often used on the hook with hemp as loose feed and the combination works very well. The tare is four times larger than hemp when cooked. It is much softer skinned and impales on the hook more easily. The fish seem to home in on this bigger offering among the smaller grains of loose fed hemp. The tare can be used in its natural light brown state or soaked in soda to blacken off and simulate hemp. The simplest way to prepare tares is to add a handful to the hemp while it is cooking. That will be ample for a session.

Baiting-up

With hemp as hookbait, a 16 or 18 hook is recommended, pushing the bend into the split where the tiny white shoot emerges. For tares, a 14 or 16 is about right, usually just lightly skin-hooking the bait. If the fish are a little shy, push the hook into the tare where a slight seam runs around one side. This only leaves part of the shank visible.

Always make sure the point of the hook is just protruding with hemp and tares to ease the task of setting it home on the strike. It can prove a devil of a job if the point is buried in the bait.

When fed correctly, hemp is capable of mesmerising fish like roach, chub and barbel into a feeding frenzy. With roach and chub, this means feeding a few grains on every cast. The bait is not always instant-acting. It might take several hours to work up a swim but it's worth the effort.

Hemp tactics for barbel are rather different. A large carpet is laid on the bottom and sometimes it takes half-a-gallon or more to pull in the fish. But once the barbel are in the swim, the hemp will hold them for long periods.

SWEETCORN

This is a summer bait linked with tench, bream and carp on stillwaters but it will also tempt chub, barbel and roach on river venues. A 10, 12 or 14 gilt coloured, eyed hook is best and a strong hooklength is advised because the bites are often quite savage.

Always leave the hookpoint standing proud of the tare.

GROUNDBAIT MIXES

Some very complicated groundbait mixes were around long before boilies made their mark and in many ways the thinking behind them is very similar. Matchmen soon discovered that complex Continental mixes seemed to draw and hold fish very well, particularly when fishing at close range with the pole.

To put groundbait into perspective, the most basic form is white or brown bread-crumb. White on its own goes a little stodgy when mixed with water. But brown turns fluffy and produces a nice cloud when introduced into the swim in the right manner. The two can also be mixed to achieve different consistencies.

Fish may be attracted by groundbait either visually or by its aroma. This gives the angler the choice of drawing fish to his hookbait by a visually attractive cloud effect or introducing a feed mix which will hopefully hold the fish while they eat their way to his hookbait.

Groundbait is a good attractor when loose feeding fails. There is a limit to the distance you can throw or catapult loose feed and that's often a drawback. Sometimes, it will go unnoticed simply because the fish are not resident in the swim. But groundbait in cloud form is much more visible and as fish are naturally inquisitive creatures they will want to investigate. It is quite normal

for water to become coloured by wave action, extra rain or boats which stir up debris. Fish associate these disturbances with finding food.

Another use for groundbait is as a carrier to deposit loose feed greater distances. And heavy groundbait will hold on the bottom of fast flowing swims when loose feed is usually swept away.

Continental groundbaits

Breadcrumb is used countrywide as ground-bait but it is easy to overfeed the fish. Crumb swells to twice its size in water and fish are quickly filled up. That's where European anglers have been very clever, formulating mixes which contain very little, if any, bread feed. Instead, they rely heavily on non-absorbing ingredients like crushed hemp and overcooked biscuit flour. Bland flours like ground walnut, peanut and coconut are also incorporated and there can be up to a dozen ingredients in the more successful Continental mixes.

On the tackle shop shelves you'll find Continental groundbaits developed for particular species of fish and with very different consistencies. Some bind well, others give a lovely cloudy effect. Some are even recommended for use with certain baits like bloodworm, maggots or casters.

CATAPULTS

A catapult is needed to feed loose offerings, boilies and groundbait at distance. A well designed, loose feed 'pult increases feeding range up to 30yd if the wind is right. On canals and small rivers this is a big advantage because you can spray casters or maggots right across to the far bank.

A good groundbait catapult is a must for bream on large, open gravel pits or big, sluggish rivers where the fishing range is frequently 40yd or more. Make sure you pick the right gauge of elastic and also check the pouch is rigid enough not to break up the ball of groundbait.

BAIT CHART

Bait	Species	Recommended hook size/pattern
Maggots	Barbel, bleak, bream, carp, chub, dace, eels, gudgeon, perch, roach, rudd, ruffe, tench.	Single: 18-24, fine wire. Double: 14-18, forged. Multiple: 8-12, forged.
Casters	Barbel, bream, carp, chub, dace, eels, roach, rudd, tench.	Single: 16-20, fine wire. Double: 14-18, forged. Multiple: 10-12, forged.
Pinkies	Bleak, skimmer bream, dace, eels, gudgeon, perch, roach, rudd, ruffe, tench.	Single: 20-24, fine wire. Double: 20, fine or forged.
Squatts	Bleak, bream (and skimmers), dace, gudgeon, perch, roach, rudd, ruffe, tench.	Single: 22-24, fine wire. Double: 20-22, fine wire.
Worms	Barbel, bream, carp, chub, eels, perch, roach, ruffe, tench.	Lobs: 2-12, forged. Brandlings: 8-16, forged. Reds: 14-18, fine wire.
Bloodworms	Bleak, bream, skimmers, gudgeon, perch, roach, rudd, ruffe, tench.	Single: 20-26, fine wire. Double: 18-24, fine wire.
Breadpunch	Bleak, skimmer bream, gudgeon, roach, rudd.	16-24, fine wire.
Breadflake and crust	Barbel, bream, carp, chub, roach, tench.	Large pieces: 2-12, forged. Small: 12-16, fine wire.
Luncheon meat	Barbel, carp, chub, tench.	Large pieces: 4-10, forged. Small: 12-16, forged.
Boilies	Barbel, bream, carp, chub, tench.	Standard: 6-10, forged. Mini: 10-14, forged.
Hemp	Barbel, chub, dace, roach, rudd.	Big fish: 14-18, forged. Roach, etc: 14-20, fine wire.
Tares	Barbel, bream, carp, chub, roach.	Big fish: 12-18, forged. Roach, etc: 14-18, fine wire.
Sweetcorn	Barbel, bream, carp, chub, roach, rudd, tench.	Single: 12-16, forged. Multiple: 8-12, forged.

LEGERING

The float should be stripped from the line in favour of a single leger weight or swimfeeder when the fish are beyond floatfishing range and you can't tempt them closer. Another signal to change is if the flow or drift prevents you holding the float tackle stationary when the fish demand a bait fished that way.

With legering techniques it is possible to more than double the range of float tackle and in flowing water you can stop a bait hard on the bottom at distances that would defeat the float.

The straight leger restores the balance of tackle presentation back in the anglers' favour when the float is in trouble. But don't just leap for the leger straight away, very often the swimfeeder will bring the fish in just as well if not better.

There are two basic types of feeder popularly known as **open-end** and **block-end**. Both are manufactured from clear or coloured plastic and are perforated with exit holes to release bait. The difference between the two is that the open-ended model is used for groundbait and the block-end purely with loose feed like maggots, hemp and casters.

Cage feeders are a more recent development and consist simply of a latticed metal framework in the shape of a cylindrical plastic feeder through and around which the groundbait is moulded.

OPEN-ENDED SWIMFEEDERS

The open-end feeder is made in several sizes with corresponding increases in weight loading and each takes different amounts of feed. Extra weight can be added with purpose-made leads which clip on the feeder body or fit underneath existing weights.

The open-end design usually has a short nylon loop at one end to which an American swivel link is clipped. The reel line is then threaded through the swivel and the feeder stopped with a splitshot or leger stop. Below this goes the hooklength.

There is little need to introduce extra links or to cover the nylon loop on this swim-

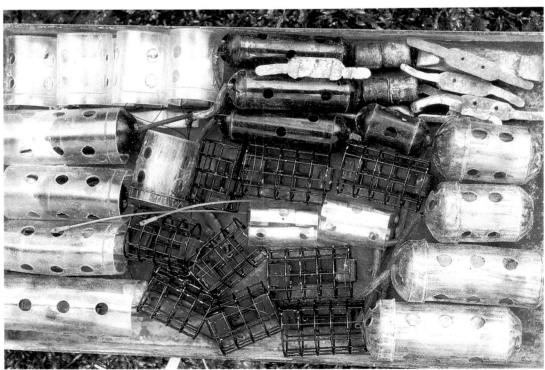

The range of feeders carried by Dave Coster to cover most demands on rivers and lakes.

feeder with silicone tubing to prevent the hooklength tangling. The rig is relatively problem-free.

Open-enders can be filled with groundbait alone – pure crumb is the favourite when fishing bread on the hook – or with a combination of groundbait and loose offerings like casters, squatts, hemp and pinkies. The loose bait is mixed into the groundbait and pressed inside the feeder or compressed in the centre with retaining plugs of groundbait at either end.

Lately, Continental groundbaits have become very popular for this type of feeder fishing. Their excellent binding qualities hold in loose feed very well for long casting.

BLOCK-END FEEDERS

Block-end or closed feeders have two end caps. The bottom one is normally permanently fixed while the top cap is removable to allow the feeder to be filled. Block-ends offer more resistance to flowing water than open-ended models and tend to roll before settling. This can cause the hooklength to twist around the nylon attachment loop on the feeder. The answer is to slip a short length of silicone tubing over the nylon link then there is nothing for the hook to catch on during the cast or when the rig hits bottom. The tendency of the block-end to tangle has resulted in some manufacturers incorporating short links made of plastic which solves the problem to some extent. Other models come complete with a swivel which is moulded in the top cap of the feeder.

Block-ends are usually filled with maggots which gradually filter out of the exit holes ensuring a steady trickle of loose offerings are spread around the hookbait. Caster and hempseed make another good combination in the feeder with caster or maggot on the hook. Like open-enders, these designs are manufactured in varying sizes ranging from tiny feederlinks which

A reasonably tangle-proof block-end feeder rig. The reel line is threaded directly through a single swivel which is partly covered by silicone tubing, or an American swivel link may be attached to this first.

are fished with small baits like pinkies through to the big block-ends for piling large amounts of maggots in the swim when big catches are anticipated.

The swimfeeder is a good method because it guarantees that loose feed or groundbait will be distributed precisely where it is wanted around the hookbait. It's a deadly technique even in the hands of a novice angler.

Generally, it's best to give the feeder a break every now and then and switch to a straight leger until the swim needs further topping up with bait. As a rough guide, use the feeder until the swim comes alive then alternate with an Arlesey bomb, the priority being to keep the bites coming.

There are, of course, venues and types of swim where the straight leger will outscore the swimfeeder. Think twice before slinging out a feeder in shallow, clear lake water or hard fished canal venues. It will do more damage than good! The feeder is also more likely to spook big fish like bream in stillwaters than it might on flowing rivers.

BITE DETECTION

There are several ways of interpreting bites when legering and each method has its strengths and weaknesses. The leading indicators are swingtips, quivertips and springtips. Which you choose depends on the swim, weather conditions and target species.

Swingtips

Bream are notoriously fickle and will spend some time playing with a bait before deciding to take it. The low resistance offered by a swingtip is much less likely to scare a fish in this sort of mood.

Another advantage of the swingtip is the wider arc of striking power it affords when fishing at distance. The rod is positioned pointing towards the end tackle instead of the 45 degree angle that's required with the quivertip.

Swingtips are sold in varying materials and lengths ranging from 5 or 6in (12.5 or 15cm) up to about a foot or so. They can be made from Sarkandas reed, cane, plastic or even carbon.

For the most positive bite indication, a length of 8-10in (20-25cm) is about right for

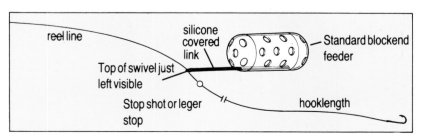

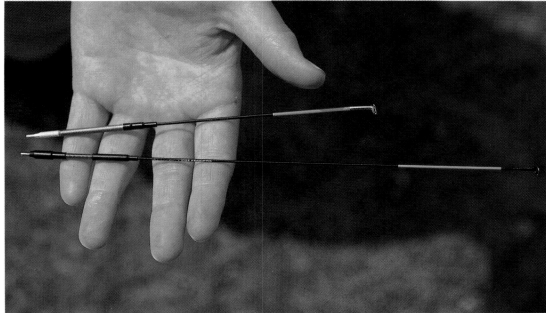

Standard springtip and adjustable model which doubles as a quiver by pushing the tip back through the spring. If your tip bends before the spring comes into play then buy a new one! The spring must collapse first on the bite otherwise you might as well resort to a straight quivertip.

***Below:** Setting-up your swingtip.*

normal conditions, using a swingtip made from a light material. To counteract drift, wind or flow, light swingtips must be fitted with special pre-formed, rigid rubber connectors. These give different degrees of flexibility and are pre-set at the desired 45 degree angle.

If a medium length swingtip is still unstable despite changing to the stiffest rubber connector, the next step is to wrap lead wire around the end of the tip or switch to a longer, heavier model.

The rod must be supported by a minimum of two rests when swingtipping to keep the sensitive tip rock steady. Make sure the rests are correctly spaced to prevent any part of the rod drooping. In rough conditions it is not out of the question to use three rests to stop the wind from making false movements on the tip.

When fishing at distances over 40yd it is probably best to point the rod in its rests towards the terminal tackle for maximum striking power. But for shorter range fishing, the rod's angle to the end tackle is increased, especially when the wind shakes the rod tip. If you can tuck the rod out of the main force of the wind or shelter it in any way, this is all to the good.

QUIVERTIPS

The quivertip is Britain's No. 1 bite indicator. The most convenient model is the

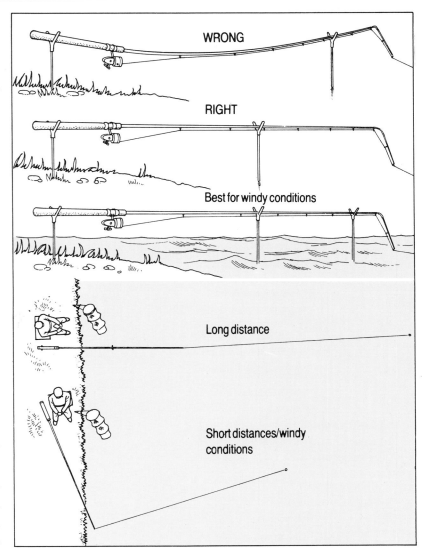

WRONG

RIGHT

Best for windy conditions

Long distance

Short distances/windy conditions

Below and right:
Today many rod manufacturers are producing custom-made quivertip rods that take up to three or four slot-in quivers. In many ways this is preferable to screw-in quivertips as a better action is achieved.

screw-in version which fits a threaded top eye. These can be fitted to most leger rods or even shorter match rods if required.

Screw-in indicators are available in dif-

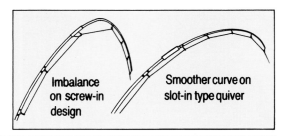

Imbalance on screw-in design

Smoother curve on slot-in type quiver

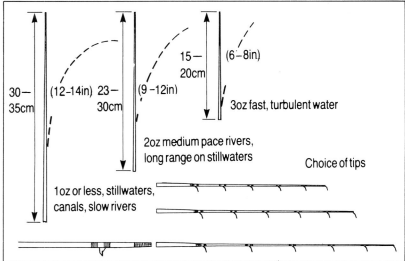

30–35cm (12–14in) 23–30cm (9–12in) 15–20cm (6–8in)

3oz fast, turbulent water

2oz medium pace rivers, long range on stillwaters

Choice of tips

1oz or less, stillwaters, canals, slow rivers

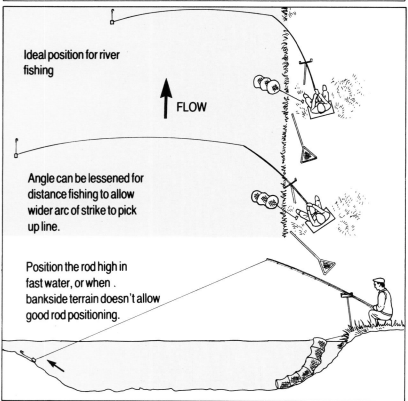

Ideal position for river fishing

FLOW

Angle can be lessened for distance fishing to allow wider arc of strike to pick up line.

Position the rod high in fast water, or when bankside terrain doesn't allow good rod positioning.

ferent lengths, tapers and test curves ranging from very stiff river models down to long, extra fine canal or stillwater designs. If your rod has a threaded top eye, it is advisable to carry several different strength quivers to deal with varying flow rates.

Many manufacturers are now producing leger blanks with two, three or four interchangeable tips which slot into the main rod. This is a superior system because there's a better relationship between the indicator and the rod. A more gradual step-down from the blank itself to the finer tip is achieved. The other option is to buy a rod with a built-in quivertip but you've got to be very sure of the rod and its intended use. This rod will probably be more powerful and robust but you'll lose the versatility of the other options unless, of course, you can afford two or three specialist rods.

The most common fault when quivertipping is poor positioning of the rod. Many anglers simply get themselves comfortable and drop the rod in to the rests without giving much thought to where it should be pointing.

Nothing is gained by pointing the rod directly at the end tackle. If there's only a small angle or no angle at all where the line leaves the tip ring on the quiver, then bites won't register correctly.

On fast flowing waters, a stiffish actioned tip must be used because the current would pull round a finer one too severely for bites to show up. The rod needs to be positioned quite high to get as much of the line out of the water as possible to prevent the flow dragging the end rig out of place.

Usually, it's preferable if the rod is pointing downstream in this situation. But you can point it upstream if the swim makes this impossible by a few modifications.

THE BOW METHOD

You can actually get away with too fine a tip in a fast flow and overcome the problems of poor bite indication. This is achieved by feeding line into the current to reduce the effect of flow or water pressure. The method is called fishing the bow. It's a brilliant technique if you can balance the tackle because the fish don't feel such heavy resistance when they pick up the hookbait. Normally, they hook themselves!

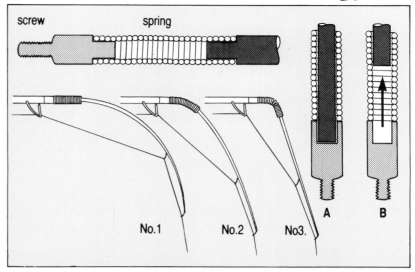

Basically, the bow method entails using lighter gear all round including a feeder that's barely heavy enough to hold bottom. Once it has landed in the swim, line is fed out into the flow. Up to several yards can be released while the rod is being placed in the rests. The line should be fed in a downstream direction but if it must be upstream then more is released to compensate.

This system is more sensitive than tight lining in flow. Really you are making the current work for you. The water pressure on the large bow of line causes the finer quivertip to pull round but not overmuch because of the line feeding process which eases the pressure.

Let's assume you've got the feeder size right and it's just holding against the bow. When a fish pulls on the hooklength the balance is upset and the feeder rolls downstream – pulled by all that line in the water. The weight of the line and feeder suddenly being released results in the quivertip dropping back sharply and at the same time sets the hook! All you have to do is pick up the rod and lift into the fish.

The line needs to be kept at an angle of 45 degrees to the rod tip when quivertipping on both rivers and stillwaters. But at great distances, the angle can be reduced to allow for the greater arc of strike needed to set the hook.

Stillwaters or gently flowing rivers require much finer, longer tips otherwise the fish feel resistance and just rattle the tip without giving any hittable bites. Here it's better to position the rod low with most of the line submerged but again always point the rod downstream of any flow or drift.

Another trick in fast flow is to hold the rod in the right hand and feel for bites on the line with the left just above the reel. This is called **touch legering** and is surprisingly sensitive to even the slightest nibble.

SPRINGTIPS

The springtip is made like a quiver but is fitted with a coiled spring just above the screw-in attachment for the rod. Some models serve as dual purpose spring/quivers by permitting the tip to be pushed back inside the spring. The idea behind the spring/quiver is that you fish with the quiver until the fish become cagey. Then you pull the indicator out of its housing to

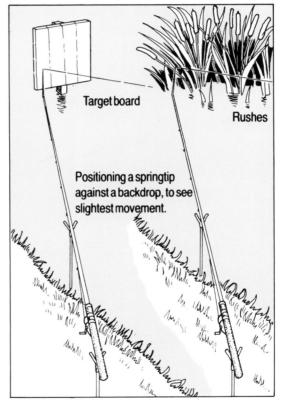

Positioning a springtip against a backdrop, to see slightest movement.

Target board

Rushes

bring the spring into play. This collapses at the slightest indication of a bite and gives much greater sensitivity without the need to break down the tackle and start again.

Avoid using too soft a quivertip because this defeats the object of the spring. If the quivertip section bends more than an inch before the spring begins to lean over, you're still quivertipping

Springtips come into their own on hard venues with little or no flow where you

Springtip
Above: 1. Tip too soft and is bending before spring.
2. Tip bending slightly in unison with the spring.
3. Tip bending before spring is effected. If you are buying a springtip go for type 3 action. With a dual purpose spring/quiver you'll probably have to settle for action 2. With action 1 you might as well be fishing with a quivertip, here the spring is only cosmetic.
A. Qivertip. Tip pushed home in the housing.
B. Springtip. Tip detached from housing.

Opposite bottom: Rod positions when using a quivertip on flowing water.

expect finicky bites. The rod is positioned low so the line leaves the springtip at as near an angle of 45 degrees as possible. Spotting bites is made much easier if the tip shows up well against the background.

Springtips register tiny indications which wouldn't be revealed on a conventional quiver and that makes the background an important consideration. With this method the terminal tackle must be free running enough not to cause any resistance before the springtip is actioned. And tighten up the line slightly once the tackle has settled so the tip moves round about a couple of centimetres. That way it will register any drop-back bites.

BUTT INDICATORS

A butt indicator offers all the benefits of a swingtip if you use it properly. The only disadvantage compared with a bite indicator fixed at the other end of the rod is that fractionally more resistance is set up with the line running through the rings before signalling a take. But this is useless if conditions are so bad that the swingtip sways continually at the rod end.

The length of a butt indicator is between 6in (15cm) and 1ft (30cm) but reckon on 9in (24cm) as being the happy medium. Anything beyond 1ft (30cm) will impede the cast.

Butt indicators are positioned on the rod with a Terry clip. The most suitable spot is midway between the reel and the first rod ring with the indicator leaning away from the angler. On some rods, the butt ring may be badly sited too close to the reel. If this is the case, a short 6in (15cm) indicator may work better fitted above it and before the first intermediate ring.

After casting out with a butt indicator, the rod is placed in two rests pointing towards the end rig. The tip of the rod is submerged a few centimetres under the surface of the water to avoid excess movement on the indicator and rod tip.

Once the tackle has settled the line is tightened up and then a little slack is given until the indicator is at an angle of just less than 45 degrees to the rod with the eye pointing upwards. This positioning allows for dropback registration which is common with this type of fishing. If weather conditions are atrocious, it is possible to position the rod at a slight angle to the end tackle – the butt indicator will remain reasonably effective.

MONKEY-CLIMBERS

The most basic bite indicator for legering is a dough-bobbin moulded from bread and pinched on the line between reel and butt ring. It hangs with sufficient play to move upwards if a fish takes the bait and runs, or drops back down if the fish heads towards the rod.

There are more sophisticated versions of the dough-bobbin made from plastic or the the much more stable monkey-climber type which is used on its own or with an electronic alarm as a visual indication of how a take is developing. The monkey-climb is a steel rod or needle between 18in (45cm) and

Below: Two positions for a butt indicator.

Below middle: Rod positions in bad weather.

Bottom: The monkey climber can be used on its own or with an alarm.

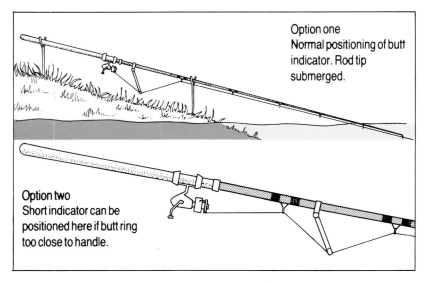

Option one
Normal positioning of butt indicator. Rod tip submerged.

Option two
Short indicator can be positioned here if butt ring too close to handle.

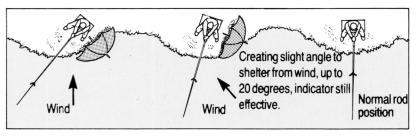

Wind

Wind

Creating slight angle to shelter from wind, up to 20 degrees, indicator still effective.

Normal rod position

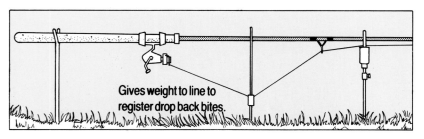

Gives weight to line to register drop back bites.

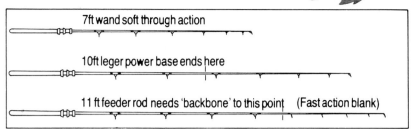

7ft wand soft through action

10ft leger power base ends here

11 ft feeder rod needs 'backbone' to this point   (Fast action blank)

36in (90cm) in length on which the plastic indicator is free running.

The monkey-climber is used for specialist forms of fishing on stillwaters and applies mainly to carp, tench and bream where long hours and possibly few takes are the norm.

Optonic alarms with compact heads that allow the volume to be adjusted have become extremely popular or you can opt for sensor heads which connect to a sounder box. This is positioned away from the rods, if required, using extension leads.

Other electronic indicators include those which rely on the line being run behind an upright arm which is usually adjustable to combat drag. Once the line tightens against the arm as the result of a bite it sets off the alarm.

Line clips

As with any form of bite indicator, deteriorating weather can cause problems with electronic alarms and it's wise to carry line clips or something similar to prevent false indications. There are two types of clip. One is fixed on the rod in front of the indicator to prevent drag creating a false alarm. The other is known as a run clip and is taped to the rod handle directly above the spool of the reel.

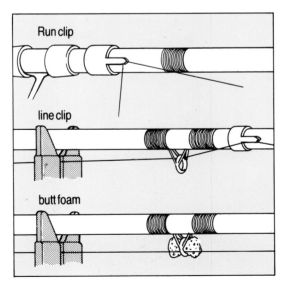

Run clip

line clip

butt foam

THE RIGHT ROD

The ideal length for a feeder/quivertip rod is 11ft. This will punch out a loaded feeder and more importantly pick up line quickly on the strike to set the hook. Leger rods of 10ft are usually designed for fishing between 20yd and 50yd out from the bank. Most happily accept a light feeder as well as normal straight leger rigs.

The majority of carbon designs have medium actions and fine lines can be used safely for shy species like bream and big roach.

Wands of 7ft or less are restricted by their length for fishing inside the 20yd boundary. But they're handy on windy days as the quivertip can be sheltered from the elements under a brolly to help spot bites. On canals, particularly, a short leger rod makes it easier to cast a light rig with inch perfect precision against far bank cover.

Although 12 and 13ft beginner's rods tend to be equipped with a threaded top eye to take quivers or swingtips, these rods are too soft to cast any distance. Their very length also makes it tough spotting tiny bites at the rod end. A 7 to 9ft rod should be restricted to fishing distances up to 30yd with a quivertip. After that 10 to 11ft rods should cover most eventualities up to 60yd. Obviously, a more rigid blank is needed once the fishing distance increases. Custom-made rods of 12ft are suited to ranges beyond 60yd but these are very fast tapered compared to match rods.

The specimen angler requires more robust rods to deal with long range casting and bigger fish. Generally, 11ft is a good length to consider for fishing up to 60 or 70yd, graduating to 12ft blanks for anything beyond. Specimen blanks are plain blanks without any form of spliced-in quivertips since they will be relying on electronic arms and monkey climb systems for bite indication. Test curves range from 1.25 lb up to 3.5lb, usually depending on the power needed for particular fish or distances.

Carbon and Kevlar blanks are the front runners in this department. There are many actions from fast tapers designed for distance work to softer through-actions for

Opposite top to bottom: Popular lake and river legering rigs.

fish like tench and small carp at shorter range. It all depends on the individual's specific requirements.

Most specimen rods are fitted with ceramic guides which are excellent and hard wearing. The one-legged models are very good on through-actioned rods as they don't affect the blank's action. There is also a trend with reel fittings to fit the screw-up types which hold the reel more securely for long casting purposes.

THE RIGHT REEL

A fixed spool reel purchased for floatfishing which has a spare deeper spool will probably adapt pretty well for straight legering and light to medium swimfeeder work if you pack out the spool with 3-4lb line. But it will not stand up to the strain of heavy feeders. A light, specimen type reel is better suited to line of 4-6 lb because it offers a good retrieve ratio and a big diameter spool to help eliminate excessive line twist.

A plastic leger stop and sliding bead carrying a non-toxic bomb – just one of many possibilities.

LINE

There is a good case for using prestretched line when legering because the lack of elasticity gives a more immediate pick-up from rod tip to hook on the strike. This also means the rod does not have to be swept through such a wide arc to set the hook. Prestretched, low diameter lines that team well with the straight leger include Drennan Double Strength and Ultima. But avoid using low diameter brands with the swimfeeder because they wear too quickly and won't absorb the shock of strenuous casting. Instead, select a more robust line like Maxima, Bayer Perlon and Drennan Specimen all of which rate as good feeder reel lines when breaking strains of 3-6lb are required.

PUTTING IT ALL TOGETHER

As with floatfishing, the reel spool must be filled to the lip for maximum casting performance. If a quiver or swingtip is fitted, check that it is aligned with the rod before threading the line through the rings. Then pull several yards off the reel and place the rod in its rests to sort out the end tackle.

First, the feeder or leger weight is slipped on the reel line followed by a small bead to act as a buffer against the stop shot or leger

stop which goes on next. Leave just enough line to knot up an 18in hooklength and tie on the hook. Snip off any excess bits of nylon protruding from the knots.

Finally, rearrange the stop-shot or leger stop if you wish to move it closer to the hook or further away. Make a habit of baiting up the hook **BEFORE** loading the feeder. If you do it the other way around then mobile baits like maggots will have more time to wriggle free from the feeder before it is doing its job in the water.

Incidentally, it's helpful to search out the swim before tying on the terminal tackle. The easiest way is to attach an Arlesey bomb to the end of the reel line. Cast out a few times and make slow retrieves and you'll soon pinpoint any snags. It could save valuable tackle.

RIVER RIGS

The open-end feeder, block-end and straight leger weight all have their days on river venues. A free-running American swivel link is fine for close-in fishing with a small feeder or Arlesey bomb. The swivel is stopped by a plastic leger stop or small split-shot – a number 6 to 8 is normally adequate – with a small bead as buffer. Always ensure the stop is positioned above the hooklength to avoid losing the feeder if you become snagged in some way.

Where the bottom is weedy or rocky, a simplified paternoster rig helps cut down tackle losses. It is easier to pull free if the bomb or feeder becomes trapped.

A stop-shot often proves a hindrance for long range river fishing as it collects bottom debris or floating weed. This can clog the swivel. Stop-shots are also likely to slip when retrieving tackle through strong flowing currents.

A superior assembly that does away with any form of stop-shot is the loop system which works superbly for open-end feeders and also meets block-end and straight legering needs.

The loop is tied at the end of the reel line leaving an American snap swivel running free within its confines. The size of the loop can be varied but 18in (45cm) is fine. At the bottom of the big loop, a much smaller loop is formed to which the hooklength is attached– it's crucial that this is formed exactly at the bottom and not slightly to one side or the rig won't hang correctly.

When cast out, the feeder rests at the base of the large loop with its weight pushing the hooklength out of the way to one side. Tangles are virtually non-existent on the cast and there's nothing on which underwater rubbish can collect. Anything that fouls the reel line comes to rest on the knot at the top of the big loop, well away from the main end rig. That loop gives enough play for a fish to register bites on the quivertip. A fish would have to pull the tip right round before the feeder hits against the top of the loop, so no extra resistance is felt.

LAKE RIGS

The Arlesey bomb is the first choice weight for swingtipping. Its streamlined shape casts well and doesn't put too much strain

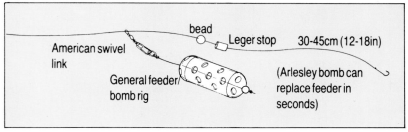

American swivel link
bead
Leger stop
30-45cm (12-18in)
General feeder/bomb rig
(Arlesley bomb can replace feeder in seconds)

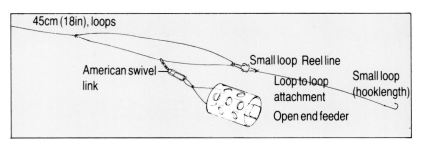

45cm (18in), loops
American swivel link
Small loop Reel line
Loop to loop attachment
Small loop (hooklength)
Open end feeder

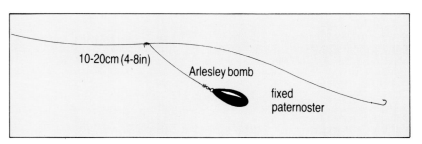

10-20cm (4-8in)
Arlesley bomb
fixed paternoster

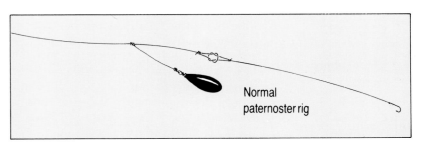

Normal paternoster rig

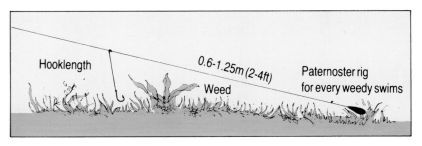

Hooklength
0.6-1.25m (2-4ft)
Weed
Paternoster rig for every weedy swims

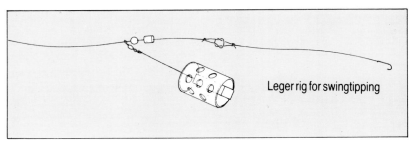

Leger rig for swingtipping

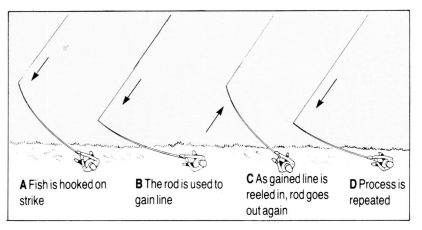

| **A** Fish is hooked on strike | **B** The rod is used to gain line | **C** As gained line is reeled in, rod goes out again | **D** Process is repeated |

How to play a fish.

for introducing groundbait. A swim is normally topped up with the feeder and then the bomb is brought in when the bites start flowing. A rig similar to the river set-up with a stop-shot, bead and swivel is used but again it can be defeated by weed.

The paternoster is the best answer for minimal weed but thick growth which reaches a foot or so off the bottom calls for a modification.

Try switching the rig around so the bomb is at the bottom and the hooklength comes off the reel line, several feet back towards the rod. Then the hookbait is left suspended above the weed and in full view of the fish.

It is also possible to adapt the paternoster system to swimfeeders in weedy water and you can take this a step further by having a running link to the feeder.

on a bite indicator when it's hanging loosely from the rod tip on the cast.

Swimfeeders are also used in lakes and bream anglers prefer the open-ended model

FISH CARE AND HANDLING

Every angler shoulders the responsibility to protect fish stocks for future generations by unhooking and handling fish as humanely as possible.

If a fish has swallowed the hookbait, simply locate the slit at the head of the disgorger on the line and keeping the nylon taut, run it down into the fish's mouth. Once the disgorger hits against the bend of the hook it normally dislodges it automatically allowing it to be retrieved. Some times you may have to gently twist the disgorger around to find a better hold on the hook. But never use excessive force. If you can't free it, the fish has a much better chance of survival if you cut the line as close as possible to the hook.

Fish naturally pick up very sharp items like snail shells which are crunched up and passed through or regurgitated. In time, a hook will rust away. And if you use a barbless pattern the likelihood is that the fish will shed the hook quickly anyway.

The best possible contribution you can make to fish welfare is to handle them with extreme care for the shortest possible time. Indeed, it's often possible to

virtually eliminate holding a fish out of water by unhooking a sizeable specimen in the confines of the landing net and transferring it in the mesh to the keepnet or releasing it immediately.

If you've got to handle a sizeable fish for a photograph, wet your hands beforehand then little if any of the protective mucus on the body will be removed. Never use a towel because it acts like sandpaper!

There are several ways of holding fish but the safest bet for the beginner is to support its head in one hand and to cradle the body towards the tail by the anal fin with the other.

If fish must be retained in keepnets, always ensure the net is staked out properly in water that's deep enough to give the fish plenty of movement. Never allow a keepnet to collapse and if possible position it in shade. The shallow margins can become very inhospitable on hot days. Also make sure your keepnet is big enough. It needs to be a minimum of 6ft (2m) in length with a diameter of 18in (45cm) and must be knotless. Water Authority bye laws state minimum sizes – so if in doubt don't use a keepnet.

ALL ABOUT THE POLE

Before setting out to chose a pole, you must know what you require of it. Basically, there are two reasons for using a pole. One is for uncluttered speed work, fishing a long line to hand. The other is for better presentation of your tackle – beyond the distance you can achieve with a rod and reel.

The crucial consideration when purchasing a pole is how long a model you require. If you fish small canals a great deal then 11 metres will put you tight up against the far bank. For lake fishing, 10-11m is fine and the same goes for river work. Most pole fishing revolves around the 7-8 metre mark but it's useful to have the extra sections if the fish move out or a big one is hooked.

Pick the longest pole you can afford – that's the best advice. But it should feel responsive and not sloppy when fully extended. It should not sag unduly either although all poles droop to some extent beyond 8m.

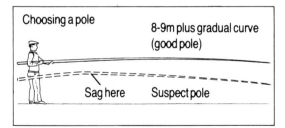

Ask your dealer about spare top sections. It can be very handy to duplicate the top three or four sections of any pole then you can have a couple of rigs made up on the bank for fishing two different lines of attack.

FLICK TIP OR ELASTIC?

There are two ways of rigging out the top sections of a pole. The simplest method is to use a flick tip which is usually a spliced-in piece of solid carbon about 18in long to which the line is attached direct. This fine carbon or fibre glass tip can also be used as a shock absorber once a fish is hooked. But there are obvious limitations.

Most pole anglers use flick tips when after small fish with baits like breadpunch, squats and bloodworm. It is more immediate for hitting finicky bites.

But where larger fish are expected then it's wise to use the elastic shock absorber. The most favoured set-up is the internal system which entails threading the elastic through the top two sections of pole. For this you will need a hollow top section or you'll have to cut the flick tip back just below where it is spliced. A PTFE bush is then fitted into the end to allow the plastic a free, smooth running passage out when under tension.

For tangle-free fishing, most pole anglers attach the elastic to a Stonfo elastic/line adaptor which has a quick-change release facility so you can change over pole rigs in seconds. Most pole elastic is colour coded now and here's a guide to their breaking strains and usages.

Colour	Breaking strain	Hooklengths
White	12oz	5-10oz
Red	1lb	10-14oz
Green	1.25lb	12oz-1.1lb
Blue	2.25lb	1.1-1.7lb
Black	3lb	1.7-2.6lb
Yellow	4lb	2.6-3.2lb

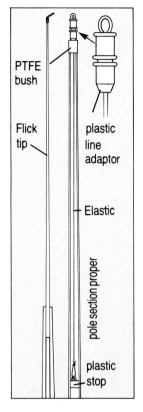

Above: *Flick tip and second section of pole fitted with internal elastic.*

Left: *What to look for when choosing a pole.*

UNSHIPPING SECTIONS

The easiest way of unshipping the sections on a long pole is to use a pole roller or your rod holdall positioned a couple of yards behind you and to slide several sections backwards at once. When using a flick tip or fine elastic shock absorber, the best way to bring the pole in, while unshipping sections, is to dip the top section under the water. This will cushion any jerky movement and helps to prevent bumping fish off the hook. This method works well for fish up to about 1lb.

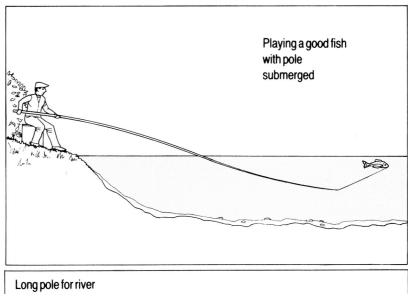

Playing a good fish
with pole
submerged

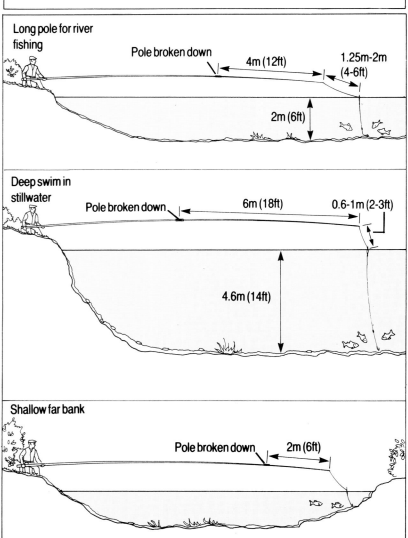

Long pole for river
fishing

Pole broken down   4m (12ft)   1.25m-2m
(4-6ft)

2m (6ft)

Deep swim in
stillwater

Pole broken down   6m (18ft)   0.6-1m (2-3ft)

4.6m (14ft)

Shallow far bank

Pole broken down   2m (6ft)

*Breaking down
different lengths of
pole for different
fishing situations.*

Obviously, it is not always possible to bring the pole back directly behind you, especially on a narrow canal towpath. If the

pole has to be brought round to the side while a fish is on, to unship sections it is probably better to keep the tip just above the water and to let the top sections and the flick tip – or elastic system – absorb any rough movements.

The only time the pole should be kept high when landing a fish is if a big specimen has been hooked and the swim is snaggy on the nearside. In this situation try and get the fish to the surface or high in the water and then bring it towards you, taking off one or two sections at a time.

The trick when fishing for larger fish against far bank snags, is to sink the pole tip very deep in the water while it is being pulled in. This often prevents the hooked fish from boring into snags overhanging into the swim.

SHORT OR LONG?

Perhaps the easiest method is fishing a short pole to hand. Matchmen often fish this way for speed purposes when there are a lot of small fish about. There are a variety of rigs you can use but the main criterion is that the end tackle can be swung in to hand without breaking down whatever length of pole you are using. Most anglers find this is best achieved with a rig which ends just short of the butt of the pole. This allows for the pole bending over when a fish is swung in towards them.

The long pole comes into its own when spot-on presentation is needed to tempt shy biting fish. On running water you can slow a hookbait down against the flow or stop it dead at far greater range than a rod and reel would allow. For this type of fishing use a longish line between pole tip and float for greater flexibility, say 4 to 6ft (1.25-2m). On stillwaters, a much shorter line is often needed – 2 to 3ft (60-100m) tightens up the control and speed at which you can lift into bites.

Another successful long pole method is fishing tight over to cover on small rivers and canals.

WEIGHTS AND FLOATS

The Olivette remains a firm favourite as a bulk weight for pole rigs. In the most popular sizes, it is now outlawed in lead but there are several good non-toxic designs.

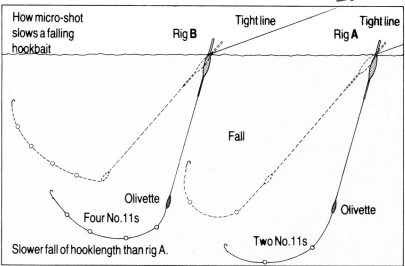

How micro-shot slows a falling hookbait

Rig **B**   Tight line   Rig **A**   Tight line

Fall

Olivette   Olivette

Four No.11s   Two No.11s

Slower fall of hooklength than rig A.

Above: How spreading more micro-shot slows a falling hookbait.

For finer presentation, Styl-leads or micro-shot are called up. The reason for using Styl-leads on a hooklength instead of micro shot is quite simple. A string of these will give the hookbait a slower descent. This has been taken a step further with very small pole floats on which Styls are now fished all the way down the rig for on-the-drop presentation.

Styls can be irritatingly difficult to apply to fine lines or dead easy – it's your choice. Without the proper Styl pinchers you're wasting your time. Even if you do fix them on the line they'll never be stable. Many anglers are put off buying Styl pinchers because they look more clumsy than ordinary forceps or tweezers. But they are just right for the job. The Styl-lead dispenser has fenced off areas for each compartment to spill out its contents. The idea is that you select those Styls which tumble out face down by picking them up with the jaws of the pinchers and then nipping them on the line. The pinchers give an even pressure along the whole length of the Styl keeping the line dead central so it won't spring out at the ends when the line is taut.

Generally, micro shot are less tangle prone than Styls so use them when a lot of fish are expected. Styls come into their own when the fishing is hard. They give just a slight edge which can make all the difference when baits like squatts and bloodworm are used.

FLOAT FACTORS

When selecting a selection of pole floats certain questions must be asked to narrow down the choice. For example, you need to ask yourself which floats will benefit your fishing. Do the different designs really offer a functional advantage or are they gimmicky?

CANE OR WIRE STEM?

Cane stems give a float better flight through the air when an Olivette is being used and that's why they're recommended for fishing to hand. This can involve fishing a very small float with the same length of line as the pole being used for close in work, say between 2 and 5 metres.

But it is also popular to fish much longer poles in the same manner for speed pur-

poses. All this requires is to beef up the float size to get the tackle out. For 5-7 metre lines use a No. 7 to 9 Olivette, 8-10 metres anything between a No. 10 to 15.

Wire stems are there purely to stabilise a float – to give the angler better control – and that's particularly welcome in blustery conditions. By losing some of a rig's weight in the float itself, it is possible to retain a high degree of sensitivity while retaining the correct weight loading to make a task like fishing a long pole a great deal easier.

The three chief styles of float can be broadly categorised as slims, body down floats and body up. There are varying

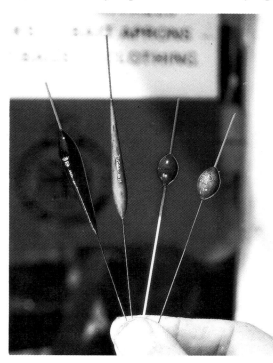

Left: Wire and cane stem pole floats with a choice of bodies.

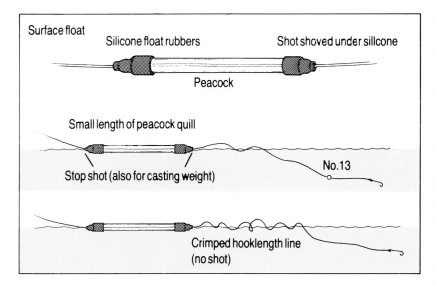

Surface float   Silicone float rubbers   Shot shoved under silicone

Peacock

Small length of peacock quill

Stop shot (also for casting weight)   No.13

Crimped hooklength line (no shot)

degrees of sensitivity within each banding but the slims are the most delicate design and are chiefly used on canals and still-waters.

The body down models take over when the slims become unstable in adverse conditions on canals or in deeper swims. The body ups are ideal for holding back in flow or ordinary trotting work.

SURFACE FLOAT

There is still a shortage of good surface fishing floats and it is best to improvise your own designs out of peacock quill. For this type of fishing the float doesn't need to be fancy. It is purely on the line to add casting weight.

Once the float has landed on the surface of the water it can be ignored! It's far better to watch the hooklength line which should be crimped up with a fingernail for better visibility.

With this rig it helps to grease the hooklength for improved floatability and visibility. Bites are easily spotted – the coils of line snake away below the surface. With an extra long hooklength, a tiny number 13 shot can be added near the hook causing the coils of line to sink very slowly. Bites either move the float along the surface or speed up the line sinking dramatically.

SHOTTING PATTERNS

Most pole floats are so sensitive that it takes quite a deal of time to set them up correctly. It's a difficult task on the bank and that's

Pincers for picking-up and fixing Styl-leads on the line.

why it's a good idea to prepare them at home, storing a good selection of ready to use rigs on winders. The diagrams above will help get you started.

RIVERS

A bulk weight is essential for the majority of river pole fishing. The easiest and least tangle prone is the Olivette. The best balance is achieved by weighting a float with an Olivette slightly lighter than the float's full capacity, leaving enough scope for the addition of two or three dust shot.

For this type of fishing a main line is used and a lighter hooklength. The Olivette is always positioned on the main line, never the hooklength. This avoids losing the bulk weight if the hook snags up. Usually, the hooklength is between 18 and 24in long to gain sufficient elasticity from the lighter, more fragile line. But sometimes you'll find the hooklength needs to be shortened considerably when fishing small fish baits like bloodworm. Here the loss of some of the hooklength's shock resistance is overcome by using an elastic shock absorber.

For trotting work the Olivette is positioned just above an 18in hooklength, stopping it with a No.8 shot with two No.8s or 10s at equal distances down the hooklength. In slow currents it can be helpful to use lighter Styl weights instead of dust shot to give an even slower rate of descent to the hookbait.

With this versatile river rig you have the option of moving the Olivette up the line as far as mid-depth to create a slow on-the-drop rig if the fish move up in the water. Or you can deepen the float and hold the tackle back hard against the flow to slow its rate of movement through the swim.

With the second rig it usually helps to add an extra shot, something like a BB, below the Olivette. This is called over-shotting and prevents the float from riding up out of the water when you hold the tackle back or edge the float through the swim. It is probably the most tightly controlled form of pole fishing and on hard days you get bites you'd never have seen on conventional gear.

CANALS

A much lighter variation of the river rig can be fished effectively on canals where the

Olivette is often used for speed instead of control to get the hookbait down quickly among the fish when they are feeding energetically. It also helps plunge the bait through to quality fish down below without it being pinched by small fry up top.

When more finesse is required a string of micro shot or Styl-leads are used in preference to the Olivette. They can be strung out in normal stick float fashion or grouped as a bulk weight where the Olivette would have been. The idea is to fish normally with this set-up until the fish move up in the water or become cagey. Then you experiment by stringing the weights out for a slower rate of descent.

Styl weights react very differently to a bulk weight. They can pick up subtle undertow and pull the tackle through more naturally, gaining vital extra bites on hard venues.

LAKES

Although the shape of float is likely to be different for lake or stillwater fishing, the weighting down the line can be very similar to river or canal rigs. In shallow water, the canal set-up is recommended while for deep water the river Olivette rig can prove useful in getting the hookbait down speedily or improving control over awkward surface drift.

Sometimes, a compromise of a high Olivette and then a string of small Styl-leads down to the hook works wonders, especially for fish like skimmers and roach which tend to intercept a hook bait just as it settles.

LINES FOR THE POLE

Forget about the lines you use for free running rigs when you switch to the pole. Your favourite waggler or stick float line may not be supple enough to give proper presentation with delicate pole floats. If you're fishing an elastic shock absorber with the pole, then you can afford to use a much lighter breaking strain. It is also possible to incorporate much finer hooklengths, down to as light as 5oz! If you're using very low breaking strain hooklengths, the main line doesn't have to be quite as heavy as you're used to on running line. For example, lines from 5oz up to 12oz tied on the hook can be matched to 1-1.5lb main lines which will hardly affect a delicate pole float. The same

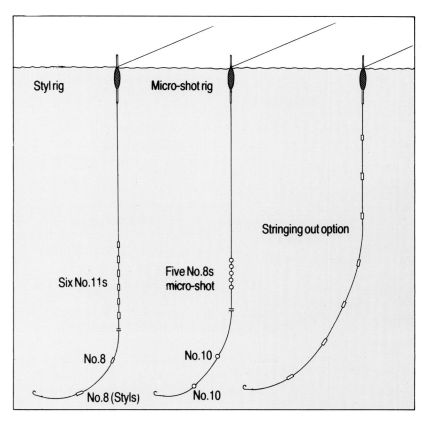

float might react very differently with 2lb line which could pull it off course and even lift the float up out of the water.

So when you come to making your pole rigs up, what breaking strains do you base them on? Well, 12oz line is very fine and hard to break with internal elastic. The elastic puts 12oz into the category of 1.5 or 1.7lb. It is also well suited to hooks ranging from fine wire 18s down to tiny 24s and for baits from plain maggots to casters, bread-

Top: Shotting pattern.

Above: All Styl or micro-shot pole rigs.

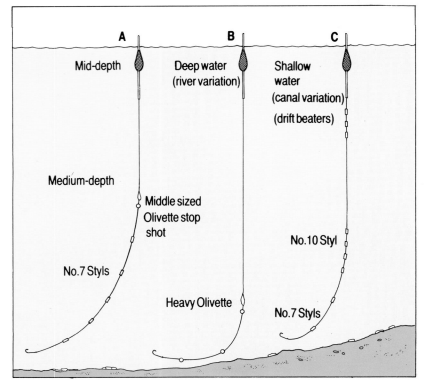

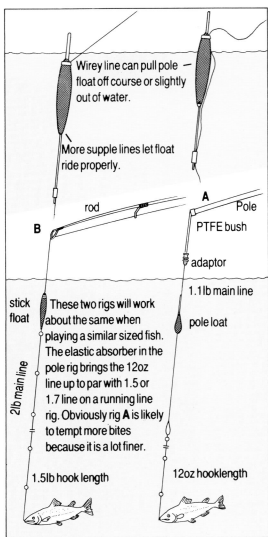

Above: Lake pole rigs.

Right: Streamline tungsten Olivettes benefit from a silicone insert to prevent any abrasion on rough edges and to act as a buffer against the micro stop shot. Frst slice through the end of a length of silicone to create a taper for easy threading. Tie nylon line to the tapered end of the silicone and thread the mono through several Olivettes. Now pull the silicone through each of the weights.

punch, hemp, bloodworm, pinkies and squatts. If you make up 50 per cent of your pole rigs to this line on the hooklength you shouldn't go far wrong.

This leaves scope to make up some extra fine scratching rigs down to 8oz or 5oz or a few stepped up 1lb and 1.7lb bottoms for those weedy swims where a big tench or small carp might put in an appearance.

HOW LONG A HOOKLENGTH?

There is quite a debate among top pole anglers as to how long a hooklength should be. The trend is to make up very short lengths down to 6in which contradicts what most line manufacturers recommend. It's a fact that the shorter a length of fine line, the less its breaking strain becomes – because elasticity is lost.

Make your hooklengths up on the long side with a minimum of 12in (30cm) up to 3ft (1m) if you can get away with it.

POLE FISHING ACCESSORIES

Winders

Once you've made up your pole rig there are plenty of different winders available to store it on. There are extra wide winders for

bodied floats and you can buy nylon clips to anchor the end of line in place. For slimmer floats which fit on thinner winders, pole rig anchors are an absolute must to hold everything in place.

Feeding aids

A small, light actioned catapult is handy for putting out squatts, pinkies and casters beyond eight metres. Another solution for spot on accuracy in flowing water is to use a small baitdropper.

The pole cup is favourite where normal groundbaiting techniques scare the fish. It consists of a small plastic open-ended cup which is fixed to the top section of the pole by a quick release clip and filled with the required feed. The pole is then manoeuvred over the fishing spot and turned over so the cup releases its contents. Excellent for

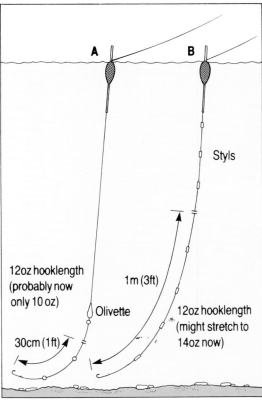

A   B

Styls

12oz hooklength
(probably now
only 10 oz)

1m (3ft)

Olivette

12oz hooklength
(might stretch to
14oz now)

30cm (1ft)

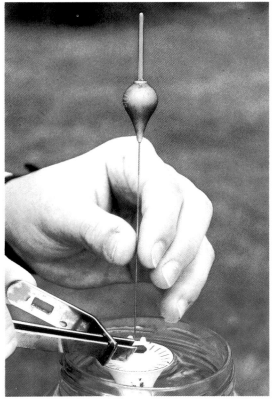

Far left: Increasing the breaking strain potential by lengthening the hooklength.

Making up pole rigs at home.
Left: This device, called a Dosapiombo makes it possible to gauge the exact weight loading required for any pole float. First clip the float inside a locking slot. Place the Dosapiombo in a container of water where it will float with the entire float standing proud of the surface. Gently drop Olivettes on the rim using tweezers or pinchers. The float will now descend to the precise depth.
Below left: *Make fine adjustments using micro-shot to submerge the float's antenna by the required amount.*

feeding baits like raw bloodworm, jokers, squatts or casters.

Rests and rollers

A good pole roller is useful because apart from making unshipping of several sections at once an easy task, it also prevents the pole from being damaged by shingle and bankside vegetation.

One of the pole rest designs which fits to the side of the tackle box can be a good investment. You can place the pole in this type of rest while you're feeding the swim. Another useful device for taking the strain out of long pole fishing is the backrest. The extendable mini pole roller fits to the back of your tackle box.

Tackle boxes

If you are going to take up pole fishing seriously then a suitable tackle box is a priority purchase. Continental boxes are in vogue because most designs have three or four drawers or lift up trays. These are ideal for housing accessories like winders.

If possible, a box which takes attachable groundbait trays is very useful, keeping groundbait or hookbaits easily to hand. Other good accessories for the box are a fishing platform for sloping banks or adjustable legs which can be bolted to the box.

THE CARP BOOM

A

B   C

TYPES OF CARP

The carp was first introduced into this country about 500 years ago and kept in monastery ponds as a food source. There are few true descendants of these fish left today because the strain has been diluted. Those that do exist are called wildies and are chub-like in profile. The wildie has small, uniform scales covering its whole body and rarely exceeds 10lb in weight. Unless you know the stocking history of a particular water where they are reported to be present, then there is no guarantee that the fish are true wildies. The slow growth of wildies inspired selective breeding from faster growing fingerlings.

King carp

The painstaking process of selection was repeated with wildies until the prolific king carp emerged. There are numerous strains of this with distinctive scale patterns. They fall into three groups which are popularly classified as common carp, leather carp and mirror carp.

Common carp have scales covering the entire body. They retain the same orderly scale pattern as the original wildie but have a more rounded body shape. *Leather carp*, also known as nude carp, have no scales whatsoever. *Mirror carp* have scales of various shapes and sizes, scattered haphazardly all over the body. There are also peculiarities among the mirrors such as the linear and fully-scaled mirror. The linear has two perfect rows of scales on each side of the body, one along the length of the lateral line and the other across the back just below the dorsal fin. The fully scaled mirror is similar to the common with scales covering its entire body but they are not of uniform

The great equalisers
The development of the hair-rig followed by the launch of commercially manufactured boilie baits brought carpfishing success within everybody's reach. Here's the recommended method for mounting a boilie with the hair trapped midway along the hook shank.

A. Hair tied from eye of hook with Nash air bead to hold boilie in place and small piece of silicone rubber slid down hook length.
B. Push silicone over eye and halfway down shank. Slot baiting needle in concave end of hair bead and push through boilie.
C. Remove bead from end of baiting needle and withdraw through bait leaving boilie trapped on hair.

size and shape. This latter scale pattern is probably the rarest of all.

FOOD CHAINS

King carp survive in just about every type of fishery, from fast flowing rivers and huge reservoirs to muddy canals. But gravel pits are the ideal location because they usually boast excellent water quality and rich weed growth. The varying depth of the gravel seams results in a tremendous fluctuation in levels and the creation of bars and troughs in which debris accumulates to trigger the start of the food chain.

This type of environment is absolutely ideal for the chief dietary needs of the carp such as bloodworm, shrimp and mussels.

THE COMPLETE CARP OUTFIT

Opposite bottom: *Two-tone common with uniform scale pattern. Carp displaying markedly different colour bands like this are relatively rare.*

You will never see me at the lakeside with all this equipment on the same day. I believe in travelling light otherwise mobility is sacrificed. But every single item of gear pictured here has been developed for a specific job, with the exception of the ice cream tubs!

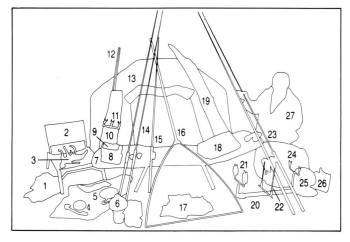

1 Nash zip sacks to retain specimen carp for photography. They will hold any size of fish in complete safety as water passes freely through thousands of tiny holes in the weave. The carp cannot see out and there is no danger of it becoming distressed while held captive in the dark. A heavy duty, waterproof zip sewn along the side of the black sack makes it much easier to place fish inside than a drawstring. The sack is tethered to a bank stick by a D ring and lanyard.

2 Fox International low chair which is ideal for short sessions or stalking. Adjustable legs and antisink, swivel feet make it stable on uneven or soft banks. Replacement parts can be obtained for all the components.

3 Feeding accessories to deal with different baits and distances. McCarthy *Pro-pult catapult* is for short-range baiting with boilies and for spraying particle baits. Wide gape aluminium frame with latex elastics and large pouch. Cobra swan-necked *throwing stick* to hurl hard, small diameter boilies up to 80 yards. Made from black anodised aluminium with rubber grip. Marksman's hunting *catapult* will fire boilies beyond 100 yards. Powerful latex elastics and slimline pouch. Gardner *Mixer Fixer,* a combined controller and bait dispenser for fishing particle floaters at long range. Gardner *Bait Rocket* also deposits particles or mini boilies beyond catapulting limits.

4 Salter tubular spring balance. Made of brass; records up to 44lb in 8oz graduations. Nash weigh-sling with nose pouch and drawstrings suitable for weighing carp to 30lb.

5 Nash dial scales record to 56lb in 4oz divisions. Moulded plastic design and very accurate. Used with Nash crescent-shaped, weighing bag which will cradle any size of carp.

6 Tea-making equipment. Tubs hold teabags, sugar and powdered milk. Millets camping kettle and Colman petrol cooking-stove complete the field kitchen.

7 Fox International Bowframe Bedchair. Heavy duty construction with adjustable legs. Positive locking system on the back frame. All four legs have swivel feet. Strong olive green canvas cover is foam-filled for extra comfort.

8 Ice cream containers for odds and ends of tackle stack neatly in tackle bag.

9 Optix Cormorant sunglasses with amber lenses to cut out surface glare.

10 Nash stalking sling. Ideal for travelling light when moving from swim to swim. Holds umbrella, bank sticks and landing net. Comfortable shoulder strap.

11 Custom-made buzzer bars engineered from high quality steel. These adjustable bars carry two or three rods.

12 Spare rod for emergency use or to fling out the Bait Rocket.

13 Nash 50in nylon brolly overwrap. Heavy duty nylon with built-in mud skirts. Double zip door has clear-view panel.

14 Long range, 2¼lb test curve rods. Custom-built 12ft Armalite blanks with abbreviated Duplon handles and Fuji FSP reel fitting. There are seven rings with the intermediates being single-leg Fuji silicone carbides. The butt is a three-legged model from the same range and the tip ring is 10mm diameter. These rods are teamed with Mitchell 300 reels which are ideal for long-range fishing because of their very even line lay.

15 Jungle stalking stick. This is made from a North Western carp blank cut down to 8ft. The 20in butt has a Duplon handle and there are six heavy-duty, Fuji eyes. The test curve is about 2¾lb.

16 Dual mesh landing net with Gardner handle and Conoflex arms. There's a slot in the aluminium spreader block in which an isotope is glued for night fishing.

17 Shelf-life Crafty Catcher boilies. The range includes King Prawn, Black Cherry, Caribbean Cocktail, Dairy Cream Fudge, Peanut Pro and Strawberry.

18 Sleeping bag rated at 13 Tog. Full length, quick-release zip, built-in head bag and groundsheet. Waterproof overbag for monsoon weather.

19 Nash Hooker holdall. Takes six rods – three of which can be already made up with reels – landing net, umbrella, bank sticks and buzzer bars. There's a full length nylon zip, carrying handle and shoulder strap.

20 Gardner Rod Pod for hard or concrete banks which bank sticks will not penetrate.

21 Super Compact Optonics with latching LED's plus volume and tone controls. Line travels over sensitive vane wheel which breaks a photo-electric cell to set off the alarm. They run on PP3 batteries.

22 Monkey climb needles and bars. Custom-made from stainless steel. Indicators have flip-tops and milled slots for isotopes.

23 Short- to medium-range rods. Tri-cast 1¾lb test curve, through action blanks with full length Duplon handles and Fuji FSP reel fittings. Fuji silicone carbide rings throughout. Normally used with Abu Cardinal 55 reels for open bale arm fishing.

24 Nash Rucksack takes everything – if you've got the back muscles to cope! Multitude of external pockets. Exceptionally robust.

25 Bucket of peanuts flavoured with maple and sweeteners.

26 Pedigree Chum Mixer. The most popular surface bait. It can be used straight from the box or soaked with colour and flavour.

27 Hardy waterproof jacket.

BEHAVIOUR & LOCATION

NATURAL FEEDING ZONES

The carp's customary feeding zones are obviously found where there is the greatest concentration of natural food. At times, the preferred food item can be so abundant that the carp feed on it exclusively. For example, carp rooting through a large bed of bloodworm become preoccupied to the point where they are oblivious of any other food source that they come across. When this happens carp are very difficult to catch.

Shady spots

Carp also love feeding under the protective canopy of trees and bushes where they feel secure. Rotting vegetation in these shaded spots attracts plenty of insects but the food supplies are often quickly exhausted. A new feeding patch might be dirty for a time but once the bottom starts to appear much cleaner then the chances of hooking a fish are very good indeed. Ultimately the feeding patch will be swept completely clean by the carp leaving no natural food there at all. When that happens the carp depart and graze the bottom somewhere else.

Weed beds

Weed beds are another environment liked by carp. They'll spend hours picking snails from the underside of lily pads and broad-leafed pond weed or browsing through dense strands of Canadian pond weed. When it's very hot they'll tend to bask in the middle of the weed and only give themselves away by tenting or by the odd slurp.

Artificial hotspots

Artificial feeding zones are frequently created on lakes and ponds by anglers concentrating their efforts in favourite swims. This is particularly true when particle-type baits are regularly introduced. Hundreds of particles sink into the bottom silt and carp dig merrily away to find them.

FEEDING TIMES

The popular belief is that carp feed more vigorously at night but I've never found this to be true. Perhaps the main reason why the night myth has developed is because carp waters are generally quieter during the hours of darkness. The carp hunter is usually sound asleep and with no movement on the bank the carp are much more likely to venture into his swim.

The only period when feeding cycles do appear to become fixed is in the winter months. In cold, wintry conditions carp barely move a muscle for hour after hour.

FISH SPOTTING

There are behaviour patterns largely peculiar to the carp which assist greatly in locating the fish.

Perhaps carps' most spectacular behaviour is their habit of leaping clear from the water and crashing back down again. It's possible these gymnasts crash into the bottom silt to disturb bloodworm and rush around to gobble them up while they are free swimming. Then once they have a great mouthful of mud and bloodworm the carp feel the need to clean their gill covers and they do this by leaping.

Bow-waving is another common sight as a fast moving fish leaves a bulge of water in its wake. This is usually caused by a carp fleeing from an area in which it no longer feels safe.

Probably the most promising location pointer of all is bubbling. Sometimes a release of natural gases from the bottom is mistaken for a feeding fish but it's easy enough to tell the two apart. Carp will not bubble in the same spot for more than a few minutes at a time. More often than not they move along at a steady rate. The trick is to sit down and line up the bubbles with a marker on the far bank and see if the bubbles start to move. If they do, they're coming from a fish.

BAITS AND PRESENTATION

BOILIE BENEFITS

The versatile and productive boilie has emerged as the nation's favourite bait because it allows us to target carp more positively and avoid unwanted species of fish. Proven ingredients include virtually every edible substance under the sun that can be ground down or freeze dried and then whisked up with eggs to form the boilie mix. Fish meals, meat meals, carbohydrates, vegetable proteins – they've all been used with varying degrees of success.

Ready-made boilies

Shelf-life or frozen, ready-made boilies are the solution if you do not have the time or confidence to produce your own. There is a massive selection on sale including neutral boilies to which you can add your own colour and flavour.

NARROWING THE CHOICE

How do you narrow it all down to the right hookbait for the job? First, you must decide if you need a surface bait, bottom bait, or even a midwater bait. Obviously, there is little point in presenting a bottom bait in 10ft of water when most of the carp are cruising on top. That calls for a surface bait and the actual choice may hinge on what other kinds of fish, apart from carp, are present in the same swim. For example, rudd would tear apart a piece of floating crust in seconds and you'd need something more resistant such as a hard floating boilie or even a sunflower seed.

If there are a lot of carp on the surface it is tactically wrong to risk hooking one and spooking the rest. Far better to get them preoccupied on a mass floating bait before risking a cast. It's amazing how little notice carp take of a hooked fish in their midst when they're preoccupied and competing for a scattering of surface baits.

If there is a lone carp rather than a shoal then it is probably better to present a single floating bait. Catapulting out particles would give it too many snacks to choose from and that then reduces your chances of a take.

The choice of bottom bait is also dictated by other species present in the swim. If the carp are grossly outnumbered by bream and tench there would be no point in fishing luncheon meat, sweetcorn or soft paste. A rock hard boilie or tiger nut would be required.

There is also a definite limit to the distance many baits can be fished. Under normal circumstances it is hopeless to try to fish a mass particle more than 30yd out. At very long range – in excess of 100yd – the only choice is a dense, hard boilie.

It is wise to keep an open mind about baits and assess each water separately. If you are unable to visit a lake often enough to test individual baits you may well have to rely on local information. But make sure that it is supported by hard facts.

POWERS OF ATTRACTION

After selecting the bait type, what about other factors such as its colour, smell, texture and size?

Is colour important?

I do not believe colour is crucial although there are times when it is beneficial to pick a specific shade. For instance, on a hungry water where fish are competing for food a brightly coloured and highly visual bait is an advantage. Conversely, where the fish are spooky in clear water it may prove necessary to camouflage the bait to make it inconspicuous and rely on smell as the chief attractor.

Colour is of no importance at all for surface baits because they all appear black when silhouetted on the surface against the sky. But colour-coded boilies are helpful for identification purposes. You'll find brown for maple and red for strawberry is a life-saver if the contents of packs get jumbled!

Why smell matters

The carp detects a great deal of its food using its powerful sense of smell and every successful bait capitalises on this fact. Bread, cheese and meat owe most of their potency to smell. The majority of particles possess individual smells, some of which can't be bettered – maples, kidney beans and tiger nuts are good examples. Other particles such as black-eyed beans, chick peas and haricots appear to work better with extra flavour added. As for boilies and pastes, the smell could almost be considered essential whether it's a natural flavour along the lines of squid, yeast and liver or a synthetic such as Tutti Frutti, Dairy Cream Fudge or Hawaiian Tropical.

Size

When possible, I like to fish baits which are half an inch in diameter or less. Carp are more prepared to accept a bait of these dimensions than an unnatural looking offering the size of a tennis ball.

As a rule of thumb, the smaller the bait the more you'll need to introduce. There's little point in trying to trick a carp with a single grain of hemp or buckwheat. The possibility of it finding such a small morsel is very remote. But introduce an extensive carpet of the the same bait, covering an area 4ft square, for example, and the chances are that several carp will move in and clean up every last grain.

But you can't apply the same principle to boilies. A single, 1in-diameter boilie which is correctly flavoured will give off the same attractive smell as a bed of hemp, and the carp will react accordingly. The size of bait is also dictated by the range being fished. It is impossible to fish rape seed any further than a few yards from the bank whereas boilies can be catapulted over 100m.

High-protein bait

Ultimately, the potential of a bait is generally considered to depend not so much on appearance or texture but on its protein content. Carp are thought to be capable of choosing between baits containing 70 per cent protein which do them a power of good and less satisfying mouthfuls with lower protein levels. That's the theory anyway,

and it's really the same principle as the carp learning by association. Over a period of time they get accustomed to picking up a certain type of bait and find they need to consume less of this food source to satisfy their bodily needs.

Unfortunately, this doesn't happen overnight and an intensive baiting campaign with a highly nutritious bait is easily undermined by somebody using a bait with the same smell but a considerably lower protein content. Food for thought there!

PARTICLE PREOCCUPATION

In the right hands, particles are one of the most devastating baits available. The

How to flavour Chum mixer
When carp become wary of floating dog biscuits, a dash of flavour can make a world of difference. Here's the most effective method. Stir 10ml of the chosen flavour into a glass filled a quarter-full of water and then pour the mixture into a plastic bag containing ½kg (1lb) of dry Mixer. Blow air into bag and shake for several minutes until liquid is evenly distributed. Leave overnight to ensure flavour completely penetrates.

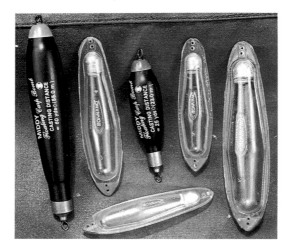

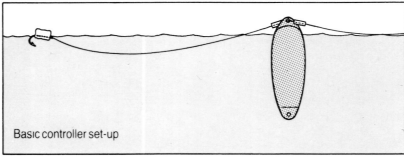

Basic controller set-up

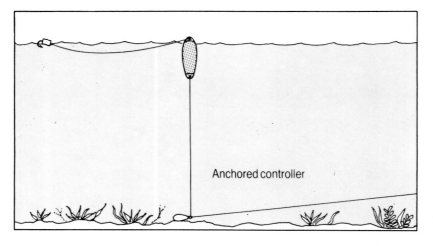

Anchored controller

Top: Controllers for staking out surface baits at short to middle ranges.

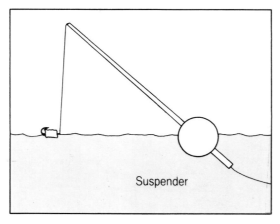

Suspender

essence of particle fishing is to substitute the carp's largest single item of food with your own chosen bait. When carried out correctly, it is possible to persuade the fish to preoccupy themselves with particles in much the same way as they would naturally feed exclusively on an abundance of bloodworm, for example.

Usually, the smaller the particle the greater the degree of preoccupation. With small seeds such as hemp, rape and dari, you might need as much as 5lb of bait per fish in the swim at any one time and that could call for 30lb of bait carpeting a small area. If the particles are larger than about peanut size I do not believe it's possible to achieve a total state of preoccupation.

You will also find certain particles are more instant acting than others and so require less baiting up. The most instant ones are maples or mini-maples. Black-eyed beans and chick peas are also in this category although they seem to work more effectively when flavoured.

The particle preoccupation has been taken to extremes on some waters, chiefly with tiger nuts and peanuts. What happens is that one or two anglers start catching well on these nuts and it has a knock-on effect. Soon everybody on the lake is fishing the same bait and it is just about impossible to catch carp on anything else. The lake's entire carp population becomes totally preoccupied with nuts. I do not like to hear of this occurring because it is detrimental to the well-being of the carp which needs a balanced diet to survive in the peak of condition.

On balance, the most consistent of the smaller particles over the seasons have been hemp, rape and dari seeds, and buckwheat. Middle-sized baits I'd recommend are tares, maples, chick peas, sweetcorn or maize, haricots and black-eyed beans. Among the larger particles, tiger nuts, peanuts and kidney beans have caught plenty of fish.

SURFACE RIGS AND BAITS

For sheer excitement you can't beat catching carp off the top. A cube of crust is the oldest form of floater but the most popular offerings are dog and catfood biscuits. They are excellent carp catchers and are cheap and convenient to use with little or no pre-

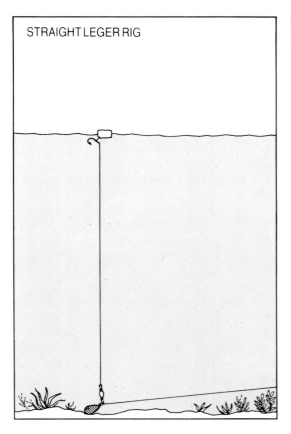

STRAIGHT LEGER RIG

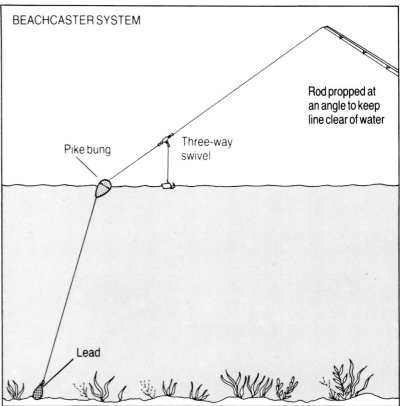

BEACHCASTER SYSTEM

Rod propped at an angle to keep line clear of water

Pike bung

Three-way swivel

Lead

paration needed. The most popular of the brands is Chum Mixer. Pet biscuits should be fished with a controller to provide casting weight.

FISHING A CONTROLLER

There are numerous commercially-made controllers but all function in the same manner. They are usually fitted with an eye or swivel at both ends and have a coloured top for visibility. A leaded bottom aids casting and cocks the controller. A controller can be fixed on the line with a couple of stops. For preference I would use silicone rubber wedged in place with a piece of cocktail stick. I position a stop either side of the controller after passing the line through the top eye or swivel.

With a single floating particle, mount it on a hair or the shank of a size 10 or 12 hook. The length of the hook link must be a minimum of 2ft and when using a nylon trace make sure it's sunk below the surface otherwise carp will see it in silhouette and take fright. If the fish finally become wary of the sunken nylon, change to a dental floss hook length. The multistranded, waxed version

marketed by Johnson and Johnson is fine. Once the floss is wet the strands separate out and resemble a soft stalk of weed floating on the surface. It certainly fools the carp for a while.

If surface drift causes problems with the controller rig then a running lead will hold the bait in position. The lead is slid on first and the end of the line attached to the bottom eye of the controller with the hook link attached at the top. After casting out, line is released from the reel once it has been buried beneath the water to allow the controller to rise to the surface.

If the carp are really spooky and avoid a hookbait fished in this manner, the answer could be the Suspender. This is a controller with a difference – the hook length does not touch the water. The device consists of a long, rigid plastic tube with a polyball and counterbalance weight attached at the bottom. Line is passed through the centre of the tube and the hook tied at the end. The length of line between the hook and tip of the Suspender is carefully adjusted so no nylon rests on the surface. The Suspender is fished on its own or with a running lead when drift or drag must be overcome.

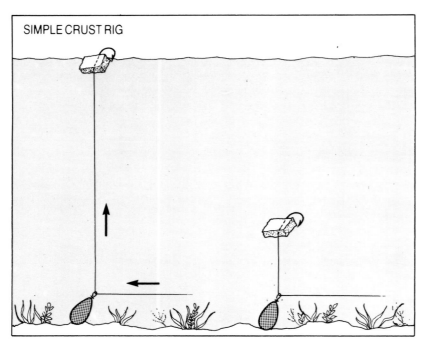

SIMPLE CRUST RIG

Beachcaster system

Another surface fishing set-up which avoids line touching the surface is the beachcaster rig. This effective method is restricted to waters no deeper than about 10ft or the length of your rod. A lead of 2oz or more is tied to the end of the main line and a pike bung or similar size float attached, to fish just over depth. The hook length is tied in about 2ft above the bung from a three-way swivel. Now the bait will sit on the surface with no line touching if the rod is propped up just off the vertical.

Straight leger

A surface rig that can be used with just about any floating bait is a straightforward leger with the Arlesey bomb running directly on the main line and a hook length that corresponds exactly to the depth of the swim. Again, this rig can only be used in swims that are less than 10ft deep or it will be impossible to cast out.

A similar method for depths greater than the length of the rod is the simple floating crust rig. The lead is totally free running and, as previously, line is buried and then released from the spool until the buoyant floater bobs to the surface. When stalking the margins or fishing at close range there is no need for any of these casting aids – the bait is freelined.

Mounting surface baits

Floating boilies are normally best fished side-hooked or with a short hair. The most widely used surface particle, Chub Mixer, is buoyant enough to fish directly on the shank of the hook or from a short hair. These round biscuits should be soaked beforehand to make them easier to mount – a needle sharp hook will blunt very quickly if you attempt to force it through a crunchy Mixer. A crafty rig idea for this bait is to mount a quarter piece of Mixer on the eye of a size 10 or 12 hook and then attach the largest biscuit you can find in the box to a long hair. Carp often swirl at Mixer to try to break it up before taking down the smaller pieces. This rig simulates that.

Sometimes carp suck in and blow out a particle floater faster than the human eye can see. This habit often develops when they've been caught frequently on baits such as Mixer, and for a period they will appear almost impossible to catch on conventional rigs. That's the moment to step in with a free-sliding surface bait. The idea is that the carp blows the bait back up the line but the hook is left trailing behind with a good chance that it will prick the fish in the lip. To construct this rig you'll need to push a short piece of small diameter rig tubing through the centre of the bait. This is easily done by first boring a hole through the bait with a drill bit or something similar. The tubing is then inserted leaving a short piece protruding either side of the floater. Slide the bait up the hooklink and tie on the hook, taking care to leave an untrimmed end of at least .25in. This untrimmed piece is tucked back inside the rig tubing to prevent the bait flying up the line prematurely on the cast. One final point: if you fish the sliding Mixer rig with a controller, you will achieve a better strike rate.

BOTTOM RIGS AND BAIT

In the days of soft paste baits all you did was mould a chunk around the hook. A strong strike easily pulled the hook free of the bait and into the carp's mouth.

Then some forward thinking anglers decided to roll their baits in little balls and boil them for a few minutes to give a tough outer skin. The main reason for doing this was to stop nuisance fish attacking and

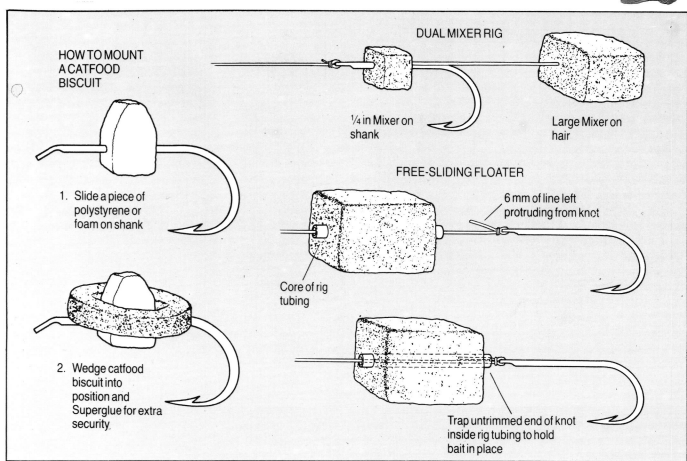

DUAL MIXER RIG

¼ in Mixer on shank

Large Mixer on hair

HOW TO MOUNT A CATFOOD BISCUIT

1. Slide a piece of polystyrene or foam on shank

2. Wedge catfood biscuit into position and Superglue for extra security.

FREE-SLIDING FLOATER

6 mm of line left protruding from knot

Core of rig tubing

Trap untrimmed end of knot inside rig tubing to hold bait in place

whittling away the more vulnerable paste baits. These new skinned baits were fine as deterrents against unwanted small fish but it was just about impossible to heave a hook through them on the strike.

Gradually, anglers started mounting baits with the point and bend of the hook exposed and the emergence of the sidehooked boilie was the first of the selfhooking rigs as we know them today.

It was observed that a side-hooked boilie fished with a front clip on the rod to combat drift produced much faster takes and a bigger percentage of fish on the bank. The hook on this rig also started to get larger with more of it exposed. I suppose this was really the start of the bolt rig.

Bolt rig

A true bolt rig comprises a short hooklink between 5-7in, with a very large, barbless, needle-sharp hook. The best hook is a Mustad Viking 94845 in size 1 and 2. These are a fine wire, forged barbless pattern with a

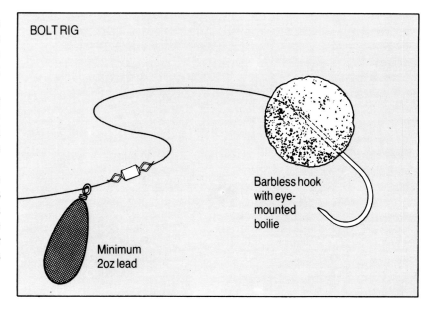

BOLT RIG

Barbless hook with eye-mounted boilie

Minimum 2oz lead

down-turned tapered ball eye. A ½-in diameter boilie is mounted directly on the eye and a heavy lead of 2oz or more must be used with the line tightly clipped up. When the carp sucks in the bait and bolts on feeling the lead, the hook drives itself home.

Above and above centre:
Counterbalanced rig for snaggy swims. The hook is made to float with a blob of foam on the bend. Hair-mounted bait is tied directly to the eye. When balanced out correctly the hook floats directly above the bait. The pattern is a size 4 Super Specimen tied to 15lb dental floss.

Above right and opposite top: Sliding pop-up. Highly successful rig which allows the ring with its hair-mounted boilie to be free running between the hook and counterbalancing split-shot. To make a ring simply cut the eye off a suitable sized hook. Once the rig is sucked in and then ejected, the bait slides up the hook link leaving the size 10 Super Specimen hook inside the carp's mouth.

Hair rig: how it works

The hair rig is simply a highly effective self-hooking method. With the hair there's a much greater chance of the free hook actually catching on a fleshy part inside the carp's mouth.

Attaching the hair

By far the most efficient place to attach the hair is halfway *along the shank*. This ensures that the hook goes in the carp's mouth, bend first. When ejected it will pivot round trying to force the hook out, eye first. That gives an excellent chance of the point pricking in the carp's mouth.

A good hook for this rig is the Drennan Super Specialist. It is fairly wide in the gape, has a chemically sharpened point and is constructed on strong wire.

The best method of constructing a hair rig is to tie the hair to the eye of the hook then slide a small piece of silicone rubber down the hooklink. Feed the rubber over the eye of the hook and trap the hair in exactly the right position on the shank.

The hair itself can be a length of 1lb Dacron which is very supple and allows the bait to move freely in an arc inside the carp's mouth with less chance of it pulling the hook out of line. The drawback with this

material is that it breaks very easily. If that causes you problems, try separating the strands of unwaxed dental floss – a single strand has a breaking strain of about 4lb.

After extensive experiments I have found that a hair length of about ¾in (2cm) between the bait and hook is the most consistent catcher.

Hair stops and beads. There are numerous ways of trapping the bait on a hair. Kevin Nash beads and stops are the easiest and most efficient way in my experience. The plastic beads are hollowed out at one end to take a purpose-made, blunt-ended baiting needle and there is a small hole at the other end through which the hair is tied. It's a simple operation to push the bead and hair through the bait with the needle and then withdraw it leaving the boilie hanging on the hair.

With the Nash stop, a small loop is tied in the end of the hair and pulled through the bait with a slender 0.75 crochet hook. Then the dumbell-shaped hair stop is trapped in the loop against the bait, holding it firmly in place on the hair.

You can use the beads with all bottom boilies and soft particles while the hair stops are a better choice for pop-ups and harder particles. The crochet needle is slightly smaller in diameter than the hair bead and doesn't damage the outer skin of

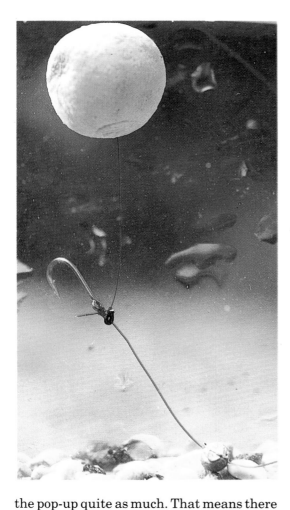

of about 12in. Lengthen it if you feel the carp hasn't got sufficient leeway to suck the bait in freely, or shorten it if it blows out without the fish pricking itself. The length of the hooklink should not be shorter than 9in or longer than 18in when fished with the hair rig.

Attaching hooks and swivels

Tying on hooks and swivels to hook traces demands great care. It is important to

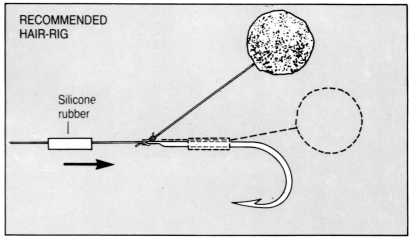

RECOMMENDED HAIR-RIG

Silicone rubber

the pop-up quite as much. That means there is less danger of the bait becoming water-logged and sinking to the bottom. It is also much easier to use a crochet hook with hard particles because forcing a bead through a hard bait soon loosens the knot attaching it to the hair.

Hook lengths. For the hook length, the leading materials are nylon, dental floss, Dacron, Kryston and Gamastrand polyethylene flosses and braids. Where links of 4-7lb are required, nylon is the first choice as there is no great advantage in using any other material in these lower breaking strains. Above 8lb I'm tending to use the Kryston type Silkworm braids in preference to the cheaper dental flosses which break at around 12lb. These new polyethylene braids are superbly limp and soft with a much slimmer diameter than the traditional Dacrons.

In heavily weeded or snaggy swims, Dacron of 15-20lb is used as the situation dictates. Providing you are not fishing over too silty a bottom, start off with a hooklink

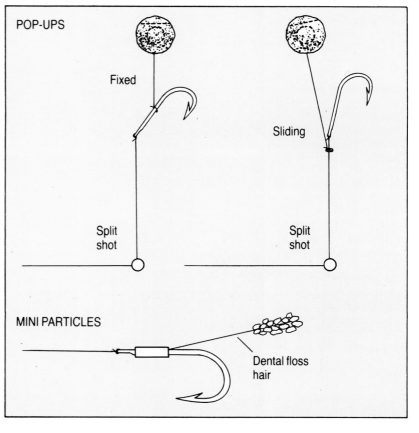

POP-UPS

Fixed

Sliding

Split shot

Split shot

MINI PARTICLES

Dental floss hair

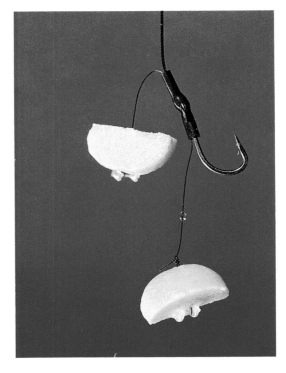

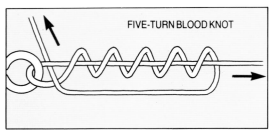

FIVE-TURN BLOOD KNOT

Above: *Bean or nut rig. Dacron hook link and hair with a size 10 Carp Catcher hook based on the Yorkshire Sedge pattern. There is no guarantee which way round the bait will be taken in and this shape of hook seems to cope best. The Brazil has been soft boiled allowing the use of a hair bead.*

Above right: *Double bait presentation. Quartered boilies are used here as particles but you could use one buoyant bait with the other being a sinker. The rig consists of a double looped hair about 3in (7.5cm) long which is slid through small bored rig tubing and down over the eye of the hook as shown. The baits are secured with Nash hair stops and the rig can be adjusted so one end is longer than the other if required.*

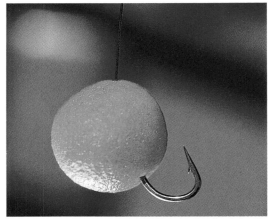

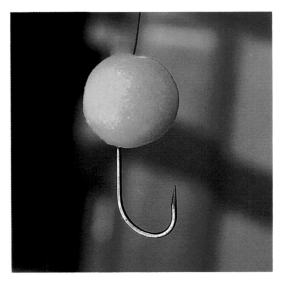

saturate the knot with saliva so that the coils bed down without burning or excessive constriction. I use a five-turn blood knot for nylon links but Dacron and dental floss only require two or three turns. Any more will make the knot unreliable.

The blood knot is the most reliable knot in fishing whatever anybody else tells you! I use it for attaching all hooks and swivels to nylon line. The tying sequence is simple. Pass the end of the line through the eye of the hook and wrap the loose end around the main line five times before feeding it back through the first loop formed nearest the eye. Moisten the knot before drawing tight.

This same knot can also be tied at night in the pitch black without too much fumbling. The line is passed through the eye by holding the hook on the tip of the tongue and prodding with the end of the line until the hole is located. Once the hook or swivel has been slid on the line, leave a longer loose end than usual. Then insert a finger against the eye and form a loop behind it, turning the loose end five times around the main line. Finally, feel for the loose end through the loop created by your finger and tighten down.

There is, however, one exception to the blood knot. This is when we are using Kryston or Gamastrand type hooklinks. These specialist synthetic materials are problematic when it comes to knotting. After extensive tests I am positive that the best knot is a five-turn Grinner, once the hooklink has been passed twice through the eye of the hook or swivel.

Pop-up rig

A bottom rig with great potential on many waters is the pop-up which I usually fish somewhere between 2-9in clear of the bottom.

Pop-ups are floaters which are made in exactly the same way as normal boilies but they are cooked in a microwave or oven to

create a watertight skin. Shop-bought boilies can be made to float by grilling but they'll need to be turned very carefully so the skin forms right around the bait.

The idea behind the pop-up rig is that when a carp swims into a baited area the pop-up bait is the most prominent and so more likely to be taken first. I would usually counter-balance the pop-up with a splitshot – a BB is about right – which is just sufficient to tether it the required distance above the bottom. When the fish are feeding ravenously and bouncing baits several inches off the bottom in their eagerness to get their fill, then you should try fishing the pop-up directly off the lead. A boilie suspended about 9in above the bed of the lake in these situations guarantees the carp will find it.

With boilies counter-balanced by a splitshot, I use two different pop-up rigs. One is much the same as the off-the-shank hair rig with about a 0.75in hair. The other is a sliding hair tied to the cut-off eye of a Jack Hilton carp-hook. The eye slides between the counterbalance splitshot and the hook, and when ejected the bait flies out of the mouth leaving the lightly pricked hook behind.

Particle rigs

The mini-particles, including hemp, cannot be fished effectively as single grains on carp tackle. The best method is to Superglue 10 to 15 seeds along a dental floss hair, leaving 0.75in between the hook and the first seed.

Medium-size particles, such as maples, can be fished on a hair in ones and twos while larger black-eyed beans and peanuts are presented singly.

When carp really get down to eating the particles they will take a hookbait as though it was a free offering. This lack of caution might result in the bait and hooklink passing right back over the pharyngeal teeth causing a phenomenon known as the bite-off. The carp swallows the hook and you lose the fish. To avoid this you should limit the length of the hooklink to no more than 9in. It is probably best fished with a heavy lead over 2oz either semi-fixed or clipped up. That should ensure that the carp bolts on feeling the lead and doesn't take the bait deep down.

If bite-offs persist after taking these precautions, then resort to a frightener on the line. Using a needle, thread the hooklink through a 2in length of plastic biro tube and Superglue it in position about 3in from the hook. The tube will hit the carp's mouth when the hookbait is sucked in causing it to panic and probably hook itself in the process.

Leger stops and weights

For 90 per cent of my legering rigs I use a swivel to stop the lead running down to the hook. It's the most reliable method and absorbs the stress of constant casting better than the plugged tube stops which weaken the rig by pinching the nylon. I've found Berkley and Kevin Nash swivels reliable in size 8 to 10s with round or diamond eyes. As an extra precaution, slip on a bead between the lead and swivel to act as a shock absorber.

The leger weights themselves are mostly straight copies of Dick Walker's original aerodynamic Arlesey bomb with a swivel at one end. Stock up with an assortment of bombs between ½oz and 3oz in half-ounce gradations and you'll meet most demands in carp fishing.

Anti-tangle rigs

Soft hooklinks of dental floss and Dacron really require the lead to be fished with an anti-tangle system. Four favourites are as follows.

Weed and silt bottoms. This rig consists of a length of stiff tubing with a bead and swivel mounted at one end. The lead can be attached directly to the swivel or on a link of nylon which is adjusted to correspond with the depth of weed or silt. Essentially it is a free-running rig, but the tubing can be wedged against the hooklink swivel with a piece of cocktail stick if you want to fish it fixed.

Hard bottoms. A distinctly different rig, with the lead mounted directly on a stiff length of tubing. The main line is threaded through the tube and the hooklink attached. This is another running rig that can be stopped with a piece of cocktail stick.

Semi-fixed rigs. There are two types of semi-fixed rigs. In the first, the chief component is a length of flexible Kevin Nash 2mm rig tubing together with a bolt bead from the same manufacturer. One side of

Opposite centre:
Side-hooked boilie. The first in a long line of self-hooking rigs. On waters where the hair-rig is not so efficient, the side-hooked bait with a hook link of between 9-12in is back in favour.

Opposite bottom:
Eye-mounted boilie. Another hugely successful method when fished with a heavy lead of 2oz and a short hook link of 5-7in (12.5-17.5cm). The lead is fixed or clipped up tightly and the hook size to boilie ratio is approximately a half-inch boilie to a size 2 hook. The hook, normally barbless, is honed to a needle point. Once the bait is picked up, the fish is pricked and bolts against the fixed lead or line clip producing a screaming take.

ANTI-TANGLE SYSTEMS

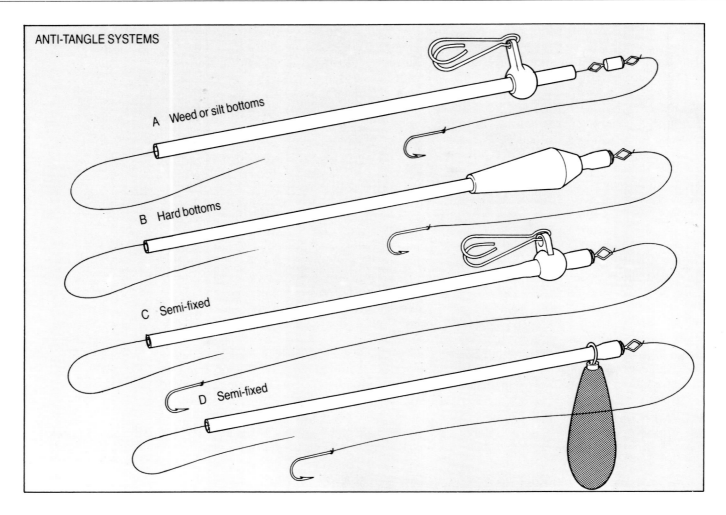

A Weed or silt bottoms

B Hard bottoms

C Semi-fixed

D Semi-fixed

the bead has a spigot on which the rig tubing is pushed. A slightly smaller spigot protrudes from the other side of the bead and this takes a short length of the next-sizedown rig-tubing which is also pushed over the stop swivel. This serves as a fixed lead but if it snags up, the hooklink can be freely pulled out. The bolt bead also carries the lead on a link swivel.

The second type of semi-fixed rig consists of a length of 1.5mm thick walled silicone tubing which is fed through the eye of the bomb swivel. The lead is pushed about ⅜in along the tubing as shown. The main line is threaded through the tube and the stop swivel attached. The end of the tube can be pushed over the stop swivel or the rig left free running.

Use these semi-fixed set-ups in preference to hanging the lead from the eye of the stop swivel. If the bomb is hung from the swivel and the line is broken above the lead then you will condemn a carp to towing a fixed lead about for several days.

Stringer systems

The use of stringers has now become a standard part of winter and long-range carping. It is the most accurate method of placing free offerings with pinpoint accuracy around the hookbait and involves the use of polyvinyl alcohol (PVA) string or thread which dissolves in water. String does not dissolve as quickly as thread but is stronger if used straight from the packet without being separated out into thinner strands.

The chief use for string is long distance fishing in summer with as many as six baits on one stringer. The boilies are threaded on a length of PVA string slightly longer than the hooklink and at roughly equal distances apart. One end of the PVA is then tied to the stop swivel and the other fastened to the hook. If used with anti-tangle tubing, the whole lot can be folded back and strapped to the tubing with two shorter pieces of PVA thread for stability in long-range casting.

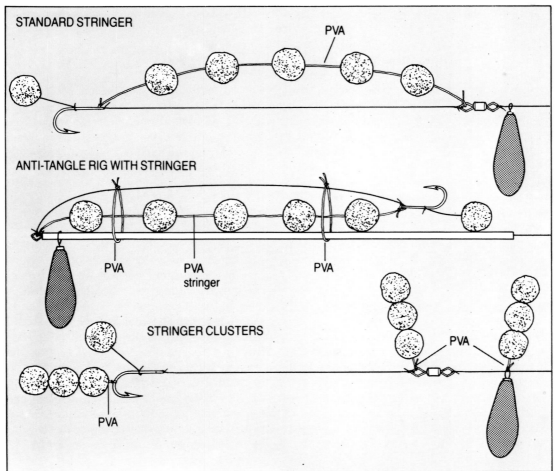

STANDARD STRINGER

PVA

ANTI-TANGLE RIG WITH STRINGER

PVA

PVA
stringer

PVA

STRINGER CLUSTERS

PVA

PVA

PVA

Above: *PVA stringer tied to the bottom eye of the stop swivel.*

PVA thread is more suitable for winter fishing. It dissolves very quickly and can be used in much the same way as string or to carry the baits in small clusters on the lead, stop swivel or hook.

Jobs for a float

I would seldom go out on a fishing trip without my two favourite float patterns; these are the Drennan Loafer and Giant Crystal.

I use a single swanshot capacity Loafer for dropping the bait in tiny gaps among lily pads, in weed beds or through trailing branches. It is fished as a slider with the line passed through the bottom end only. Sufficient shot to cock the float are fixed about 4in from the hook and a Billy Lane sliding stop knot is tied on the line at the required depth. This is a very compact rig and casts neatly into tight corners or it can be inched back into position after deliberately overcasting.

The 3AAA Giant Crystal is used for stalking fish where there is more room for manoeuvre. Two locking shots fix the float at the appropriate depth and the remaining weights are bunched close to the hook if I'm looking for a lift bite or very early warning – for example, when particle fishing. The shots are spaced out in descending size towards the hook if it appears the bait needs presenting on-the-drop style. These floats might seem heavy for the job but remember they will probably be fished on 15lb line in snaggy swims. Use anything smaller and the rig will be totally unbalanced.

FISHING OVER SILT

The worst silt problem I have ever experienced was on a shallow lake where long distance casting sunk a 2oz lead as much as 18in into the soft bottom. If you fished a 12in hooklink on that lake the bait vanished from view. There are several ways of overcoming this.

Depth of silt

The first job is to discover just how deep the lead is burying in the silt. You can quickly take a precise measurement by securing a bomb to the end of the main line and then running a 6ft length of white wool from the lead swivel back up the line and tying it off. The bomb is cast out and quickly retrieved with the rod held high all the time. What happens is that the bomb drags the white wool down into the silt and you can judge the depth by the length of wool that's discoloured by the silt. The dirty length of wool will be slightly deeper than the layer of silt penetrated by the bomb because of the angle of retrieve, which is to your advantage when assembling the rig.

Paternoster rig

Make up a running paternoster rig starting with a lead link that is approximately 12in longer than the depth of the silt. Attach the lead at one end and the running swivel at the other. Slip this swivel on the main line and then attach a stop swivel followed by the hook length which should be roughly one third of the bomb link. For example, a 36in bomb link equals a 12in hooklink. Experience has shown this to be the most tangle-free ratio.

The rig can also be fished fixed but if that is your choice use the same breaking strain line for both main line and hook length with a weaker bomb link. That way the bomb link breaks first if you get snagged solid. The same dimensions can be used as before with a Drennan welded ring or swivel at the junction of main line and bomb link. If you're using a swivel, attach the hooklink on the bottom eye. Nylon hooklinks are preferred with this rig but anti-tangle tubing can be fixed above the bomb swivel with a soft Dacron bottom.

Bait for silt

Rigs for silty bottoms should be used with a fairly light bait or one with a large, flat surface. Flat-sided particles such as kidney beans are better than maples. If you prepare your own boilies they are better flattened before boiling to make them penny-shaped. This will stop them sinking into the silt. If you are fishing at long range and round

boilies are preferred then a pop-up would be an advantage.

FISHING IN WEED

Rooted water-plants are often no different in construction from any other type of plant. Most tend to be thin with straightish stems fanning out into large dense heads. Weed viewed from the surface might appear tight packed but down on the bottom the stems are often several feet apart. Blanket or silk weed is rather different in make-up as it is unrooted and its thickness and position changes daily depending on weather conditions.

Rooted weed is the easiest of the two to tackle. It is chiefly a question of penetrating the surface canopy to reach the less dense area below. One answer is a Dacron anti-tangle rig with the hooklink strapped along the tubing at two or three points using PVA thread. The lead forces the surface fronds of weed apart, allowing the PVA parcelled rig to brush through without getting snagged up. The PVA melts leaving the baits presented among the roots. It is important not to attempt to move the rig after casting because the main line will immediately foul the surface canopy.

Blanket-weed rigs

Presenting a bait over blanket weed can be done on a paternoster type rig with a pop-up or flat-sided bait. If the carp are cruising just above the layers of weed use a pop-up on a 9in hooklink. The length of the bomb link is determined by the weed layers.

This rig can also be fished with a flatsided bait, such as sweetcorn, which stands out clearly on blanket weed. Carp love mooching up and down sucking off the odd morsel or two and when they are feeding in this manner try a paternoster with a 12in hooklink. As before, the length of the bomb link is decided by the depth of weed and it should be weaker than the main line or hooklink. Both recommended rigs for swims containing blanket weed must be fished with tight lines to ensure that the bait is in the correct position.

On waters where carp will not tolerate tight lines, I switch to a very slow sinking rig constructed with floating green putty which is obtainable from most tackle shops.

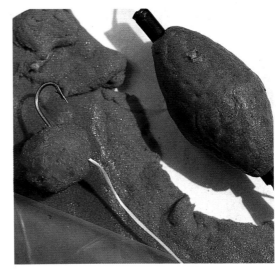

Rig tubing comes in handy yet again. This time you will require a short length of 2mm diameter. Mould the putty around the outside leaving about an eighth of an inch of exposed tubing at each end. Then push some split-shot into the putty until it just about sinks. The length of tubing and quantity of putty depends on the distance you need to cast. The main line is threaded through the tubing and a stop swivel attached followed by the hooklink. If fishing at short range you can use a silicone rubber as a stop with a piece of cocktail stick inserted.

Where the blanket weed is exceptionally wispy and the hook is continually masked then it needs suspending with a piece of rig foam on the bend. A similar method can be

Left: *Green floating putty moulded around a short length of rig tubing makes a good controller in heavily weeded swims. You'll find it doesn't snag as readily when inching it back through pads to position the bait.*

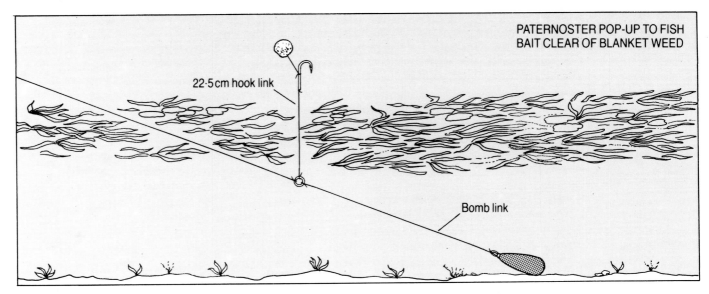

PATERNOSTER POP-UP TO FISH BAIT CLEAR OF BLANKET WEED

22·5 cm hook link

Bomb link

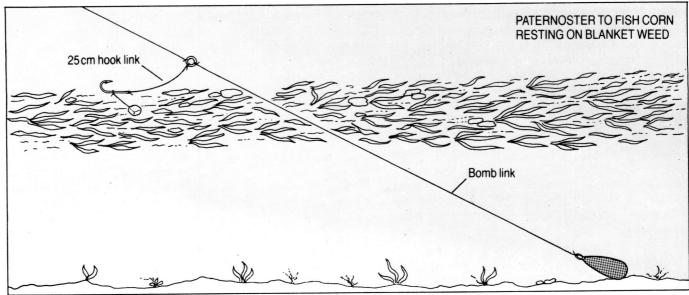

PATERNOSTER TO FISH CORN RESTING ON BLANKET WEED

25 cm hook link

Bomb link

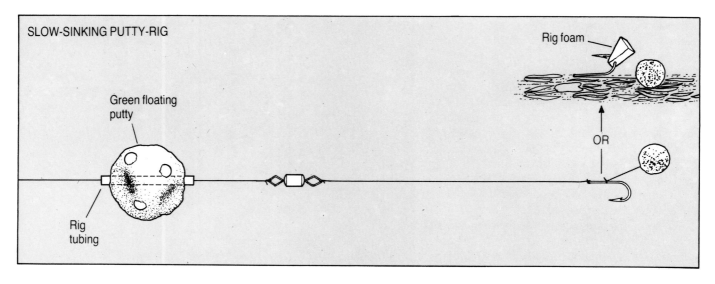

SLOW-SINKING PUTTY-RIG

Rig foam

Green floating putty

OR

Rig tubing

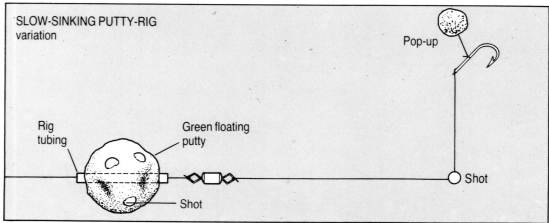

SLOW-SINKING PUTTY-RIG
variation

Pop-up

Rig tubing

Green floating putty

Shot

Shot

used with pop-up boilies when fishing for carp that are cruising just above the blanket weed.

PICK OF THE BOTTOM BAITS

Tinned meats, paste baits and boilies are the leading bottom baits. Pork luncheon meat and Bacon Grill lead the league of favourite meats. The rule with pastes is the stronger the better. Gorgonzola and Danish Blue stand out and the best meat pastes are luncheon meat, liver and beef. Old favourites such as dog-food and catfood pastes remain good stand-bys but I prefer fish pastes: sardine, pilchard, squid and anchovy seem most potent. Boilies divide into four groups: fish, meat, birdseed and milk protein mixes. If you are adding your own flavours the most consistent catchers are maple, cream, strawberry, blueberry, caramel, malt, liquorice, clove, bun spice, sweetcorn, black cherry, peanuts, mivi, salmon, shrimp, anchovy, blue cheese and honey. Use them alone or blended together. Favourite shelf-life boilies include dairy cream fudge and king prawn.

BITE INDICATION

Plastic indicators sliding on steel needles and buzzer bars are now the nation's choice – and they've improved our efficiency by 101 per cent.

Starting at ground level and working up, here are my recommendations for the chief component parts of the modern rod support, indicator and alarm system.

BANK STICKS

The choice in bank sticks is between cheap, aluminium ones which need replacing several times during the course of a season or those made in stainless steel or heavy aero-aluminium which should last for years. You'll find lightweight aluminium sticks which buckle first time out a poor investment. They're just not sturdy enough to be hammered into hard ground.

So choose a stainless-steel model with an extending inner rod for height adjustment. Check that the adjusting thumbscrew is large enough to lock up the inner stick securely. Some thumbscrews are too small and with cold fingers you'll never get sufficient purchase to tighten them down. It follows that the inner rod should slide freely with no signs of corrosion which could cause it to jam against the outer sleeve. The standard three-eighths BSF thread on the bank stick will take a lot of punishment and must be made of stainless steel or brass and not aluminium which corrodes too quickly.

BUZZER BARS

A buzzer bar is screwed on and off the bank stick repeatedly through the season in all kinds of weather. Again, the only choice of material for strength and reliability is stainless steel.

Let's look at a simple two rod assembly. I prefer to position both rods at the same height above the ground with the rear buzzer bar narrower than the front. That makes it possible to fish a much straighter line towards the leads assuming the hookbaits will mostly be just a few yards apart.

The rear buzzer bar is fitted with high sided, cupped rod-rest heads. Screw-in types are all right but for my money you can't beat the push-on, flexible rod-rest heads. These slide over brass studs screwed into the female threads on the bar. Whichever type you choose, the rod butt must sit snugly within the rest so it cannot be knocked off. Incidentally, an advantage with the stud and push-on fitting is that it's much easier to line up the rod. With a screw-in design there's always the worry that the thread might bottom out leaving the rod-rest head at the wrong angle.

The front buzzer bar takes the electronic alarms or V-shaped rod-rests with a central channel which allows the line to flow freely. Where the terrain is too soft for a bank stick to hold steady, a stabiliser is the answer. This twin-spiked accessory locks on the bank stick giving the same sort of grip as though you were forcing the prongs of a garden fork deep in the ground. With a buzzer bar carrying two rods it's only necessary to stabilise the rear bank stick as the weight of the rods will do the rest.

The bank sticks holding the buzzer bars are staked about 2ft apart with the reels positioned just inside the rear rod-rest heads leaving most of the butt sections overhanging.

MONKEY CLIMBERS

Choose your monkey climber with care because there are some diabolical models on the market! The needle must be made from quality stainless steel that won't rust. The tip is normally flattened to prevent the indicator flying off but feel for any jagged edges which will be lethal on line. The same applies with monkey bodies – some injection moulded models are left with small burrs where they have been ejected from the press. Among the best commercially-made indicators is the Grease Monkey. It has a stainless steel needle coated with black PTFE to reduce friction and special care is taken to ensure there are no dangerous

Above: The ideal set-up with stabiliser on the rear bank stick to hold everything rock steady.

Right: Flip-top monkey body moulded from PTFE with isotope chamber for night fishing.

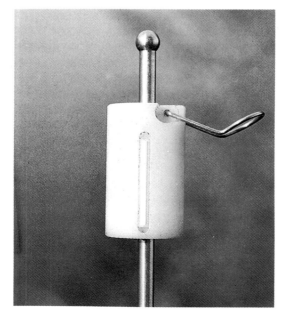

Setting up a monkey climber

The most direct way of setting up a monkey climb system is to push the needles straight into the ground just below the rod, either between the first and second ring or a couple of inches in front of the reel. But this is asking for trouble. Needles are soon damaged on gravel banks and there's always a temptation to bend them so that they line up correctly with the rod. After a few sessions of that sort of treatment the needles will look more like corkscrews.

By far the best method is to lift the needles clear of the ground by screwing them on a supporting bar which is firmly pegged in place with one or two spikes. Alternatively, fit an adjustable 'T' bar to the front or rear bank stick which again has lockable needle holding devices. The beauty of this is that once the bank sticks are securely positioned nothing else has to be driven into the ground.

Remember that monkey climb systems are not maintenance free. It is essential to keep the needles spotlessly clean. A fleck of grit splashed up by rain could find its way between the needle and the bore of the monkey body resulting in seizure. To give complete protection against splashing even in the heaviest downpour, lay a rod mat on the ground through which the bank sticks and needle bars can be inserted.

ragged edges. The body of the indicator is moulded in three take-apart sections allowing weight adjustment to suit conditions.

Most indicators are sold with a fixed line clip but the flip-top type of monkey body is better. On reaching the top of the needle, the retaining wire clip falls back completely free of the line, eliminating any possibility of snagging.

Line clips

Front and back line clips are small items but they're of major importance. Shop-bought plastic clips snap neatly around the rod but you can easily make your own from slithers of carbon with the edges smoothed down.

The butt clip goes immediately above the spool of the reel and is strapped in place with electrical tape. Secure the front clip between the first and second intermediates down from the tip ring on the top joint. If you're right handed then the line clips should be on the left hand side of the rod – that way you can reach them more quickly from your sitting position.

The front clip serves as a wind and drift beater with a free-running rig. Clip up with the bare minimum of tension to overcome the conditions and set the monkey climb at the base of the needle. I don't recommend front clipping with a bolt rig because a vicious take smashes the monkey body into the rod and can damage it.

Bolt rigs should be firmly back clipped to create resistance and help set the hook. In this case, the needle is normally fished just in front of an open spool with the monkey climb up high. When a carp belts off with the bait, the line bursts from the clip and the monkey body drops an inch or two on the needle before hovering on the spot as line continues to peel from the spool at a quite furious rate.

The same approach is also adopted with a fixed lead, especially when fishing against an island or the far bank. At these times, the carp usually run towards you, slackening the line between the lead and rod tip. With a front clip you'd get no indication at all from the angler's side of the rod tip unless you were lucky enough to spot the line go slack. But with a back clip and the monkey at the top of the needle, there's a very positive drop-back. Add as much weight as possible to the monkey body to provide the earliest possible indication.

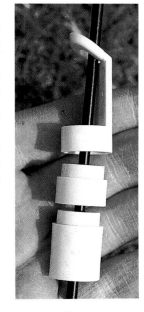

Above: Greased monkey with snap-apart indicator. Probably the best buy among commercially-made indicators.

Left and below: Clipping down, this is how you'd set the indicators when fishing the rods high over weed or with a free-running bolt rig. It's also the system for strong winds and undertow. The line is held in the front clip only.

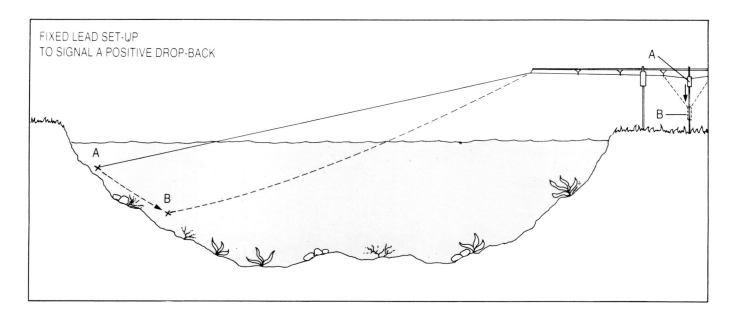

FIXED LEAD SET-UP
TO SIGNAL A POSITIVE DROP-BACK

Above: Clipping up the correct way when fast runs are expected on bolt type rigs incorporating a fixed lead.

BUTT FOAM

This foam is useful in a variety of situations. When it's necessary to keep as much line as possible off the water to prevent it scraping a gravel bar or snagging a weed bed, then a wad of foam stuck in the first or second ring of the rod will do the job. It maintains constant tension on the line raising it above the obstruction even after a run has developed.

Another time to use foam is when strong winds create heavy undertow. Line tends to belly out in undertow as a hard running fish pours line from the spool and the time taken to wind down and make contact is prolonged. That could be time enough for the loose line to foul a snag in the swim. Foam solves the problem by maintaining direct contact with the fish at all times.

When using butt foam, trap the line against the bottom of the rod ring and not at the side or top. If the line is pressed against the top of the ring it could possibly get damaged as it digs down into the foam under the pressure of a hooked fish.

ELECTRONIC BITE ALARMS

Staring at a static monkey climb all day strains the eyes and makes it impossible to scan the lake effectively for signs of fish activity. A reliable electronic bite alarm permits you to keep your eyes peeled and get on with other things such as baiting up and rig tying without any fear of missing a take.

Antenna alarms and Optonics

The most basic alarm is the antenna type where the line is drawn around an upright arm. Once it tightens as a result of a run, a pair of contacts are drawn together completing the circuit and sounding the alarm.

These alarms can be adjusted to register a slight increase in pressure on the line but they will not react to a loosening of the line.

The best-selling indicator is undoubtedly the Optonic with its rotating vane wheel on which the line rests. Any movement of the line spins the wheel and cuts through a photo-electric cell giving off a bleep.

The top of the range Optonic has adjustable tone and volume with two light emitting diodes (LEDs). One LED glows all the time the vane wheel is turning and the circuit is being broken. The other LED is latching and regardless of whether or not the run is continuing it will stay alight for several seconds. This is a great help when fishing multiple rods. A slight pucker of the line signalling a twitch or line bite is often encouraging news and it's good to know on which rod it occurred.

The Optonic bleeps whichever direction the vane wheel rotates and responds immediately to drop-back bites, unlike antenna alarms.

STRIKE AT A NODDING ROD TIP

It's impossible to legislate for every kind of take. For instance, there'll be times when the bites are very indecisive no matter what kind of line clip and rig you're using. These nudges at the bait might only show up as a slight nod of the rod tip. But strange to report, if you time the strike correctly the finicky fish are often very easily hooked!

PREPARING FOR EVERY RUN

The power and speed of a run clearly depend on the rig and distance being fished. These factors determine how the indication system is pre-set and it's important to get it right otherwise good chances may go begging. First, here are summaries of my three main lines of attack depending on distance.

Margin fishing

This calls for an open bale arm approach because carp hooked in the margins will make a blistering run. Fishing with a closed bale is simply asking for trouble. Front clips are unnecessary because undertow shouldn't have much of an effect. There is also little point in fishing the monkey climb at the top of the needle in anticipation of a drop-back as fish are unlikely to charge straight at the bank. A tight line between rod tip and lead would also spook them.

The first move is to position the rods low to the ground with just the tips projecting over the water's edge. Leave a fair amount of slack line in front of the rod and do not clip up in any way. Select the lightest monkey climb body and locate the needle a couple of inches in front of the open spool.

Medium range fishing

At medium range in open water the approach is similar to that for the margins except that the rods are slightly higher and they need to overhang the water as much as possible. Clip up if there's any undertow or with a semi-fixed lead. Fishing at this range, fast takes are still possible and providing there's no immediate danger from snags then an open bale arm is favourite.

The speed of the take will be much reduced when fishing tight up against an island or the far bank. The carp will move right, left, or straight towards your own bank and that means back clipping with the indicator perched at the top of the needle. Fishing the bale arm open or closed is a matter of personal preference in this situation.

Extreme long range fishing

Beyond 100yd I like to use a running lead rig. The fish could move off in any direction and line pulled through a stationary bomb is easily recognisable. When forced to fish a

Top of the range Super Compact Optonics fitted with ears to hold the rods steady in very windy weather.

semi-fixed lead at extreme range I select the heaviest monkey body in my box and will even add extra weight in bad weather. With so much line out, a carp can tow a bomb quite some distance before registering an indication at the rod so, if you fish a light-weight monkey climb, that carp could be in the margins before you realise what's going on! Point the rods as far out over the water as possible and directly at the leads. If a shallow bar intervenes, fish the rod tips much higher than the butts – it's not unusual to elevate the tips by as much as 5ft above the ground.

Reel churner fishing

The three methods of attack described above allow you to sit back at your leisure. But at other times you'll need to hover over the rods ready for a quick strike followed by a rapid wind-down to stop a fish ploughing into trailing branches or other obstructions. So position the rods at a comfortable height for an instant strike. Fish with a closed bale arm and keep the line as taut as possible but without clipping up as this might spook the fish more than is necessary. Try to avoid a fixed lead for the same reason. Position the needle a couple of inches behind the Optonic so there's a fair distance between the reel and the monkey climb. This is an important point because a run will probably spin the reel round a couple of times before you've had a chance to grab the rod. The oscillating movement of the line just in front of the reel would certainly jam a monkey climb if it was fished tight up to a closed bale.

This type of set-up is often described as reel churner fishing. Reacting to a run is simply a matter of picking up the rod with one hand, grabbing the spinning reel-handle with the other and holding the carp on a tight line as hard as possible to prevent it reaching the danger area.

HOW HARD SHOULD YOU STRIKE?

Whack into a carp fleeing from the margins and the end result is likely to be a snapped line and lost fish. Instead of slamming into a fish at close quarters, close the bale arm and let it run off against a correctly pre-set clutch. Striking carp at medium range is less of a problem. There's a fair amount of room for error and an over enthusiastic strike will not normally do any harm. Fishing an open bale arm at medium range with no imminent danger from snags, close the bale and strike firmly while continually winding. If carried out correctly, you will feel a solid thump at the end of the rod as it comes to an abrupt stop when the hook is driven home. After conducting many experiments with striking at fish at distances over 100yd, I know it is a total waste of time. A powerful strike will barely move the bomb a couple of inches and that's not sufficient to drive a hook into a carp's mouth. It's far better to pick up the rod and wind down until you feel you can't retrieve any more line. Hold the rod as high as possible and pull it back over your shoulder maintaining a tight line at all times. The fish will only be lightly pricked at long range and the hook needs to be worked in deeper by constant pressure. Stalking fish at short range demands a firm strike. Make sure you are fishing with tackle equal to the punishment it will receive.

SPOTTING THE LINERS

Carp often bump into the line between the rod tip and lead resulting in false runs known as liners. It's more likely to happen in shallow water or over bars where the fish will be swimming very close to the lines for a great deal of the time. Distinguishing between a liner and the real thing is easy enough when you're not clipped up. The line normally catches on the fish's dorsal or tail fin for a second or two before falling free and the effect on the indicator is a slow rise followed by an equally steady descent to a point on the needle just short of its original position. If you're striking at what appear to be slow, confident takes and completely missing them, restrain yourself and wait to see if the indicator falls back. The chances are that you're striking in vain at liners. When fishing clipped up, it's much harder to detect a liner. Sometimes the line will immediately ping free, simply causing the rod tip to nod. But when the line is pulled clear of the clip the indicator will be sent flying up and down the needle several times under its own inertia. Delay the strike for a few seconds to check if the run develops properly – that's the only solution.

TACKLE AND TECHNIQUES

PREBAITING PRINCIPLES

The need for a pre-baiting programme largely depends on the amount of fishing which is being done. The carp in many lakes do not require any persuasion to show interest in hookbaits. This certainly applies on hard fished waters where baits are going in constantly and the fish instantly recognise coloured little balls as a food source.

Prebaiting becomes essential for consistent results on waters which are only lightly fished. It should be carried out regularly and, if practical, on a daily basis. Start off by scattering free offerings as widely as possible because carp are great wanderers and you want to be certain that they'll bump into your bait.

Steadily build up on the amount going in rather than piling in thousands right at the outset on a virgin water. If baits are left uneaten for days they could go off and repel the carp and the process would have to be repeated from scratch.

After a week or two of prebaiting the whole area, narrow it down to selected spots. Even on small waters it's a good plan to bait up about a dozen different swims to increase the options.

Points of interception

On a featureless water it is difficult to pinpoint the precise point at which carp will enter the swim but bait up in a diagonal pattern and your chances of intercepting patrolling fish are dramatically increased. The same method works well on gravel pits where carp follow the troughs between bars, usually sticking to one side rather than ploughing through the centre. Try to cover three bars if possible.

When fishing across to an island, bait each end instead of the middle and you're more likely to intercept carp moving in and out. Finally, if you're tackling a known hotspot it is just a matter of concentrating the free offering as tightly as possible around the hookbaits.

FEEDING ACCESSORIES

There are various baiting aids to help you propel the chosen bait the required distance.

Catapults

There isn't a catapult made that will deal with all baiting tasks. For single boilies, cubes of luncheon meat and anything similar, a small pouch offers more firepower. Spraying particles or catapulting several boilies simultaneously, calls for a larger pouch. The quality of the latex elastics is the key to performance and with heavy use these might require replacement two or three times a season.

Baiting up with large boilies at extreme range is a job for the Marksman hunting catapult which is used in the United States to kill small game. A sturdy steel frame, wrist support and very powerful latex elastics make it possible to fire single baits in excess of 100yd.

Throwing stick

A throwing stick is the best tool for hurling hard, small diameter boilies up to 80yd. It's surprising how quickly you can distribute several hundred boilies with a well designed model such as the swan-necked

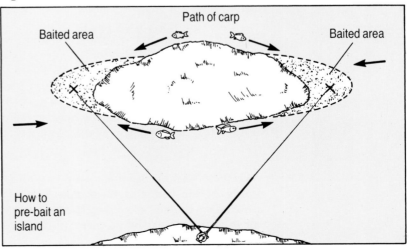

Path of carp

Baited area

Baited area

How to pre-bait an island

Wrist-grip catapult powers hard boilies beyond 100 yards.

Cobra. Baits leave the throwing stick at great speed and they'll travel furthest when skimmed just above the surface.

Bait dropper

Feeding particles at distances beyond about 50yd is way beyond the capacity of a standard catapult. This is a job for the bait dropper. I've found Gardner Tackle's Bait Rocket ideal for slinging out a handful of particles or mini boilies beyond 60yd. The dropper is cast out on a beefy rod with a test curve of around 2.5lb and on hitting the water it turns turtle, spilling out the particles. Incidentally, use a 15lb shock leader with the dropper to avoid a potentially dangerous crack-off.

MARGIN TACKLE

Now to the choice of tackle, starting with that for margin and mid-range fishing.

Rod and reel

The right rod for margin to mid-range fishing is a through-action 12ft model made of carbon or a Kevlar mix with a test curve between 1.5 and 2lb. There are many excellent blanks on the market and the development of lightweight reel fittings and friction-free rings makes these softer rods a great pleasure to fish.

Carp hooked at close range put the whole tackle under tremendous stress. The rod must be capable of tolerating the first surge of power from the fish and through-action is the only choice.

As most margin to mid-range work demands an open bale arm, my choice of reel is an Abu Cardinal 55 fixed spool. These reels offer a superbly reliable bale arm mechanism which closes at the first time of asking. The clutch at the rear is very positive and won't seize up at critical moments. A smoothly operating roller completes a fine reel.

Line and hook

It follows from the above that the line needs to possess plenty of stretch. So make sure you steer clear of the low diameter, pre-stretched nylons which would be too unforgiving. Reliable brands include Maxima and Sylcast but do not use a breaking strain of less than 8lb.

Finally to the choice of hook. The best pattern is a forged, round or crystal bend, medium shanked model. Test every hook before tying it on and reject those which bend out of shape at the slightest pressure. A highly recommended pattern is the Drennan Super Specialist.

MARGIN METHODS

Methods of margin fishing are as varied as the situations which demand them. Whether it's the dramatic heaving of a carp out of lily pads or the tense excitement of sitting quietly at night listening to the carp getting closer and closer in. Let's begin with bubbler fishing.

Chasing bubblers

Tackle a bubbler by casting the hookbait a few feet in front of the anticipated path of the carp. Where it's difficult to cast accurately, intercept the fish by baiting up several yards in front of it with the hookbait left among the free offerings.

But before deciding on your approach, spend some time observing the speed, direction and regularity of the bubbling. You must be absolutely spot on with the cast because carp love feeding in a straight line and are most unwilling to make detours.

Fishing in lily pads

Extracting a carp from the centre of lily pads can be played in two distinct ways: by

brute force or by stealth. The heavy-handed method is short lived but dramatic. The sequence is to strike, wind down and possibly step back a few paces – all in one movement – without giving an inch of line. The carp is turned over on its back in a cascade of weed and water and bundled into the net before it realises what's happened. Any reduction of pressure is likely to end in disaster.

With the softly, softly approach, the carp is permitted its first powerful rush. This builds up weed on the line, exerting enough weight and pressure to bring the fish to a halt. The weed is certain to festoon the carp's head, masking its vision and forcing it to slow down. There'll be a few heavy lunges as it attempts to bury itself still further into the weed bed but now is the moment to gently increase the pressure, moving the rod from side to side. This sawing motion on the line should free some of the weed and when back in direct contact with the fish again its head is forced round at a different angle. That will provoke it to bolt in a different direction and the procedure is repeated. Eventually, the fish will run out of steam and you can then coax it into the net.

The rough and tumble of pad fishing makes it imperative to fish as simple a terminal rig as possible – swivels and leger weights have a habit of catching up on lily roots.

LONG RANGE TACKLE

The ability of your tackle to reach those few extra yards can make all the difference in long range fishing. Your tackle must be robust too for those moments when the pressure is really on.

Rod and reel

A stiff, fast tapered rod fits the bill for long distance, and tip-actioned models built of Kevlar are justifiably popular. For the record, my 12ft blanks are fitted with seven rings for long casting purposes and the test curve rating is 2.25lb. They're fine for fishing at 100yd but at extreme range – say 140yd – then 13ft rods with a 2.5lb test curve are better.

I have tried all kinds of reel but can't find anything to match the Mitchell 300S and Shiman series for evenness of line lay. There is no bunching at the front or back and the wide spools can be overfilled quite safely to achieve extra distance.

Line

Low diameter, pre-stretched lines are ideal for long casting and my preference is for Bayer Ultima Super Strong. Remember there's very little give with these monos and they are nothing like as abrasive resistant as standard lines.

A long range outfit with leger weights up to 3oz is a lethal weapon. Crack-offs could kill. For that reason, a shock leader or bumper as they're sometimes called *MUST* be used. A minimum of three rod lengths of non-stretched 15lb line is tied direct to the reel line with the stop swivel at the end. That gives a greater margin of safety when winding up to a big cast.

The most reliable knot for attaching the shock leader to the main line is a five-turn double blood. Trim the loose ends of the knot back to within ½in and they will be less likely to catch up in the rod rings and so impede line flow.

Shock leaders are also a good safety measure when fishing over gravel bars. This is because the reel line near the leger weight is roughed up continually by the coarse bottom and therefore will be severely weakened.

Hooks

Suitable hooks for long range carping are the chemically sharpened Kamasan B980 and Drennan Super Specialist. They're similar designs with a small, neat barb and relatively wide gape for their size. But Kamasans are forged on a finer gauge of wire than Drennans which gives easier penetration at 100yd where the power of the strike has little effect.

Tie on the more robust Drennan Super Specialist if you think the pressure has to be piled on at long range to prevent a fish from reaching snags.

LONG RANGE METHODS

The biggest problem posed by fishing at extreme distance is the effects of drift and drag on presentation.

Drift and drag

Casting into a stiff cross wind puts a huge belly in the line which should be straightened out as much as possible before the bomb splashes down. This is done by braking the last few yards of the cast with the forefinger on the open spool, a technique known as feathering. But don't stop the line flow completely because the lead will suddenly bounce back on itself in mid-air, tangling the hooklink around the main line.

Once the bomb strikes the water, bury the line immediately by thrusting the rod tip beneath the surface, closing the bale arm and gently tightening up. Try not to overdo it and so move the lead.

Most nylon lines are naturally buoyant but they will sink very quickly if previously soaked. Detach the loaded spool from the reel and leave it to soak overnight in a solution of washing-up liquid and cold water. One squirt of liquid to a couple of pints of water is the right level of dilution. Once there's a straight line between bomb and rod tip the line clips and butt foam will keep it that way. But take the trouble to test every knot in your rig after three or four casts. Hurling the terminal tackle long distances imposes a lot of strain, particularly on the stop swivel knot which receives the most battering.

ACCURATE CASTING

The ability to cast consistently to the same prebaited spot is an obvious priority at any range. A short cut is to carefully select the weight of bomb that will just reach the swim with a powerful cast. That way you know a strong cast cannot overshoot the mark. A given weight should cast roughly the same distance every time if the propulsion remains constant. It is easier to judge the power of a cast by exerting full compression rather than holding back. As a direction finder, line up with a bush, tree or bank of reeds on the far bank and aim to one side or the other to coincide with the prebaited area.

Casting at night

If you can consistently cast to the right spot in daytime, there is no reason why you shouldn't achieve the same degree of accuracy at night. As a guide, once you've cast out mark the line in front of the rod tip for about 3ft with Tippex or coloured nail varnish. That will serve as an accurate distance marker for the night session. In fact, when the marked line shoots through the rings you will hear it clearly. Feather the line at the same time and you'll also be able to feel it. Immediately you hear or feel the marked line, brake the cast.

Casting beneath trees

When casting tight to overhanging trees clip on a much heavier weight than is required to reach the distance. The reason for this is that a heavier weight will obviously drop much faster when braked fairly hard as it reaches the correct range. The lead should dive very quickly, achieving the right sort of low trajectory to take it beneath the trees. Feather the line as the lead nears the overhanging branches and slacken off completely once it hits the water. This ensures the bait is presented as far under the foliage as possible.

Swim markers

Some carp hotspots are only a few feet square and in these cases it's a good idea to use a floating marker consisting of a spent film canister or a polyball. Attach the marker to a length of line that's slightly longer than the depth of the swim and tie a leger weight at the other end. Then secure the marker line to the reel line with PVA tape and cast out. There should be just enough time to manoeuvre the marker into position before the PVA melts. Don't forget to retrieve it at the end of the session!

LONG OR SHORT SESSIONS?

The bivvy is the enemy of efficient carp fishing, at least for short sessions. If your hours on the bank are limited, then leave it at home. The disruption of moving swims with a bivvy is too great to contemplate when time is precious. A 50in umbrella provides all the protection necessary for a single night on the bank and if the fish start crashing out at the other end of the lake then you're mobile enough to take advantage.

If I'm on the bank for more than 48 hours and the swim allows me to cover most of the lake then I'll slip an overwrap on the brolly.

PLAYING AND HANDLING

PLAYING THE FISH

The limitations of the tackle must be uppermost in your mind while playing fish. But whatever the strength of the rig constant pressure must be maintained on the fish to avoid the line going slack.

Retrieve line by a pumping action. Wind the rod tip down towards the fish until it reaches the 10 o'clock position. Then hold the reel handle steady and pull the rod back over the shoulder to about 1 o'clock. Repeat this action until the fish is within netting range. At some stage in the fight, the fish will probably win line against the pre-set clutch unless you screw it down tight and allow the reel to rotate backwards. Backwinding, as it's called, is the method preferred by most big fish anglers.

Kiting

One tricky manoeuvre you'll certainly face is when a fish dashes straight towards the bank against a tight line and starts dictating matters – a problem known as kiting. To regain control, the carp's head must be pulled round by applying heavy side-strain so that it is pointing back towards you again. Keep the rod low to the water on a horizontal plane and this will increase the pressure against the side of the carp's mouth, forcing it to turn in an arc.

If the carp stubbornly resists this pressure and there's a danger of it running into snags, such as overhanging bushes in the margins, thrust the rod tip deep into the water to keep the line as near the lake bed as possible. That way there should be less chance of it fouling trailing branches.

Gravel bars that rise steeply from the depths are a serious hazard as carp often run along the bottom of troughs grating the line where it runs over the lip. Common sense should tell you to raise the rod up high, lifting as much line from the water as possible so it enters at a more acute angle. If there is a high bank behind then it's better to play the fish from there.

SAFE NETTING

When the fish is played out, don't let someone else net it for you unless you're confident of their ability. Sink the net well before steering the tired fish over it and don't try to scoop it out at full stretch.

Always bring the carp right over the sunken net until its mouth is almost touching the spreader block. This guarantees it will go in first time. Do not stab at the fish or chase it with the net.

The right net

It follows, of course, that the net itself must be right for the job. It should have a sturdy handle of between 5ft and 6ft and arms of about 42in. Strong fibre glass is as good for the frame as lightweight boron and carbon because when the net is wet they all seem to weigh the same. A drawstring tensions the arms once they have been sprung into the aluminium spreader block.

A dual mesh net about 4ft deep should swallow the largest carp you're likely to meet. The beauty of the dual mesh design is that the micromesh in the base of the net gives the fish greater protection.

CAREFUL HANDLING

The safest way of lifting a carp from the water is to gather the meshing together just below the arms of the landing net. This takes the strain off the arms and the spreader block which could be smashed by the combined weight of the fish out of water and the wet net.

Find a soft patch of ground on which to gently lay the carp or use a purpose-made unhooking mat. Whatever happens, do not put the fish down on hard ground. In an emergency use your bedchair or even spare clothing.

If the carp starts to thrash about at this stage do not attempt to pin it down against the hard ground. It is virtually impossible to restrain a carp in this manner without using excessive force and damaging the fish. Slip your hands underneath the fish instead and cradle it against your body. Again, you must avoid exerting undue pressure.

Moving carp with bare hands is fraught with potential dangers because a sudden kick from the fish could easily tear it free from your grasp. For that reason, it must be held as low to the ground as possible.

THE UNHOOKING CODE

A fish hooked just inside the mouth or in the scissors will cause very few problems. It is a simple matter to grip the hook between thumb and forefinger and gently tease it out. When it is beyond the reach of the fingers, use a pair of forceps.

Where the real difficulties start to arise is when a hook is not easily freed because it is deeply embedded and has taken a very secure hold. In these cases you must cut the hooklink and then gently rotate the hook within the fleshy part of the mouth where it is secured and extract it point first. Removing it in this fashion prevents the barb being dug deeper into the skin. Snip the eye off the hook and repeat the same procedure when the hook has been driven deeply into the bony extremities of the lip.

If the hook has been swallowed so deep that it is out of sight, do not try to drag it back into view by the hooklink. It is better to leave well alone and cut the line as close to the hook as possible. The carp will eventually discard it.

WEIGHING THE FISH

Regardless of the type of scales you use, a purpose-made weighing sling is essential to provide the carp with the support it needs out of water. The sling should always be soaked in lake water to avoid removing protective mucus layers from the body of the fish.

Once the weigh sling is soaked, wring out the excess water and hang it on the scales to zero in the pointer. Follow this procedure and you will not have to worry about subtracting the weight of the sling once the carp has been on the scales.

Lay the carp on its side in the sling if there's any possibility that its body will be bent by its own weight once it is suspended

from the scales. The weigh bags I prefer are made by Kevin Nash. The first accommodates carp up to about 30lb and is made from black nylon with heavy duty drawstring handles. It also has a built-in nose flap for extra security. My other bag will hold any carp that swims in this country.

Scales are once again a matter of personal choice but I favour the Salter tubular spring-balance that records up to 44lb and the Kevin Nash 56lb dial scales. Both are easy to read and zero in a wet weigh sling.

RELEASING AND RETAINING

If the catch is not going to be photographed then it is best to release it immediately. Carefully lower the sling containing the carp into the lake and allow the base of the sling to sink free from the fish. Support the fish in an upright position with your hands, steadying it until it recovers and is ready to swim away. A freshly released carp frequently bolts off at great speed and its head must be pointed towards the middle of the lake otherwise it could injure itself by crashing into the margins.

Choosing and using a sack

Fish caught at night can be retained until daylight for pictures if sacks are allowed on the water. There are some excellent designs on the market and I'd recommend that you purchase one made from industrial nylon rather than the keep-net type of close weave meshing.

Clearly, it must be possible for water to circulate freely through the weave of the sack for the safety of the carp. The best ones empty almost immediately when lifted from the water. Others drain very slowly and should not be used. Sacks are machined with top or side openings fastened by a drawstring and in some cases a heavy duty zip. A strong lanyard for staking out to a bank stick is another important feature.

As with the weigh sling, sacks must be thoroughly soaked before they come into contact with a fish. Never put more than one carp in each sack. Doubling up results in two very sick-looking carp and a lot of loose scales in the bottom of the sack.

Always think carefully before positioning the sack. Deep, shady margins are the ideal resting place.

PIKE FISHING

The pike is revered by some anglers but feared by many more – and that's a great pity. Historical records reveal how this fear of pike has been responsible for creating the most ridiculous myths and legends that have persisted right up to the present day. In 1988 a Russian claimed to have rescued his son, alive, after a pike had swallowed the child. Then in 1989 a marauding English pike is supposed to have bitten large chunks out of a dog! What follows is a realistic discussion about pike and pike fishing.

The pike has been on this Earth for about 80 million years, much longer than man. When the Americas drifted away from Europe and the Atlantic Ocean was born, I believe that two populations of pike became separated. Those in North America eventually gave rise to our own pike, *Esox lucius*. At a time when a land 'bridge' across the Bering Strait joined Siberia to Alaska, they migrated to Europe.

PREDATORS AND PREY

The role of the pike in freshwater ecology is not as threatening as the myths would have us believe. Carp-like species have also been on Earth for millions of years – again, long before man – and the pike has never managed to eat them all. The function of a predator like the pike is to *control* the numbers of prey, not destroy them. After all, a species that consumed all its prey would be consigning itself to oblivion.

The weight of pike a fishery can support depends very much on the productivity of the water. Most experts maintain that a ratio in the region of 7-10:1 is about correct. That is, for every 7-10 tons of cyprinids about one ton of pike can be supported. In really rich fisheries producing a high standing crop of cyprinids like roach and bream, I believe the ratio can be as low as 3-4 to 1 and still remain a viable and healthy ecology.

Now it's a fact that waters which are left fallow for a decade, with no interference by man, are seldom teeming with pike, what-

ever the ratio of prey fish to predators. Most of the pike biomass is contained in a relatively small number of big fish, which also control the numbers of small pike by eating them.

I fish one water where the annual spawning produces a great many pike of about 1lb in weight. As the weed dies, in November, they become vulnerable to big pike, and by January or February almost all the little pike have gone. This water is rarely fished, has a small head of big pike, and some of the best roach and bream fishing that I know.

It follows from this that humans are bad news for pike ecology. Fear of the species results at best in misconceptions of the pike's role and at worse in a blood-letting. Far too many pike are removed and killed, when they should be left in the water.

But pike anglers themselves cannot escape criticism. Heavily fished pike venues usually deteriorate into poor waters, with few decent fish, and often a large head of jack pike. Later in this chapter I'll explain how to deal with pike in a way which ensures their good health and survival.

Left: *Like many efficient predators, the pike is built for fast acceleration over short distances. Barrie Rickards captured this streamlined specimen from the middle of a weed-bed where it was waiting in ambush.*

Above: *Even modest pike boast an impressive set of teeth but they are not intended for biting humans or dogs!*

SELECTIVE FEEDING

There is one other matter concerning the role of pike and prey that is worthy of mention. Research shows that where a particular prey species exists in large, healthy numbers then pike will selectively prey on them and other species may escape relatively unscathed.

In Irish waters pike may feed almost exclusively on perch and eels where these have not been commercially netted or longlined. In some Fenland and Broads fisheries the bream is the fish that occupies the pike's mealtimes. Elsewhere it is the small pike.

In many trout waters, the cyprinids present act as the 'buffer' species and protect the trout. Remove the cyprinids and the pike focus on trout. Only at times of artificial and abundant stocking of trout can the pike's head be turned!

HOW PIKE FIND THEIR FOOD

The pike seems to use all its senses to capture its prey. It can certainly see extremely well in clear water – but manages to intercept spinners in the dark too! It surely detects vibrations with its sensitive canal system of pores in the head region and along the lateral line. There is a weight of evidence that a pike will home in on vibrations when it's on the hunt. It can also smell out its food, and is prepared to scavenge on fish or parts of fish it finds on the bottom.

In fact, the three senses, and feeding responses, determine the three basic piking methods used today:

- Sight and vibration means we can spin for them.
- Sight and a main food item means we can livebait.
- Smell and the scavenging role allows us to fish a deadbait for them.

The pike is, therefore, designed to hunt live or dead fish, and this makes it especially vulnerable to anglers. Offer a fish and, in the end, a pike will succumb to the temptation. The manner in which it feeds also makes it vulnerable to bad handling by anglers. For all these reasons the pike is a special case for conservation care.

Many ordinary pike anglers and, increasingly, coarse anglers in general, are giving the pike the care it needs and deserves. But there is a long way to go yet because fisheries managers in general, and trout-water managers in particular, seem unable to shake off their fear and loathing of the pike.

RECAPTURES PAINT A
FALSE PICTURE

Sometimes we get a false idea of the number of pike in a water because they are recaptured. Studies demonstrate that certain fish are for some reason particularly prone to recapture. Others manage to avoid the angler totally.

Where the same fish are netted possibly several times in a season, it gives an inflated impression of a water's potential, and in some instances persuades clubs to carry out unnecessary culls. Repeat captures should indicate that all is well and that the anglers are treating the pike correctly. Indeed the recaptured fish allows an inspection to be made of the standard of previous handling techniques.

ALL WATERS SUIT THEM

Pike are capable of adapting to all types of water: they are found almost everywhere, from fast trout streams and big, slow rivers to gravel pits and canals. The vast lochs of Scotland and Irish loughs produce very large fish and, sometimes, good fishing. But big pike also occur in relatively small gravel pits of a few acres. There will not be so many of them, but their sizes may not be dissimilar.

Inexplicably, certain regions have a history of breeding big pike or of good pike fishing. Any Fenland drain wider than 10ft

A lean pike hooked from the Shannon system by Paul Harris of the Irish Tourist Board. This vast network of navigable river and loughs always offers the real chance of a monster fish.

and at least 2ft deep can produce pike in excess of 20lb; the same size water in Yorkshire does not.

There must be few areas of the country where a 10lb fish is not possible. But pike of 20lb are a different proposition. Even in good pike country it is noticeable that 20-pounders are not captured as frequently as 20lb carp are taken from good carp territory. It is possible that there are fewer of them, of course.

Technically, it is not difficult to catch pike, though they are as easily disturbed by noise as other species. The infrequent capture of 20lb-plus pike may simply reflect the fact that a predator at the top of the food chain is present only in relatively small numbers.

THE THREE BASIC METHODS

My preferred piking technique is static deadbait fishing. But by far the most successful technique is livebaiting simply because that is what a pike usually feeds on. He will find it hard to refuse a small live fish for very long.

Livebaiting goes back hundreds of years, and is certainly not restricted to pike fishing. But the use of small fish for bait has always bothered some individuals. I would certainly not take umbrage at any angler opting for lure fishing and deadbait fishing – just as long as he doesn't tell me his results are unaffected!

Deadbaiting and lure fishing can be highly effective. In the warmer summer and autumn months I'd back lures against deadbaits any day. But in the depths of a cold winter, when pike may creep about slowly on the bottom, lure fishing can be ineffective and static deadbaiting highly successful. Livebaiting is good all the time.

That puts the three approaches in perspective – but I like to have all three strings to my bow, and I probably put in more days lure fishing than I do fishing baits.

HOW PRESSURE AFFECTS PIKE

After plotting thousands of pike captures I am convinced that, if the barometer is low

You can try deadbaits in all shapes and colours and most will tempt pike including such exotic offerings as dyed sandeels. Mackerel tail, chunks of eel, herring, sprat, smelt and sardine are all well proven baits which can be fished with confidence.

and steady, you are far more likely to get runs on deadbaits than livebaits. But if the barometer is rising or remains high, the opposite is the case.

On shallow waters a rising pressure may result in all methods working, but there is still a strong tendency for the pike to chase moving baits. I do not fully understand the reactions of pike to lures in different pressure regimes. They certainly *will* feed when the pressure is low, but this apparent contradiction is perhaps explained by the fact that at such times it is the smaller pike which take the lures most readily. Presumably the bigger pike are creeping about mopping up deadbaits or scavenging, and their smaller brethren feel safe up top!

DEADBAIT SELECTION AND RIGS

Today there's a huge range of deadbaits available from the fishmonger's slab. Almost all sea fish are good. Many of them seem more effective than the water's natural fish such as roach and perch.

My favourite baits are sardine and mackerel, with smelt and herring a close second. I wouldn't worry if I never had any other deadbait than these, but I've caught pike on most species of freshwater fish, including trout and eels, and on cod, plaice, flounder, whiting, haddock, weavers, dragonets, bass, and quite a few others. I still use small codling regularly, and I suppose if I had a third choice bait it would be sprats.

How do we fish deadbaits? The rigs and systems are relatively simple but highly effective. Too many anglers fish needlessly complicated rigs.

First, let's consider the line itself. I

generally opt for line of 11lb or 12lb when the water is more or less snag-free. If I'm afloat or fishing in the vicinity of serious snags I step up to 18lb. I rarely use lighter or heavier line than these. The strong line will not help you once a fish reaches the snags, but it's a great help when you are attempting to bully it away from the danger zone.

I have used Platil line for over 30 years and can also recommend Sylcast, Omni and Maxima. A word of warning. Test all lines at the beginning of a day's fishing by giving them a good pull at the business end. Take a coil in the left hand and another in the right and pull them firmly. It should be impossible to break 12lb line like this. If you can do so you must immediately inspect further along the line. If I find a line has gone weak – and they do this quite suddenly – then I load with a fresh spool immediately.

At the business end you must always use a wire trace. There are good commercially made traces in the shops, such as those marketed by Middy or Shakespeare, but I prefer to make my own. The trace length should be about 12in, with a swivel at one end and a link swivel at the other (Fig.1).

HOW TO MAKE UP A TRACE

There are basically only two types of wire that you can use – the rather fine variety which is too stiff to twist with the fingers, and slightly thicker, softer and more pliable wire which can be twisted by hand. I prefer the latter, and use PDQ or Alasticum.

I attach it to the swivel by passing it twice through the ring and then twist the two lengths closely together, by hand, for about an inch. A tiny blob of Araldite where the overlap finishes, is ideal, not a smear, because the latter will not stop weed and debris snagging on the twisted end of wire.

The link swivel is attached in the same way, as is the treble hook on the end of the snap tackles that I use. The snap tackles are also about 12in long (Fig.2) with a second treble, known as a Ryder hook, loosely sliding on the wire. It is so loose, in fact, that if you move it along quickly it does not put a kink in the wire. Finer wires do not perform well in this regard.

The snap tackle can be added to the link swivel of the trace wire (Fig.3) when you are bait fishing, or removed and replaced by a spinner, spoon or plug if necessary. You will notice that when bait fishing there are then two lengths of wire. This is important because deadbaits occasionally flip back while being cast out and would tangle with the main nylon line were it not for the second trace.

The same applies when livebaiting or suspending deadbaits. It is wise to eliminate any chance of this happening by using two lengths of wire in this way. Then if a pike does take a flipped-back bait it gets its teeth around wire and not around monofil.

RODS AND REELS

Now let's consider the rod. I think the ideal in carbon is 12ft of through-action, with a test curve of about 2.5lb. There are some good 3lb test-curve rods about, and you can go down to 2lb, but 2.5lb is about suitable for anything. In glass-fibre I aim for the same test curve but a length of 10ft is sufficient. There are many brands of high-class rod on the market today. My advice is to go to a tackle shop that sells a fair bit of big-fish gear, as it's likely they will stock a good pike rod.

Reels? What a difficult question! I use a variety of fixed spools: as long as they take 200yd of 15lb monofil and they are not obviously cheap, I know they will suffice. I use Mitchells, Ryobi Ceratec, and Shakespeare reels; but many others are good too. Normally, of course, you need less than 100yd of line.

WHERE TO FIX THE LEGER WEIGHT

There are two ways of attaching a leger weight. You can hang it on the link swivel between the snap tackle and the back trace,

Below: A commercially made snap tackle from the Middy stable. When fishing bait you'll also need an up-trace.

Below right: There are numerous ways of storing snap tackles including foam rolls with a protective wrap-around.

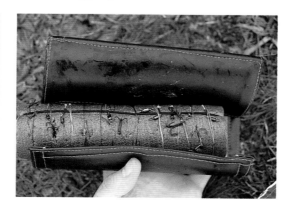

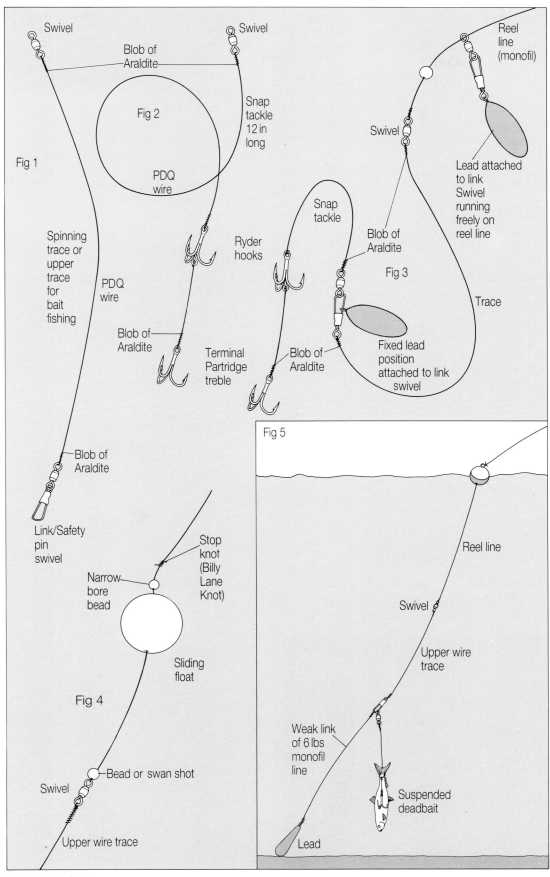

Swivel

Swivel

Blob of
Araldite

Reel
line
(monofil)

Fig 2

Snap
tackle
12 in
long

Fig 1

PDQ
wire

Swivel

Lead attached
to link
Swivel
running
freely on
reel line

Snap
tackle

Spinning
trace or
upper
trace
for
bait
fishing

PDQ
wire

Ryder
hooks

Blob of
Araldite

Fig 3

Blob of
Araldite

Trace

Blob of
Araldite

Terminal
Partridge
treble

Blob of
Araldite

Fixed lead
position
attached to link
swivel

Blob of
Araldite

Fig 5

Link/Safety
pin
swivel

Stop
knot
(Billy
Lane
Knot)

Narrow
bore
bead

Reel line

Sliding
float

Swivel

Fig 4

Upper wire
trace

Weak link
of 6 lbs
monofil
line

Bead or swan shot

Swivel

Suspended
deadbait

Upper wire trace

Lead

Correct positioning of the hooks in a whole bait.

so that it is fixed. Alternatively, you can make it free running by putting a link swivel on the line above the back trace, and attach the lead to that.

In weedy waters I always use a fixed lead because it increases my chances of connecting quickly and directly to the fish when a run occurs. The actual weight is decided by the casting distance or the need to hold against the current.

For float legering you add a sliding float above the trace wire. I usually stop this float with a small bead, which then runs against a stop knot (Fig.4). Normally I use simple, round floats ranging in size from small, ½-inch pilots up to models with a 2in diameter. But there are now many excellent pike sliders on the market, such as those made by Drennan and Middy. I'm sure they're every bit as good as mine.

This outfit is quite versatile. It can be adapted for free drifting a deadbait simply by setting the float stop-knot shallower than the depth of water. It can be changed to paternoster by doing the same and then adding a weak link of line to the link swivel between snap tackle and trace, and putting an anchor lead of appropriate weight on the other end (Fig.5). The deadbaits, incidentally, are just as effective hung vertically, and it is unnecessary to spend time setting them horizontally.

POSITIONING THE TREBLES

I prefer hooks between sizes 6 and 10 for all my piking, even when wobbling deadbaits. I use quite a few brands, including excellent

patterns like Eagle Claw; but most of the time I use an appropriate Partridge hook.

With most deadbaits the movable Ryder hook should go in the very root of the tail, or through the lips of a head end of mackerel or herring. The fixed tail treble is positioned about halfway along the flank of the deadbait. The hook halfway along the flank is the main hooking treble. This is where the pike will grasp the bait when it takes it crosswise in its jaws.

The firm hooking in the tail root aids smooth casting and distance, greatly enhancing the aerodynamic profile during flight. If this hook was further forward it would more easily lose its hold as well as adversely affect smooth casting. This is especially important when casting mackerel and herrings.

I treat sardines differently, using a large single hook instead of a Ryder, fixed in position. This goes through the eyes of the bait. With sprats I may use a single hook rig only, and in this case it doesn't matter a lot where you hook it.

FLOAT OR STRAIGHT LEGER?

I generally use a float when legering because it tells you just a little bit more about what is happening down below. A straight leger is more likely to find snags you didn't know were between you and the bait. When fishing from a boat, it also helps map out the depth variations accurately.

You may, of course, decide to fish a deep hollow on a sunken float. This gets the bait to exactly the right position above the bottom irrespective of variable and perhaps unknown bottom contours. It isn't quite so informative as fishing a float on the surface, but it has its uses in gravel-pit complexes where the depths vary from yard to yard.

It is quite possible to use long, cigar-shaped floats and to set these so that the slightest touch on the deadbait tilts the float. You cast out, fishing overdepth slightly, place the rod in rests, and then gradually tighten the line until the float cocks and holds.

I do straight leger often enough, but there are times when the pike seem able to move the bait some distance without the rod's indicator system registering a take.

Precision-made plastic floats from the Drennan range including sub-surface models.

BITE DETECTION SYSTEMS

Bite detection when legering is nowadays a fine art. I prefer a belt-and-braces approach that was devised by my friends. I use an electronic bite alarm and fish with an open pick-up, tucking the reel line in a clip directly above the spool. It needs to be clipped as lightly as wind and water currents allow. Then, between the first two rod rings, but before the front rod rest, I hang an indicator to show up a slack line bite as well as a normal pull. Drop-arm indicators are fine – but they are not for me. Once released by a fast forward pull they tell you nothing further about the bite. I have also known them freeze in position!

With my belt-and-braces approach you hear the buzzer and see the light, whether a drop-back bite or a straight pull is indicated. The drop-back is shown as the indicator falls slowly towards the ground.

I used to use washing-up bottle tops as indicators but have switched to white plastic tubes about 2in long. They are split along their length so that they can be quickly hung on the line or removed. The way to obtain them is to buy ordinary plastic bottles of various weights and diameters, and cut them with a pair of scissors. It takes only moments to prepare one.

Mine are not only of different weights but also of different colours. I add Sellotape in colours like fluorescent orange or bright green. Choose the correct weight for the day and set it so that it hangs down perhaps a foot or so below the horizontally set rod. This will give a nice rising bite or a drop-back, provided the rods are a couple of feet above the ground.

If the rise is slow you can remove the line from the clip on the rod to eliminate any resistance it may cause. Like floatfishing, this system gives a very early and clear indica-

tion of a bite, especially if any slack line to the lead has been gently taken up before the bite indicators have been set.

YOU MUST STRIKE
QUICKLY

Why should we want a very early indication of a bite? The answer is that the pike has a large mouth, as suits its predatory nature. It often swallows its prey very quickly and it is necessary to strike while the bait is still in its mouth. Any bite indicator system which tells you immediately the bait is taken is a plus.

With small baits of all kinds – say, under four ounces in weight – you should strike immediately. Spot the indication, check that the line is running or the float moving steadily, wind down until you feel the resistance of the fish and then strike.

You may need to give the pike a little longer with a larger bait like a chunk of mackerel or a whole herring. But if the hooks are positioned on the bait as described, then 15 or 20 seconds is the longest that you need to give a run. *Never wait for a run to stop and then restart* – this can be fatal for the pike. It almost always results in the pike swallowing the bait.

Self-cocking Pencil deadbait floats and sliders manufactured by Middy together with one of their mid-depth patterns.

Left: *Bite alarm and indicator system preferred by Barrie Rickards. It's a belt and braces approach that leaves nothing to chance.*

Below: *Drop-arm mechanisms are highly visual indicators and many pike anglers swear by them.*

Barrie Rickards maintains a tight line all the way to the bank and that's essential whatever size of pike you are playing.

STRIKING, PLAYING AND NETTING

To strike, simply wind down quickly and smoothly until the resistance of the pike is felt. Then, with the rod pointing at the fish, sweep it back until it takes on a real bend. *Keep it bent!* Under no circumstances slacken off at this point, even if you have to give line.

Pike anglers fall into two schools of thought with regard to the angle of the rod during the strike. I strike upwards, but a majority strike sideways, leaning the rod into the corner of the pike's jaw. I do not know which is better, but both work in practice.

The reel has a slipping clutch which can be set to just below the breaking strain of the line, so that giving line to a running fish should be easier. I find it smoother and more efficient to backwind on the reel, or allow the pike to do it for me, trailing my index or second finger on the flyer of the spool. I have the clutch wound up tight to eliminate any chance of slippage on the strike.

I cannot advise you on the playing of fish, as this really comes only from experience. During the warmer months you may well take 15 minutes to land even a fish of 10lb. Under all circumstances, try to net the fish as soon as possible, before it is tired. The quicker the better. It is a question of striking a balance between hustling a fish too quickly and risking it coming adrift, or being too slow, which also increases the risk of loss.

Nowadays everyone uses a landing net to land pike. I think a large, round model is more efficient than the triangular net, but nobody takes any notice of me! The important thing is to have a big net – 30in in diameter if it's a round net, or with 40in arms if it's triangular. Place the net in the water and draw the pike over it. Then lift the frame so that the fish is enveloped in the mesh, grasp the mesh and lift to the bank. Do not over-strain the frame of the net.

The landing net mesh needs rethinking for pike angling. Micromesh is fine for most angling but not for piking. The trebles are sure to get badly tangled in such fine mesh and you can spend longer unhooking the hooks than you do unhooking the pike. The pike is more difficult to unhook when this happens, and the traces easily get damaged. Furthermore, a micromesh net in a river current can be a nuisance and occasionally dangerous.

I use 1in mesh netting of knitted (*not* knotted) material. It rarely causes a tangle, and even when lure fishing I do not hesitate to land a fish. With micromesh netting the prospect of tangles puts you off sometimes and you try to beach fish or pull them out by hand. This defeats the object of having a net in the first place. I bought my net by mail order from the USA.

UNHOOKING MADE EASY

Once on the bank the netted pike should be lowered on to soft ground, grass or an unhooking mat. In a boat the floorboards need covering with sacking or a similar material. I use polythene packing material with all the little air pockets. It is extremely kind to fish. You can use this on the bank, too, of course; for me it is less fiddly than the unhooking mats.

There is no need to be fearful of unhooking pike. Gone are the days of prodding and poking, with a gag holding the pike's jaws open. Just as far gone, in fact, as the days of the gaff. I shall describe what to do as though you were a right-handed person. Simply reverse the procedures if you are left-handed.

If you've got a large fish lying on the unhooking mat, then put the underside of the fish to your left. Kneel astride it gently, perhaps stretching some netting over its body and kneeling on that. The idea is that the pike is held down firmly, yet gently. It's easy to do.

Now put a soft, thick glove on your left

hand, drying your hand first. I use gardening gloves with a soft leather finish or cheaper, plastic ones, equally soft, from Millets. Lift the upward-facing gill cover (the fish's left gill cover) and slide the gloved fingers beneath it but above the gill filaments. Move the hand forwards until your fingers fetch up against the point where the two sides of the lower jaw merge. You need a glove to do this because there are teeth on the gill-filament arch supports to stop small fish escaping through the gill covers once they are inside the mouth.

Then grip the left jaw of the pike with the palm of the gloved hand and lift the fish's head off the ground. Quite often its mouth will open at this point; if it does not, you can give it a little encouragement by pushing the tip of the upper jaw with your gloved thumb which is free and positioned to do this. It all sounds complicated but actually is very quickly accomplished. I would say that 30 seconds is rather a long time for the total act of unhooking a pike.

You can, if you wish, follow exactly the same procedure with a small pike. But an even quicker approach is to take the glove hold I have described and lift the pike quickly off the floor – its mouth usually opens and it is not in a position to flap very much. Should either a big or a small pike flap about (you can usually sense this is about to happen), simply take a tight grip with the gloved hand and wait for it to stop. This is why soft gloves are used – for the pike's protection as well as yours.

Back to the unhooking! Hold the forceps in your right hand – but do not put your fingers in the handles in the way you normally would with scissors: if the pike spun suddenly, you could break a finger. Now simply look for the hooks. If you can reach them easily from the front, do so. If not, close the jaws of the forceps and slip them into the mouth through the gill cover opposite the one you have a grip on. Grip the shanks of the hooks and turn them upside down, bottom hook first. If the hooks are small, they'll pop clear of any tissue easily enough.

BARBED OR BARBLESS?

I have deliberately left any discussion of barbless hooks to this point. Barbless or semi-barbless hooks come out more easily

Above: *A well padded glove and a pair of forceps . . . that's all you require to remove hooks from pike.*

Above left: *Grip the jaw of a pike in this way and the mouth will obligingly remain open.*

than barbed hooks. My preference is for very small barbs. In careful hands I'd leave the choice to the angler. I feel I have good reasons for disliking barbless hooks, but I urge you to try both and make up your own mind. My own view about big barbless hooks – size 6 and larger – is that they are dangerous to pike, but 10s and 8s should be fine. Microbarbs are what we need, and one day we shall have them.

All this unhooking should be quick. If it isn't, then something has gone wrong at the time of the bite. If you intend taking photographs, the camera should be ready before you get a run. An unhooked fish can be sacked up before photography, but do remember that it will quickly recover and be more of a handful then. I take my photographs at capture, but do it very quickly, the emphasis being on the pike's welfare not on the quality of the pictures.

When weighing a pike, the same principle applies: get everything ready before you catch one. The commercially-made weighing slings are excellent, but remember to zero the balance with the weighing sling on it. I see no harm in hanging a pike momentarily on a weighing hook. It is really no different from the hand-unhooking method for small pike and does them no harm at all. You must, of course, be careful always to weigh fish over soft ground.

Most of the pike I return to the water swim off strongly, immediately. I do not remember the last one that didn't. Nursing a fish actually indicates that something has gone wrong. If it happens, then carefully reappraise your techniques and procedures. It is all-important to our future piking.

The rich tints of autumn traditionally trigger many pike anglers into action but it's a mistake to ignore the mean fighting fish of mid-summer.

THE DELIGHTS OF LURE FISHING

Lure fishing for pike is a whole new ball-game. If you are taking it up for the first time, do not begin in the depths of winter. The summer is best, but pike are still active to lures in September and October. In late December and January you need to know your waters well.

The basic equipment is similar but only one trace is necessary now. The rod needs to be rather lighter than bait-fishing rods, not only because you have to carry it but also it will be used for casting lighter baits. Many artificial lures are quite small, and usually no heavy lead or float is involved.

I use the same range of line breaking strains and reels. Several firms make spinning rods and the only ones to avoid are those with a test curve of 2.5lb or more. I'd go for a test curve of between 1.75 and 2lb. The rod needs a slightly more tippy action than for bait fishing: a lot of casting is done with a flick of the rod top.

As a rule I prefer a 9ft or light 10ft rod, but I have used them as short as 4.5ft. With the short, so-called baitcasters – a misnomer if ever there was one! – the handle is usually designed to fit a multiplying reel rather than a fixed spool. You should avoid multipliers until you really have the hang of lure fishing. After that stage has been reached, such reels add a new dimension to your fishing: you gain accuracy and efficiency, if losing a little distance.

Pike will attack fish their own size as this spoon-caught jack demonstrates.

One of the great delights of lure fishing is the lack of heavy tackle. You need a rod, landing net and a small rucksack or bag into which can go the following: waterproofs, food, drink, camera, unhooking gear, spring balance – and lures. Do not stint on the last item: take 20 or 30.

Another great pleasure for the lure-fishing enthusiast is roaming the banks. So avoid big tackle boxes, especially those supposedly custom-built for lure anglers. They were, in fact, invented for North American boat anglers, for whom the cantilevered box is ideal. But when roaming the banks, leave them in the car. The choice of rod also relates to the venue. Long rods are best from reed-fringed banks, and shorter rods are preferable from boats.

CHOICE OF PLUGS, SPOONS AND SPINNER

Choosing lures is what really throws the newcomer, just as the wealth of flies may give the new fly fisher some headaches.

There are essentially three types of lure: plugs, spoons and spinners. The last two almost always sink. The plugs may float and dive shallowly on retrieve, float and dive deeply, sink or work across the top.

Spoons look like tablespoon blades, or modifications of that shape. A majority wobble on the retrieve. Spinners have blades which spin around an axis, the latter often a bar of wire to which the hooks are attached.

Basically, what you need is a range of types, to enable you to fish all the water available, as the fancy takes you. And for each lure type you need a range of sizes and colours. A big lure for pike might be 8in long, a small one 1in. I go for three sizes myself – roughly 2in, 5in and 7in long.

Colours? This is a little easier. Anything pikey, perchy, silver, copper or brass works well. Add to them a few jazzed-up colours such as red or bright yellow or white, and you can cover most eventualities. I recommend always having a red flash somewhere on the lure: I believe the pike target it, so on long spoons have it at the back end of the blade by the trailing treble.

LURES SHORTLIST

If I was forced to pick four favourites in each type, this is how I would make my shortlist. First of all, for summer fishing, you need a surface popper, the floater that you can work in spurts across the weed beds and between lily leaves. Then I would have a shallow diver in several colours, like the Big S – and perhaps its kid brother, the Little S. A shallow diver like this can be converted into an effective sinker by putting a Wye lead at the head of the trace, between trace swivel and line.

A buoyant floater like the Big S can also be fished in very deep water on the paternoster, where the bottom is known to be relatively free from snags. Add about 2-3ft of line to the head swivel on the trace and a suitable lead to the other end of the paternoster link. After the tackle sinks to the bottom, the lure itself will be buoyant above the lead, and the retrieve then causes it to dive. It can be fished sink-and-draw, naturally. So with the Big S you get several for the price of one!

An out-and-out small plug that I would never be without is the Sweeper – or its American counterpart, the Quarterback.

This has a very fast action and fairly shallow retrieve that is highly desirable sometimes. Finally, perhaps, I would take the tried and trusted Yellow Tiddler.

Spoons are, in a way, a simpler choice. First on my list would be variations on the Norwich spoon theme. Vary the length, wobble, and colour, but the basic Norwich shape is a winner. My four spoons would simply be of different lengths, with a range of colours. Possibly the 5in model might be in heavy metal and light metal.

My favourite spinner is a buzzer or, more correctly, a spinner bait. This is probably the best all-round lure in existence. It would be followed in my list by various barspoons, such as the Jet or Kilko, Pearl or Dorado (in different weights and colours), and perhaps a Rooster Tail or two. I'm sure I've exceeded the four we gave ourselves as the limit – but it is easy to get carried away when lure fishing.

Top: Four superb plugs from the Shakespeare series (from left): Little S, Yellow Tiddler, Red and Silver Popper and Sweeper.

Above: A brace of Norwich type spoons with Fishtail and Ladybird spinners alongside.

*The spinner bait (**right**) looks a strange construction but its fluttering action is irresistible to pike (**below**). Barrie finds it most effective worked across the surface through weed beds (**below right**). Pike will literally stick their heads out of the water to intercept it.*

Fishing with a reasonable selection of lures in your bag gives a potential diversity that is enormous. But as well as trying different types of lure you should also vary the retrieve speed from steady to erratic, fast to slow. Work out the optimum performance for each lure. Always, but always, cast with confidence. Never get into that boring round-the-clock routine of casting. Cast to where you think the pike might be lurking.

I change my lure every few minutes until I hit upon the pattern for the day or the hour. The slightest change in retrieve style can transform the day.

Lure fishing simply adds to the versatility of the piker. There are more complicated things you can do when fishing for pike such as balloon fishing, drifter rig fishing, or trolling. But follow the advice in this chapter and you will be ready for anything.

SEA FISHING

Both fishing from the shore and from a boat are
covered in this comprehensive section. Here is your basic
guide to selection of a basic beach outfit, baits,
rigs and casting methods while the essential tackle and rigs
needed for a day on a charter boat are covered, with
advice on crucial matters like safety.

FREEDOM OF THE SHORE

The prolific seas around our wild coastline contain a multitude of species and present the adventurous shore angler with a wide choice of target fish for most of the year. And there's not a penny to pay for the privilege of fishing among some of the most rugged and spectacular coastal scenery to be found anywhere in the world. No licences or permits are required to fish in saltwater and access remains unrestricted with the exception of a few isolated beaches which are privately owned.

In real terms the cost of beach tackle has fallen and it's possible to buy a complete outfit for well under £100. Just how much to invest ultimately depends on how seriously you want to get involved. The choice is yours.

TIDAL INFLUENCES

A thorough understanding of tides, the effect of their rise and fall, and of weather conditions on the feeding behaviour of different species is of fundamental importance.

During each 24-hour cycle there are normally two high and two low tides. Exceptions to this include marks such as the Solent and Southampton Water where a peculiar tidal phenomenon results in a second high water in each tidal phase, usually one hour after the first high water.

Highest and lowest tides

The height and fall of tides is determined by the gravitational pull of the moon and varies from day to day. The actual high tide time advances by approximately 55 minutes in each cycle. The highest tides in any month are described as springs and occur at the time of maximum gravitational pull when there is a full or new moon. At the other extreme, the smallest tides, known as neaps, fall midway through a moon phase when the moon and sun are pulling in opposing directions resulting in a weak gravitational effect and little movement in

the tide. The interval between one high water and the next is about 12 hours 25 minutes.

Tide tables

Tide tables giving the precise times of high and low water are obtainable from local clubs and tackle shops. There are critical differences in these times even along comparatively short stretches of coast because headlands, sandbars, estuaries and other features can all substantially hinder the free passage of tidal flows. That makes it a good idea to obtain tables for those areas you intend fishing regularly as it avoids laborious calculations based on regional or Tower Bridge, London, charts. Mind you, these are reasonably simple to understand because all it involves is adding or subtracting the stated difference for your fishing patch from the high water times listed.

Feeding times and tides

Generally, a young flood tide is the prime fishing time especially on a shallow beach where there is a large rise and fall of tide. As the water starts to flood back over the sand, flatfish move in and feed on small crabs, worms and shrimps dislodged by the inrushing tide.

Many species feed most heartily in the fiercest of tidal flows. This is certainly the case with cod, smoothhound, bass, whiting and even the humble dab. The stronger the tide, the more food items are ripped from the seabed and carried along to the waiting fish.

Although a flooding tide through to high water is the peak feeding time for many species, there are a few localised exceptions. These are chiefly in areas renowned for experiencing strong tidal flows on the ebb but very little movement on the flood.

Feeding habits and weather

During settled spells in summer when the sea is flat calm and clear, many fish feed by sight and stay in deeper water making the angler's task more difficult. They can become extremely finicky and bait presentation is then even more critical.

But stormy weather gives the beach angler a real break! Fish move close inshore to gorge on the free harvest of food disturbed by the turbulent wave action and caution is thrown to the winds.

Discoloured water forces the fish to feed by scent rather than by sight and they become easy pickings at close range.

Piers cast a spell on the young and old alike offering a safe, comfortable platform for fishing.

ALL KINDS OF MARKS

The coastline around the British Isles provides every imaginable kind of fish habitat. Each type of mark has its own brand of attraction. Let's have a look at the main categories.

Sandy beaches

These might look flat and uninteresting but they're home for a wide variety of species. Bass are the No. 1 quarry from many south-west-facing storm beaches. When the sea is whipped up into a terrifying cauldron by gales, these silver kings of the sea feed in the surf, often just behind the second breaker and within comfortable casting range of any angler.

Plaice and flounders are the chief summer catch from many sandy beaches on day tides while night sessions are almost guaranteed to produce nocturnal sole on fresh ragworm. In winter, shoals of cod and whiting move in – particularly along the east coast – and the dab swap places with the plaice and sole. Lug and ragworm are probably the top baits for sandy beaches but sandeel and peeler crab also score heavily.

Estuaries

The shelter of an estuary provides the angler with a refuge whatever the weather on the open sea. Flounders are the mainstay of sport for much of the year and in summer there's the chance of eels, mullet or even smoothhound. Coalfish provide extra entertainment at northern venues.

Shingle

Flat shingle beaches invariably produce

similar results to sandy shorelines. Once the tide starts to ebb, you'll find the shingle more often than not gives way to a sandy bottom. The basic difference between many shingle and sandy beaches is the strength of the tidal flow. Shingle beaches are exposed to faster torrents producing superior fishing in winter for codling and whiting.

Rock

There are areas of rocky foreshore where the seabed is actually relatively clear with sandy patches but often the rocks extend out for some distance with the additional complication of heavy kelp beds. Heavy tackle is a must. Species which prefer this rough terrain include wrasse, conger, rockling and pollack. Rocky marks which give way to broken ground are easier to fish and they hold a greater number of species, with rays, dogfish and cod frequently putting in an appearance.

Steep shelving

The 16 miles of shingle that make up the mighty Chesil Bank in Dorset is probably

Ballan wrasse bite hard but spit out the bait or run you into kelp incredibly quickly. Even the tiddlers bend a float rod until it creaks!

the best known example of a steep shelving beach. These deep water marks undoubtedly offer the best chance of a record catch or an outsize fish more usually associated with boat fishing. Turbot, ling, bull huss, rays and trigger fish have all figured in the action at Chesil.

For sheer variety the steep shingle beach takes some beating. Normally, long range casting isn't necessary with deep water almost under your feet.

Piers, groynes and harbours

The numerous Victorian piers, groynes and harbour walls protruding from our coastline again give the shore angler the advantage of reaching deep water with minimum casting effort. They are excellent, safe marks for novices of all ages to learn the ropes. In summer the strong currents around many of these man-made structures provide superb light line floatfishing.

THE BASIC OUTFIT

This modest mound of tackle represents virtually all the gear I need to take on anything that swims around the British coastline. I always try to travel as light as possible.

1 11ft carp rod to get the maximum fun from mackerel, garfish and scad on light float tackle.

2 Abu 9ft spinning rod for pollack, bass and coalfish.

3 Full length chest waders. I find they're essential for fishing storm beaches when a big sea is running.

4 Miner's headlight for nightfishing. More versatile than static paraffin or petrol lamps which are no help when you are wading into the surf to grab a late night cod.

5 Anchor pressure lamp used on the coldest of winter nights

6 A selection of reels.

7 Bulk spools of 10,12,15 and 25lb Maxima nylon.

8 Filleting knife for gutting fish and cutting up bait.

9 Heavy duty rucksack for carrying tackle on long distance hikes to remote marks.

10 Cantilever box.

11 Bulk spool of 50lb Maxima for shock leaders, 60lb Daiwa mono for the main trace line and 25lb Sylcast which I use to tie up hook snoods

12 Home-made measuring stick to check that fish are sizeable according to local regulations.

13 Groundsheet to prevent small items of tackle being lost in the sand or shingle.

14 Selection of weights including 5oz Breakaways, plain torpedoes, long tailed bombs and flat leads for rock fishing.

15 Small cantilever box.

16 Strong gaff capable of beaching 40lb conger. A cord on the handle is looped around the wrist to stop a powerful fish wrenching away the gaff.

17 Landing net for use when floatfishing from rocks and groynes.

18 Rig wallets to store terminal rigs.

19 Brolly sheet to prevent wind and rain gusting under the sides.

20 Zziplex 12ft, NG2 lightweight carbon beachcaster for bass and pollack fishing.

21 Daiwa 12ft, high performance HPB-12M carbon beachcaster for lightweight match fishing.

22 Zziplex 13ft, 2500M carbon beach-caster. This is my all-rounder and deals with most general fishing demands on the beach.

23 Zziplex Quatra match rod to tackle conger. I have cut 3in off the tip to beef it up.

24 Ian Golds Supermatch Tripod. This superb rod stand will take one or two rods.

REELS ON PARADE

1 DAM Quickfly 90 fly reel for mullet fishing with maggots.

2-4 Daiwa Millionaire 6HM multipliers with the level winds removed. They are loaded with 10, 12 and 15lb Maxima plus 50lb shock leaders for fishing sand and shingle marks.

5 Ryobi S320 heavy multiplier reel containing 20lb Maxima for ray and conger fishing over semi-rugged ground.

6 Daiwa Millionaire 6HM multiplier fitted with level wind and loaded with 25lb Maxima to cope with heavy weed.

7 Daiwa Millionaire 6HM with level wind removed. Filled with 18lb line and 50lb shock leader to help lift fish up the sides of breakwaters and harbour walls.

8 Ryobi two-speed TS4 fixed spool. Ideal for pollack and bass spinning with 12lb line.

9 Shakespeare Omni fixed spool loaded with 5lb line to floatfish for mackerel, wrasse, pollack and garfish.

10 Abu 7000 heavy duty multiplier takes 30lb line to deal chiefly with conger.

THREE-TIER CANTILEVER BOX

1 Mustad DC Easy Links, Aiken quick-change swivels and Taylor and Johnson Rapier split rings. All are used to connect rigs and sinkers.

2 Sharp, surgical scissors to trim bait, flounder spoons (Chapter 7) and spare set of coasters to secure reel on rod.

3 Beads used in the make-up of traces and as fish attractors Roll of knitting elastic to lash soft baits like crab

on hook. Toothbrush for cleaning sand and grit from inside reels while on the beach.

4 Berkley heavy duty swivels and packet of size 2, gold coloured Mustad Aberdeen hooks used for flounder fishing.

5 Cox and Rawle Uptide, chemically sharpened hooks, size 2/0 to 7/0. Ideal crab hooks when cod fishing.

6 Size 1/0 and 2/0 needle point Kamasan hooks used for dogfish and bass.

7 Small Berkley McMahon snap links to connect sinkers.

8 Large McMahon snaps used for quick-release clips on traces.

9 Packets of size 1 and 2 Kamasan hooks. I use them as general-purpose patterns.

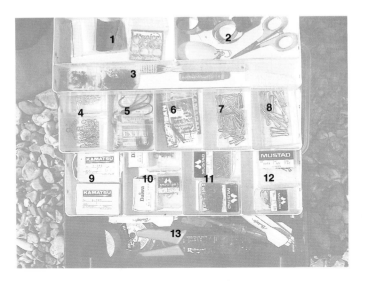

10 Selection of Mustad and Daiwa size 1 and 2 fine wire, Aberdeen hooks for flounders and dabs.

11 Spade end, size 2 Mustad Limerick hooks with wide gape that are perfect for using peeler crab when eel fishing.

12 Mustad Limerick, size 3/0 and 1 eyed hooks. These are a fairly soft pattern and easily bend out making them a good hook at marks where there's plenty of snags.

13 Baitsafe capsule to protect soft baits, wire trace line, crimping pliers, screwdriver, roll of tape.

TWO-TIER CANTILEVER BOX

1 Breakaway lead lift to help keep lead high in water over rough ground and reduce tackle losses.

2 Bullet weights which I use occasionally when floatfishing in rough water. Plummet weight, with cork insert for hook, serves as depth finder alongside harbour walls and groynes.

3 Dispenser of AAA split-shot to cock Drennan No.4 Piker float

4 Plastic and stainless steel spoons for flounders and plaice,

5 Wire booms to fish down the side of piers,

packets of size 14 Mustad, Dippa and Sundridge specimen-hooks used for mullet and small eels.

assortment of Avon and stick floats for mullet, wrasse, mackerel and garfish in calm conditions.

6 Sundridge size 8 specimen hooks. Used as extra bait-securing hook in certain rigs.

7 Lead bombs up to 2oz used when pollack fishing with spinning gear.

8 No. 4 split-shot for holding small bait on seabed, even when legering with heavy tackle.

9 Taylor and Johnson split-shot, small Avon floats.

10 My mainstay Drennan No. 4 Piker floats with several other larger floats, spools of Sundridge line and a handful of odd lures.

HOOKS AND BAITS

HOOK SIZES AND KNOTS

The majority of sea hooks are manufactured with eyed- or spade-ends for attachment to the nylon hook trace or snood. With an eyed hook, simply thread the line through and tie a half-blood knot. Trim the loose end of line with scissors or nail cutters to form as neat a tying as possible.

The traditional spade-end knot is trickier to tie, but persevere as this style of hook is a must for small crab baits.

The size range of sea hooks is very extensive but most demands will be met between a small size 4 and a 7/0 which is the largest a beach angler is ever likely to use.

POPULAR HOOK PATTERNS

Hooks are relatively cheap and you should tie up new ones for every trip with the exception of large, stainless steel conger hooks which can be sharpened and used again. There are four leading patterns: Aberdeen, Limerick, Uptide and O'Shaughnessy. Within each of these classifications there are significant differences between competing brands. To avoid any confusion here are my precise recommendations for each pattern.

Aberdeens

I use two types of Aberdeen, the traditional fine wire versions and the more robust patterns sold under the Kamasan label. My preference in the fine wire Aberdeens are the Mustad 3262 and Daiwa pattern. But I rarely use anything over a size 1 in this group because the fine wire bends easily on a decent fish. The problem is magnified in the larger sizes which have a wide gape.

A small size 4 or 2 fine wire Aberdeen is ideal when fishing for dabs, sole, flounders and pout. The Aberdeen's long shank and fine wire is perfectly suited to top flattie baits like small, fragile harbour ragworm but they need to be threaded on with care otherwise they'll disintegrate. Both the

Mustad and Daiwa versions have extremely sharp points and prominent barbs giving excellent penetration and holding powers. Kamasan long shank Aberdeens with their chemically sharpened needle points are slightly thicker in the wire and are much stronger than standard patterns. They are the hook to trust at venues where there's a chance of picking up a weighty fish.

Limericks

The Mustad Limerick is a wide gape, short shank hook which teams well with small peeler crab baits when fishing for the likes of eels and pouts. This design of hook is needed with a bulky crab bait which would tend to slide down a long shank hook and mask the point. If the long shank hook had a narrow gape as well, then the problems would be compounded leading to poor penetration.

The short shank Limerick allows the top half of the crab to be lashed securely in position with knitting elastic to prevent it sliding down and clogging the gape. But even if the crab did slide you'd still be fishing effectively because it would not completely shroud the point because of the generously wide gape.

Hooks to trust. If conger are in your sights then you will require the big O'Shaughnessy hook on the left. The other patterns in the top row are a Kamasan Aberdeen, traditional fine-wire Aberdeen and Mustad-eyed and spade-end Limericks for crab baits. On the bottom row are a Cox and Rawle Uptide pattern and smaller stainless-steel O'Shaughnessy.

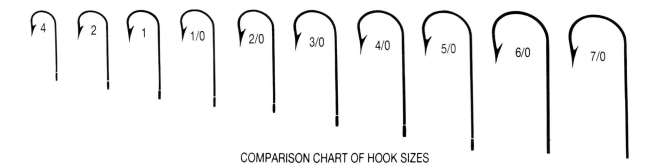

COMPARISON CHART OF HOOK SIZES

The Mustad Limerick is obtainable in eyed- or spade-ends, but the eyed hook is made from relatively soft wire and bends easily. I much prefer the spade-end which is stronger and the ideal all-rounder for small crab baits. Whichever Limerick you choose, I would not recommend using sizes above 2/0. I normally stick to size 4 and 2.

Uptide

A more robust hook is necessary for larger crab baits when after cod, smoothhound and bass. The Cox and Rawle high tensile Uptide pattern fits the bill. This wide gape, short shank hook is extremely strong even in the larger sizes. The 3/0 and 5/0 are cracking hooks to use with big crab baits when the cod are running.

O'Shaughnessy

Freshly dug ragworm look sturdy but the tail end is brittle.

The O'Shaughnessy design is an extremely strong hook made from stainless steel with a medium length shank and average size gape. My preferred patterns in this range

are the Mustad 34007 and Daiwa Superstrike. It's the hook to use for powerful fish in rocks or kelp as it will withstand considerable punishment.

I use the Mustad in a size 1 for wrasse. I've never had one of these hooks bend out of shape even when a large fish has got me stuck solid in kelp.

The Daiwa Superstrikes in sizes 5/0 and 7/0 are my trusted conger irons. The hook is 100 per cent reliable, with a razor sharp point. That's important because conger are often finicky feeders.

BAIT CATEGORIES

The natural diet of sea fish consists chiefly of worms, small prey fish and shellfish. In bright, clear conditions fish usually feed largely by sight and are more inclined to take prawns, sandeels and crabs. When the water is rough and coloured, scent plays a major part in food location and shellfish, worms and peeler crab are more readily taken.

It is virtually always essential that the bait is fresh but there are some, such as slipper limpet, which work better if they are a few days old.

VERSATILE WORMS

Of all the natural baits, worms will be accepted regardless of weather conditions and they rate as the most prolific catchers of sea fish because they figure so prominently in their diet.

RAGWORM

The common red ragworm with its distinctive, centipede-like paddles running along both sides of its body serves as nourishment

for a wide range of species. It is carnivorous and feeds on small invertebrates and other tiny particles that it filters from mud, shingle or fine sand. Normally, only the giant king ragworm, which can grow to several feet in length, are found in sand with the smaller worms preferring mud or shingle.

It is worth pointing out that worms dug from mud keep better than shingle rag and they're a far firmer bait, probably because they are not so watery. Collecting ragworm is a back-aching task especially in winter when they burrow deeper to escape the cold. Invest in a wide-pronged potato fork if you intend digging your own and that will eliminate a lot of the sweat.

It is relatively simple to locate the most prolific areas of worms. Walk carefully across the mud keeping an eye open for little jets of water squirting from small holes. That's a sure sign that ragworm are in residence and then it's just a case of digging where there is the greatest density of worms.

Ragworm should always be handled with care. Grip them near the head as the tail end is brittle and breaks easily. Also these worms can inflict a nasty bite with powerful, horny-like nippers which protrude from the jaw. It's not unknown for them to draw blood.

Over the years, I've found that ragworms of 5-6in produce the best results. I would sooner use half-a-dozen small rag with lots of tails dangling attractively from the hook than a single, big worm.

Mounting rag on the hook

Ragworm should be threaded on the hook head first. Feed the hook through the body, gently drawing the worm around the bend, up the shank and past the eye until the tail is left hanging free below the barb. The only exception to this method is for sole living on muddy bottoms. For reasons I have never fathomed they want their rag threaded on tail first with the head around the point of the hook.

Storage techniques

It's possible to store ragworm in a tank of aerated sea water and many anglers find this a satisfactory method. The water must be kept cool and any dead worms removed immediately. Tanked rag are best taken from the water 24 hours before you intend using them and left to dry on newspaper. But I have got to admit that I regard this technique as inferior to storing worms in a fridge. Untanked rag make a much better bait.

My system of storing rag is to lay the worms in trays lined with newspaper and then cover them with seaweed. The trays are kept in a fridge with the temperature set between 40-45 degrees Fahrenheit. Freshly dug ragworm will remain in perfect condition for several weeks but if the temperature rises and they start to die there is little that can be done to save them. Never retain broken and whole worms together otherwise they will quickly deteriorate.

Transporting ragworm on short trips is easy with a covering of seaweed in a plastic bucket. But if you're travelling a long distance, a cool box will be needed.

WHITE RAGWORM

No angler worth his salt would enter a major competition without a supply of lively whites which are markedly different in appearance from red ragworm. In fact, they are not true ragworm at all and their colour

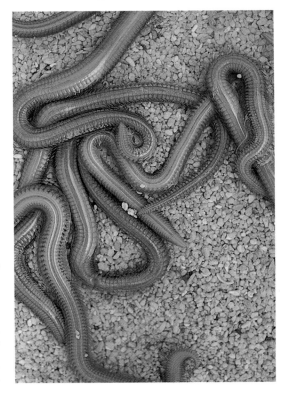

White rag will remain lively if they are stored in coral sand and sea water in the fridge.

varies from a pearly white, among the bigger specimens, to a dirty grey depending on the sand or gravel they frequent. All white rag have a pronounced vein running just under the skin from head to tail. They are ferocious cannibals which often kill red rag on sight.

Whites are extremely active and wriggle violently when handled, eventually forming tight coils or even breaking in half.

The exact location of many white rag beds is kept secret but areas of small stones or coarse sand containing a large population of tube worms are a favourite habitat, especially if the sand is fairly wet. They like liquid sand because they can travel through it at a rate of knots searching for unsuspecting prey.

Large pearly white snakes can only be collected on a big spring tide. Look for a small ridge of coarse sand as close as possible to the low water mark. As a rule you do not have to dig too deeply to gather smaller whites because they live in the top 6 in. But the larger worms tend to be much deeper.

Average size whites can be dug on smaller tides but don't expect a bucketful. About 60 an hour would be good going but you would have to excavate getting on for a ton of spoil!

Smaller fish show a distinct liking for small, white ragworm on a fine wire, size 2 Aberdeen hook. Larger snakes are a superb cod bait and can be used singly on a size 2/0 Kamasan.

Storage techniques

White rag must be left in a bucket of sea water for 24 hours to clean themselves before being stored in the fridge. Never mix them with other types of worms or retain broken ones – they will quickly foul the water.

For best results, store in a fridge, on a tray containing coral sand and covered with 2in of fresh sea water, a maximum of ten worms to a tray. The fridge temperature should be set at 45 degrees Fahrenheit. In transit, pack the trays in a cool box after pouring away the sea water.

HARBOUR RAGWORM

Harbour rag look similar to normal red ragworm but there's a pronounced yellow vein running along the whole length of the body. This most delicate of all worm-baits seldom exceeds 3in and is favoured by the match angler for snatching small fish. Their beds are found near the high tide mark in estuaries and harbours and they can be gathered on the smallest of neap tides.

It's possible to collect a dozen or more with a single forkful of mud or gravel and they will even live in brackish water.

Superb for flatties

A fine wire, whipped or spade-end hook is required to present these small worms, with a size 4 tied to a snood of 5-10lb nylon fitting the bill. Thread a dozen maddies up the line and you've got a superb flattie bait.

Storage techniques

Storing maddies poses no problems. First wash them thoroughly in sea water as soon as you have finished digging. Then lay them on damp hessian or newspaper in trays and place them in a fridge set at 45 degrees Fahrenheit. They can also be retained in weed or an aerated tank.

LUGWORM

The popularity of lugworm puts most other sea baits in the shade. It is widely distributed and produces fish consistently, particularly at the country's big cod marks where it is often the only bait worth using. There are three categories of this worm classified as the common blow lug and the black and yellowtails.

BLOW LUGWORM

These are found in all types of terrain from sandy storm beaches to muddy estuaries. But it's the sandy venues which offer the easiest and most productive digging opportunities.

Blow lug live in a U-shaped burrow with a coiled cast of sand revealing their presence. Look carefully and you'll also see a small hole a few inches from the cast which is the other end of the worm's burrow. The casts are discharged by the lug as it filters the sand for food. They appear as the tide starts to ebb and the biggest concentration will be located at the low water line, especially on a

big tide. This is also where the largest worms will be found.

A thin, wire type hook baited with four small lug is fine for plaice and whiting but cod demand slightly larger and stronger hooks with bigger worms.

Storage techniques

Once again a wide-pronged potato fork is the most efficient tool for digging up these worms in wet sand and mud. I normally drop freshly dug lugworm into a bucket of clean seawater, separating out any broken ones to avoid killing the lot.

I try to dig three days before the worms are actually required. I leave them in water for the first two days giving them time to wash through sand and debris in their system. Then I place the worms on a sheet of newspaper for 20 hours to dry. This hardens them up and results in a far better hookbait.

One additional tip, which will help keep your lug in the best condition, is to place damp hessian over them while they are laid out on newspaper.

Never keep blow lug in a hot room or direct sunlight otherwise they will do exactly what their name suggests and blow. A cool, darkened room or fridge set at 45 degrees Fahrenheit is the right climate.

BLACK AND YELLOWTAIL LUG

These worms come into their own for cod and will outfish blow lug every time. But their beds are extremely limited. Kent and North Wales hold the biggest stocks.

Unlike blow lug, black and yellowtail live in a burrow which goes straight down for several feet. Their casts also differ in that the coils of sand are completely symmetrical.

Yellowtails can be trench dug with a potato fork in summer on the Kent coast but a bait pump is a more practical solution for big black lug. The pump is pushed into the beach directly over a cast and, hopefully, sucks up the worm along with sand.

Storage techniques

Yellowtail lug will happily survive in tanks of water, twisting themselves into tight coils. But keep them cool and don't store too many in a container.

Another method of retaining yellowtail and black lug is to gut them as soon as they are dug by squeezing out all the sand from their insides. Wrapped individually in newspaper, they will keep for several days or can be frozen. Frozen black lug is a great bait for dabs at deep water marks like Chesil and Dungeness.

CRABS

All crabs must shed their shells from time to time in order to grow and during the moulting period they give off a scent which acts as a powerful stimulant to fish. Crabs in this state are described as peelers.

Peelers

What actually happens during a moult is that the crab fills itself up with water forcing its shell to crack and fall off. The old claws and legs are also discarded leaving a soft, new green skin underneath which enlarges and takes several days to harden. When they are moulting or soft the crabs become lethargic and vulnerable to predators.

Edible crabs, the velvet swimming variety and common shore crabs are all of interest to the shore angler. But the velvet swimming crab is the hardest to obtain because of its preference for deep water.

How to recognise peelers

Peeler crabs shelter under boulders or along the edges of groynes and harbour walls, often burying themselves under the sand

Lugworm are the only bait worth using at many of the big cod marks.

Peeler Presentation
Top left: Kill the crab before removing the legs and all traces of the shell.

Top right: Cut away the gills.

Above: Cut body in two, mount on hook and lash tight with knitting elastic.

for extra protection. When they've actually shed their shells, the shore crabs cannot be mistaken for anything else but a softie because they are literally extremely soft to the touch. Peelers are less obvious but there are several tell-tale signs that the crab is in the process of a moult.

To check if the crab is a peeler or not twist and remove an end leg segment. If a soft, brightly coloured new skin is revealed underneath the old shell then it's definitely a peeler. But if white muscle and tissue is found then the crab is not moulting.

At an advanced stage of moulting, the crab's shell will start to split away, with a crack appearing along the side of its body. These crabs are in prime condition for fishing. As a general rule, crabs that are a dull matt colour or covered in barnacles are more likely to be peelers.

In early summer, the smaller female crabs begin to moult. Some of these hide away in silt but more often than not they

will be carried underneath a male. If the female is being carried the correct way up then the crab will be a peeler. But if it is carried upside down it will be a softie mating with the male crab above.

A second moult of the large cock crab occurs in autumn just before they move off into deeper water at the first hint of cold weather.

Storage techniques

Live peelers must be retained among weed in a fridge set at the mandatory 45 degrees Fahrenheit. They should be checked daily and any dead ones removed. Every second day, place them in saltwater for about one minute. That's just long enough for them to wet their gills without taking in too much water and will ensure they remain in first-class condition.

Mounting on the hook

Before mounting a crab on the hook, kill it as humanely as possible with a pointed tool. Lift away the top shell and remove the legs and claws. Strip off all the remaining shell including the bits around the mouth before cutting out the gills with scissors.

The crab is now ready to use, although it may need to be cut in half depending on its size and the type of fish you are seeking. The legs can be used on their own or for tipping off other baits once they've also been peeled to expose the new soft legs underneath.

The wide-gape, spade-end Limerick is ideal for smaller baits while the Cox and Rawle Uptider pattern is suited to larger

mouthfuls. Lash the crab on the shank with knitting elastic if necessary, to help hold it in place during the rigours of the cast.

When fishing for smaller species I find half a crab is more than adequate. Cutting it in half allows the juices and scent to flow more freely. This also holds true when using a whole crab for cod, bass and smoothhound on a size 2/0 Cox and Rawle Uptider. I find catch rates are increased by cutting the crab three-quarters of the way through before threading it on the hook and whipping it with elastic thread.

One useful tip, particularly when smoothhound fishing is to tip off the bait with a couple of peeled legs. This certainly increases the catch rate. Peeled legs and claws are also effective for tipping off worm baits. They are tough and sinewy which prevents crabs stripping a bait too quickly.

Freezing peelers

Strange as it may seem, correctly frozen peelers can yield better results than fresh baits. Frozen peelers release scent and juices far more quickly and that's often an advantage in a match. The best time to freeze crabs is during the spring moult when a flush of big cock crabs peel simultaneously making collection easy. But crabs must be in prime moulting condition with the shell just starting to split away. Dead or hard crabs are totally useless for freezing.

Remove all the shell and the gills as already described. Failure to cut away the gills could turn the crab black and render it useless. Once the peeler has been completely cleaned, wash it in fresh water and then dry with paper kitchen towel. Wrap the crabs individually in clingfilm, making sure each packet is totally airtight, before placing them in the coldest part of the freezer on a flat tray. It's a good idea to date stamp each container. The legs and claws can also be frozen but keep them separate from the bodies.

Incidentally, tinfoil is not as good as clingfilm because it's difficult to get airtight and the crabs will eventually dry out making them less potent.

Transporting peelers

Frozen crabs must not be allowed to thaw out until just before they are needed as hookbait and should be transported in a large Thermos flask. Place the flask in the freezer the night before your trip to ensure the crabs travel in a perfect frozen state.

On the beach, remove no more than five or six peelers at any one time from the flask and tighten the lid immediately afterwards. Tipping out all the crabs at the start will make some of them useless as hookbaits before the session is finished.

HARDBACK CRABS

Surprisingly, anglers achieve very little success with hardback crabs even though they are regularly eaten by many inshore fish. The reason remains a mystery. Wrasse and smoothhound are the only two species which are enthusiastic about hardbacks presented on the hook. Small crabs about the size of a 10p piece work best but the presentation is critical.

Mounting hardbacks

First remove the claws before mounting the crab by passing the hook through its body approximately half-an-inch from its jaw. There's no need to tie the crab with elastic thread unless you are distance casting. The O'Shaughnessy pattern rules supreme for wrasse and smoothhound when using hardbacks. Tie on a size 2 for wrasse and a 3/0 for smoothhound.

Storage techniques

Collect small hardbacks from any rough ground just below the high-water mark. Store them in a cool, darkened shed with a good covering of weed. Keep them well away from heat and direct sunlight. They will need a daily soaking in saltwater but the length of time they spend in the water is not important.

HERMIT CRABS

These make excellent baits for many species, including cod and smoothhound, although they are extremely soft and difficult to cast. Unlike other crabs, the hermit does not moult in order to grow. It lives in a vacant winkle or whelk shell and scouts around for a larger shell when it outgrows its current home.

Above and opposite: *How to Cut up a mackerel. Cut a fillet away from your body.*

Good-size hermits are not commonly found in the intertidal zone. The most effective way of collecting them is with a weighted dropnet baited with a piece of smelly fish and lowered from a pier, breakwater or harbour wall.

A small hammer is needed to crack the shell to release the hermit. But do not smash it too hard or you will be left with a pulped crab. Apart from its main claw, the body of a hermit is too soft for distance casting. A 2/0 fine wire hook will hold these delicate baits and provide a good bait for a decent cod or smoothie.

Hermits must be retained in a cool, aerated tank of seawater. They won't survive for very long out of water and damp weed will only sustain them for a short period.

PRAWNS AND SHRIMPS

High sea temperatures in summer tempt prawns and shrimps inshore but they soon scurry back into deep water as colder weather begins to bite. The heaviest concentrations are usually in the vicinity of harbour walls, rocky outcrops and the base of seaweed covered piles.

Collecting these shellfish presents few problems with a purpose-designed pushnet. As the tide ebbs away, the net is worked over rough ground or weed and apart from prawns you'll also catch a good number of small fish.

The alternative method is to use a dropnet baited with fish or meat. The net must have a top which closes as soon as it is lifted out of the water from alongside a pier or harbour wall otherwise the prawns will be able to escape.

Most inshore fish take prawns, including wrasse, bass, pollack and flatties. Light float tackle is the most pleasing method for using this bait. Stick a size 6 short shank hook in the prawn's tail so it can move naturally.

Prawns will only stay alive if they are kept in a bucket of seawater with a portable aerator. They quickly perish once left out of water. If you want to keep prawns for long periods the water temperature will need to be far higher than that for most other baits, somewhere in the region of 55 degrees Fahrenheit. Regular changes of water are also necessary as bacteria multiply quickly in the warm water.

Slipper limpets

Unlike other shellfish, the slipper limpet gathers together in clusters with as many as a dozen stuck together. The largest ones on the bottom of the stack are always females and anchor the community to a stone. After a southwesterly gale, large quantities of limpets get washed up on the high tide mark. Some estuaries hold a good stock and oyster fishermen regularly dredge them up.

Once the limpets have been prised apart, a soft, yellowish flesh is exposed which can be scooped out and used as bait. Although many species accept freshly collected limpets, catches will improve by using stale, smelly baits which are at least two weeks old. Storage is simply a matter of placing them in a damp hessian sack in a cool corner out of direct sunlight.

Winter specials

Slipper limpets will catch fish for most of the year but I rate them indispensable in late winter when storms present the flatfish with a harvest of shellfish disturbed by turbulence. A size 2 Aberdeen crammed with six limpets takes fish after fish at these times. Although they are not a recognised cod bait, limpets are frequently effective during December and January when they're capable of singling out heavyweights.

Freezing method

To freeze slipper limpets, shell some week-old ones and place the fleshy parts on absorbent paper to dry. After a couple of hours transfer them to a sheet of newspaper, sprinkle on some salt and leave overnight. Remove any surplus salt the following day before packaging the limpets in batches of 40 ready for the freezer.

Most shellfish salted and frozen in this manner will become significantly tougher than the natural bait and that adds up to problem-free casting.

RAZORFISH

Although razorfish can be collected after a big storm in the same way as slipper limpets, they are also seen sticking out above

the surface of the sand at the low-water mark during spring equinox tides. They must be approached stealthily because they disappear in an instant. And don't pull too vigorously because they anchor themselves in the sand with a toe and break easily.

On some beaches, razorfish will emerge at the surface if salt is sprinkled down their hole. It's thought this tricks them into believing that the tide has started to flood.

The razorfish is another delicate bait and like limpets they'll produce better results when they're a few days old. Most flatfish take razorfish along with bass, cod, eels and pouting. Like any other shellfish, the peak time to fish them is after storms. A size 2 Aberdeen hook is more than adequate.

They are an ideal bait to freeze. Just wrap them individually in newspaper and pop them in the freezer. To make them tougher, salt and freeze in the same manner as slipper limpet.

OTHER SHELLFISH

Along the north-east coast mussels are highly rated for cod and flatties. Elsewhere, few anglers seem to give them serious consideration.

The mussel's soft, fleshy contents will not withstand casting in the natural state unless used on light float tackle. To harden up the mussel, it must be salted, like limpets, although freezing isn't necessary. Mussel becomes very tough once salted and serves as a superb cod bait. Hook choice varies depending on the type of fishing.

SANDEELS

Sandeels are a premier bait for bass but many beach anglers shy away from using them because of the difficulties of collection and storage.

Fresh sandeels usually outfish frozen bait with the exception of doggies which display no preferences. Few tackle shops have the facilities to keep live sandeels. If you can't collect your own buy some which have been blast-frozen as they're always of the highest quality.

Catching sandeels

For the angler living close to the coast, netting is the easiest way of catching sandeels in numbers but the outlay on equipment is not viable unless the costs are shared between friends.

The alternative method is to go out and dig for them. It's relatively easy under the right tidal and weather conditions. The most prolific sandeel spots are on sandbars where large numbers can be dug on warm, muggy nights during a big spring low-tide.

As the tide recedes, many sandeels bury down in the sand for a couple of inches and the only equipment required is a fork and a bucket filled with sea water. A portable aerator is essential if you want to keep them alive. Fork over the top three or four inches of sand, moving backwards. All you will see of the eels as you fork them out is a flash of silver as they try to bury themselves again.

Freezing techniques

There's a method of freezing that allows sandeels to thaw out as good as new – but they must be kept alive right up to the last moment. First, rinse the eels in freshwater and dry individually. Then lay them out separately on newspaper. Deposit them in the coldest part of the freezer and, once frozen, package them as required.

Hooking methods

I like to fish sandeels in the tidal stream on a light spinning rod with a 1oz ball weight and 3ft flowing trace. For light line or float work, the hook is passed right through the head by the eye and then out again about half-an-inch further down just behind the gill cover. Make sure the point of the hook is not covered.

Presentation is not quite so important when bottom fishing for rays and doggies but I favour passing the wire hook directly through the eel's mouth, down through the body and emerging approximately 1.5in from the eel's tail. To prevent the eel being ripped off while beachcasting, whip it on securely with elastic thread.

MACKEREL

This is one of the outstanding fish baits. It is a major food source for many larger sea species but Eastern Bloc factory-ships ripped a hole in its numbers through overfishing in the Western Approaches.

Trap the mackerel fillet in position with a second, smaller hook on the snood.

Cut small strips as shown and then slide filleting knife along backbone to remove them all.

Catching mackerel

The three main methods of catching mackerel are feathering, floatfishing and spinning. Feathering is the obvious choice if you want to catch them in numbers purely for bait. Mackerel shoals are easy to spot as they move inshore to chase small fry which boil on the surface in mad panic. Terns and gulls also hover just above the shoals to feed on any small fish breaking the surface.

Once a shoal has been sighted, it's just a case of heaving out a string of six feathers and working them back through the shoal with repeated, quick sweeps of the rod and a steady retrieve.

Freezing mackerel

If you want to freeze mackerel they must be gutted immediately after capture. That's the only sure way to guarantee a firm bait. Rinse the fish in freshwater as soon as possible and when dry wrap them individually in clingfilm before storing in the coldest part of the freezer. After a couple of days pack the mackerel in a heavy grade plastic bag with as much air expelled as possible. The bags should be tied to make them airtight. Bait frozen in this way will last for some time.

Presenting mackerel

Most beach rods are capable of casting a good sized fillet sliced from one side of the mackerel. Remember to cut away from your body with the mackerel resting on a flat surface. Hook size depends on the size of the fillet but a 5/0 O'Shaughnessy is more than adequate.

The problem with these bulky fillets is that they slide down the shank on the cast and cover the point of the hook. This can be avoided by using a smaller, second hook like a size 2 Kamasan or something similar to

trap the fillet in place. Slide this smaller hook down the snood until the bottom third of the hook rests over the top of the bait. Then twist the snood around the shank several times to secure the hook. Finally, set the Kamasan firmly in the top of the fillet and the bait will hold fast to it.

Worm baits tipped off with small strips of mackerel are a useful ploy. To prepare these small strips make a series of deep cuts approximately quarter-of-an-inch apart diagonally across the flank of the fish. Then slide the sharp filleting knife along the entire length of the backbone until all the fillets are removed. These will be the right size for tipping off or can be used as bait in their own right.

SQUID

Squid is one of the top attractors for double-figure cod in winter. Pollack, rays and conger also like a whole squid, and smaller species, such as whiting and dabs, take it in thin strips.

Frozen squid can be bought from most tackle shops in 5lb packs. Thaw out a box just sufficiently to break the squid apart into smaller packs for re-freezing. Grade the squid at the same time. Larger pieces which are too big for casting should be kept together for cutting into strips. Do not thaw out the squid completely because it quickly deteriorates. If the flesh turns a pinkish colour then you've got problems – the bait is starting to go off.

Whole squid are mounted in a similar way to mackerel on a 5/0 hook. Once again a small bait-holding hook needs securing on the snood to hold everything rigid.

HERRING

The oily herring leaves a superb scent trail on the seabed and its applications are similar to those of the mackerel. It works well in small strips either as a single bait or for tipping off worms in winter.

There are several other fish offerings, like sprat and pout, which are basically used whole as big fish baits for conger, rays and bull huss. In the case of pouting, a good fillet from an 8in fish or the head and guts make cracking conger fare. A secondary, bait-holding hook is always required for these presentations.

Whole squid is one of the best attractors for double-figure cod.

LINE, WEIGHTS AND RIGS

MONO SAFEGUARDS

Swinging a heavy lead sinker on the seashore is a potentially lethal exercise. Sensible precautions must be taken to avoid the nylon monofilament snapping during casting and possibly hurtling the weight out of control towards other anglers. Clearly, safety-first measures start with the choice of a suitable line. For general legering there are three distinct considerations.

First, there is the reel or main line which should be at least 10lb breaking strain as an absolute minimum. This is followed by a shock leader of 50lb nylon to absorb the stresses imposed by casting. The shock leader is not optional – you owe it to fellow anglers on the beach to think of their safety. Then comes the short length of main trace line on which the snoods or hook lengths are hung. For the trace I use 60lb Daiwa which is both strong and supple.

The trace is heavier than the casting leader to compensate for the weakening effect of knots used to assemble the terminal rig. Remember that every time you tie a knot in nylon it reduces the breaking strain.

REEL LINES

Apart from breaking strain, the diameter of the line also has to be taken into account when selecting a main reel line. There are significant differences between manufacturers on this score, with the same line strengths in rival brands varying considerably in diameter. Anglers with a good casting technique will certainly benefit by using lines with a lower diameter as they'll achieve longer distances. But these lines tend to be fairly stiff and knot strength is not all it could be. For the average angler, the larger diameter lines provide more secure knots and smoother casts. Recommended reel lines include Maxima, Drennan Beachcast and Shakespeare Superjet.

Jumbo spools of line are the most economic buy.

Neat leader knot slides easily over the tope eye of the rod.

Economic bulk spools

Bulk spools holding 600 yards or more are the most economic buy for reel lines and I carry stocks of 10lb, 12lb, 15lb, 18lb, 25lb and 30lb. Colour does not really matter although brown or fawn snood lengths appear to outperform traditional blue lines.

SHOCK LEADERS

A 50lb shock leader tied to the reel line permits a thinner reel line to be used without fear of cracking off while casting. When preparing to cast, the leader should be long enough to run from the terminal trace back to the reel with half-a-dozen turns on the spool.

The shock leader is tied to the main reel line with the standard leader knot comprising a uni-knot and half-hitch. For extra security, it can be strengthened by doubling the loose end of the reel line back through the half-hitch. Dependable brands for leaders are Drennan and Maxima.

HOOK SNOODS

Inevitably, hook lengths take a hammering when they're repeatedly retrieved over rough bottoms and crunched by fish with sharp teeth. Supple rather than hard nylon is preferable for snoods as it will withstand abrasion far better. But it also needs to be strong enough to deal with a decent fish.

You will hear conflicting opinions on the most suitable breaking strain for snoods but I reckon between 20lb and 25lb is fine for most beach work. This may seem rather hefty for a hook length but lighter snoods have a tendency to twist and kink, often spinning fish from the hook on a fast retrieve.

The actual length of the snood is dependent on tidal conditions and fish movement but you won't go far wrong if you follow my specific suggestions for the various rigs which follow later in this chapter. The brand of line I prefer for snoods is 26lb Sylcast.

WEIGHTS

Shore weights or sinkers are moulded from lead. Their principal task is to provide casting weight for the baited trace and then anchor it to the seabed.

Plain torpedo leads

The profile of a sinker determines its casting efficiency and in this regard nothing compares with the aerodynamic shape of the torpedo lead. It offers minimum wind resistance as it cuts through the air, resulting in smoother, longer casts and more bait left intact on the hook.

Most leads are designed to grip the seabed but plain torpedo or bomb-shaped sinkers will tumble along with the tide covering a wide area and often producing better

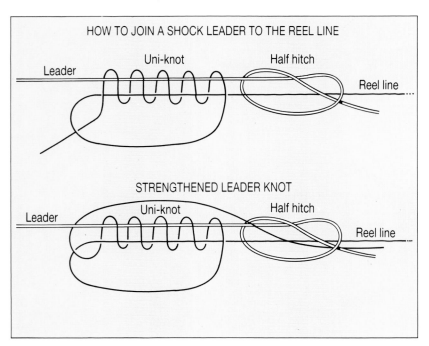

HOW TO JOIN A SHOCK LEADER TO THE REEL LINE

Leader — Uni-knot — Half hitch — Reel line

STRENGTHENED LEADER KNOT

Leader — Uni-knot — Half hitch — Reel line

catches than a static weight. This tactic works well at deep water marks like Chesil for plaice and dabs. The torpedo design is the one to use when shy feeding fish are deterred by the resistance of a grip lead with wires that dig into the seabed.

Long-tailed torpedo

The long-tailed torpedo has a 3-4 in wire tail instead of the customary loop connector and it anchors the terminal tackle more effectively. It also stabilises the lead in flight and helps achieve greater control during the cast.

Breakaways

The popular Breakaway sinker with its collapsible grip wires is the weight for rough or windy conditions. The grippers hold fast in a moderate tide until you make a strike or a good fish takes the bait. Then the four wires spring clear of their fixed positions and swivel backwards out of the way so they don't impede the retrieve.

Breakaways often result in fish hooking themselves without any need to strike. Species like cod and pout are inclined to seize the bait with such force that they automatically pull the hook home against the firmly anchored Breakaway.

Long-tailed Breakaways are available for enhanced casting performance.

Fixed grip leads

These were widely used before the introduction of the Breakaway but nowadays they are only really called up when the strength of the tide makes it difficult to hold bottom with any other sort of weight.

Torpedo sinkers are the most aerodynamic and tumble along with the tide. The long-tailed version is more stable in flight.

Grip lead for fast tides.

Latest versions of the Breakaway feature a more robust loop connector and trimmer beads.

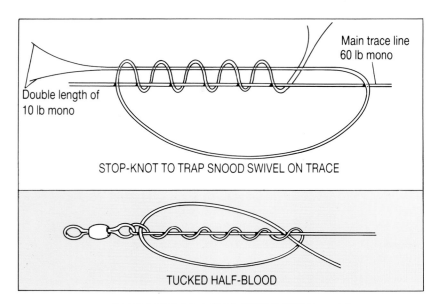

Double length of 10 lb mono

Main trace line 60 lb mono

STOP-KNOT TO TRAP SNOOD SWIVEL ON TRACE

TUCKED HALF-BLOOD

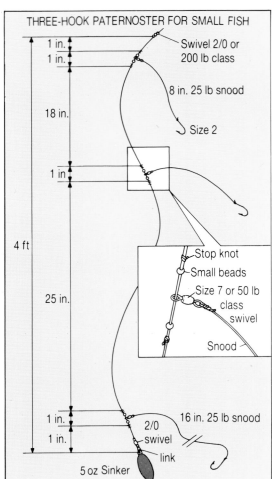

THREE-HOOK PATERNOSTER FOR SMALL FISH

1 in.
1 in.
Swivel 2/0 or 200 lb class

18 in.
8 in. 25 lb snood
Size 2

1 in.

25 in.

Stop knot
Small beads
Size 7 or 50 lb class swivel
Snood

4 ft

1 in.
1 in.
16 in. 25 lb snood
2/0 swivel
link

5 oz Sinker

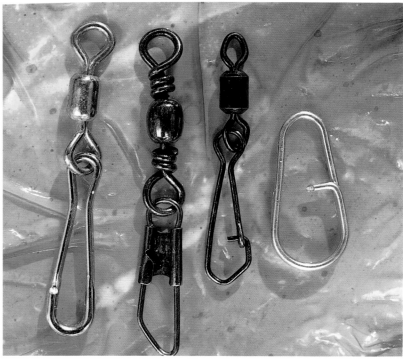

Above: The Berkley McMahon snap (left) or Mustad Easy-link (right) will hold the sinker securely during casting – but the American snaps in the centre can open up.

As their names suggests, fixed grip leads bite into the bottom at all times, even when retrieving. If a fixed grip won't hold then, it's a case of sitting it out until the pace of the tide subsides.

ATTACHING SINKERS TO THE TRACE

Never tie a heavy lead weight direct to the nylon trace because the knot will rapidly weaken when dragged over shingle and through pounding surf. It will even quickly

deteriorate on flat, sandy beaches and after a couple of retrieves you'll run the risk of a crack-off. The weight must hang from a robust connecting link such as a Mustad DC Easy-link, O-ring or a Berkley McMahon snap. Never use the American type snap links which can open up during the cast.

SIZES TO CARRY

All rods have a minimum and maximum payload and the combined weight of the trace and sinker should never exceed the upper limit. The payload normally ranges between 4-8oz for most 12ft beachcasters. You'll find a range of sinkers between 3-6oz will cover most eventualities.

SWIVELS

Invest in stainless steel swivels made by top companies like Mustad and Berkley and quality is guaranteed. Brass swivels are a false economy because they quickly corrode.

The sizes are classified in much the same way as hooks, or in poundages to indicate the sort of loading they will tolerate. But there's no standardisation of sizes between brands and that causes a certain confusion! As a rough guide I use 2/0 or 200lb class swivels at the top and bottom of my terminal traces with No.7s (25lb) to hold the snoods.

BEADS

There are many uses for beads and they're an important component in many of my rigs. Haberdashery or art and craft shops are the best source for packets of small beads. Expect to pay around 50p for a packet of 500!

TERMINAL RIGS

Basic paternoster

Arguments always rage about the most efficient types of rigs but you can take it from me that the three-hook paternoster without frills reigns supreme. The hook snoods hang from the trace on swivels which are allowed a certain amount of free movement between stop-knots. It's the most tangle-free system yet devised.

Paternosters are usually made up with size 2 or 4 hooks to seek out flatties and other smaller species like pout, whiting, eels and rockling. But the rig will catch many other species of fish and if the chances of a heavyweight are high then I'd recommend the stronger Kamasan irons. But let's run through the construction to make matters abundantly clear.

Assembling basic paternoster

First, take 4ft of 60lb mono and tie a 2/0 swivel to one end using a tucked half-blood. This is more secure than the orthodox half-blood and is recommended for those parts of the trace exposed to maximum stresses. Thread a small bead down the trace followed by a small, size 8 swivel and another bead. Repeat this operation twice more before tying another 2/0 swivel to the remaining loose end of the trace with a tucked half-blood.

Next, you need to trap groupings of two beads with a swivel in between at the positions on the trace indicated on page 120. The safest method is to tie stop knots on either side of the beads as these will not damage the trace.

The beads allow the snoods to pivot more freely and act as buffers to prevent the swivels rubbing against the stop knots. There should be approximately 1in of free play for the swivels and beads between the stop

knots. It's customary to position the top two snoods close together with a longer snood on the bottom to drift in the tide flow.

Finally, tie the hook snoods to the three small swivels with tucked half-bloods. Again, follow the dimensions in the diagram making sure the snoods do not overlap one another. If this happens and a pair of hooks lock together the rig will get into an almighty tangle.

Cod and bass paternoster

As a starter rig for cod and bass, simply remove one of the snoods from the three-hook

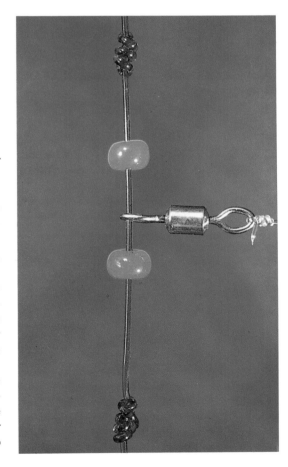

Let the snood swivel around the trace and the risk of fish spinning free on the retrieve is reduced.

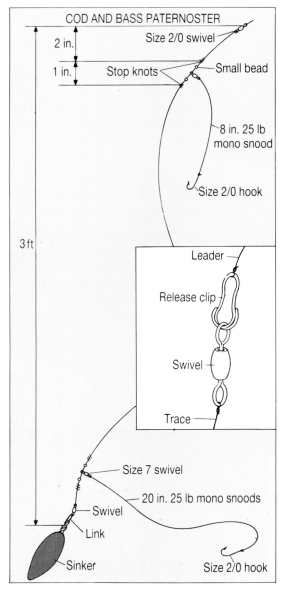

COD AND BASS PATERNOSTER

Size 2/0 swivel

2 in.

1 in.   Stop knots — Small bead

8 in. 25 lb mono snood

Size 2/0 hook

3 ft

Leader

Release clip

Swivel

Trace

Size 7 swivel

20 in. 25 lb mono snoods

Swivel

Link

Sinker   Size 2/0 hook

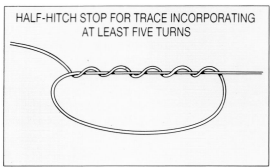

HALF-HITCH STOP FOR TRACE INCORPORATING AT LEAST FIVE TURNS

paternoster. Then you can use larger hooks like 2/0s and bigger baits without impairing casting distance.

Quick release clips

The casting leader can be tied direct to the 2/0 swivel at the top of the paternoster trace. Alternatively, use a quick-release clip like the McMahon snap, Aiken's spring-loaded model or the Mustad DC Easy-link. The quick-release clip is tied to the end of the casting leader and means you can maintain a ready-baited, spare paternoster in reserve to replace the one you've retrieved from the sea. Using this system, it is amazing how much time is saved on the beach.

Spacing snoods with half-hitches

Another method of making up the three-hook paternoster is with half-hitch stop knots tied in the trace itself. But there must be at least five turns in the knot. Anything less and the trace will constrict on itself and snap during the cast.

Assembly is much the same as before, starting with the initial 2/0 swivel. Then tie a half-hitch with five turns a couple of inches down the line and slide on the bead, small swivel and another bead. Position the second half-hitch within 1in or so if you can manage it. Repeat the sequence to achieve the correct spacing between snoods.

Ring the changes

Occasionally, fish may only take the top baits on a paternoster leaving the bottom one untouched. When that happens reposition the snood lengths so they all hang above the sinker. In windy or stormy conditions it's wise to cut the paternoster down to just two hooks to improve casting distance. These can be fixed above the lead or one above and one below.

ROUGH GROUND WRASSE RIG

A specialist rig is necessary to tackle the rock and kelp terrain preferred by wrasse. I eliminate as many swivels as possible and offer a simple set-up that is least likely to snag among the boulders. A heavy reel line of 30lb is fished straight through from reel to trace to help heave the tackle out of trouble.

Constructing wrasse rig

A 3ft length of 60lb mono is the backbone of the trace. As some losses are inevitable in the tackle graveyard of wrasse country, you can tie one of the cheaper 2/0 brass swivels to one end. A stand-off loop is tied about 2in down the trace followed by a second stand-off a further 18in away. Attach a 2/0 brass swivel to the bottom of the trace and short 6in snoods of 20lb or 25lb mono to the stand-off loops. Give wrasse too much room for manoeuvre and they'll dive among the kelp in a flash.

Size 2 Mustad O'Shaughnessy hooks are the most suitable pattern but always have a small file handy to sharpen up the points because of the blunting effect of the rocks. Incidentally, the bottom hook on this rig should always be at least 6in above the sinker to avoid snags.

Rotten bottom

There are two ways of attaching the weight. If the seabed is particularly hostile then you'll need a length of weaker line linking the bottom trace swivel and sinker – a ruse known as a rotten bottom. Tie on around 8in of 25lb line and this lighter nylon will break first if the sinker becomes trapped, allowing the rest of the trace to be recovered. I tape around the top part of the weight and the first couple of inches up the line to give added protection over rough bottoms. It also saves using swivels and links on the sinker which are often lost to the depths.

Anything goes for weights over rough ground. You can make do with old spark plugs if necessary to avoid losing expensive lead sinkers. I normally use flat leads which I make at home to plane the tackle to the surface and find losses are normally at acceptable levels.

Lead-lifts

Instead of the rotten-bottom, a Lead-Lift can be incorporated in the trace when fishing a semi-rough seabed. This fin-shaped strip of plastic is about 2½in long with a stainless steel wire running through its entire length with loops at both ends. The larger loop holds the weight and the smaller connects directly to the trace.

Surprisingly, Lead-Lifts have little effect on the cast and this is certainly the case with heavier lines. On the retrieve, water pressure on the side of this device forces it to the surface very quickly bringing the tackle

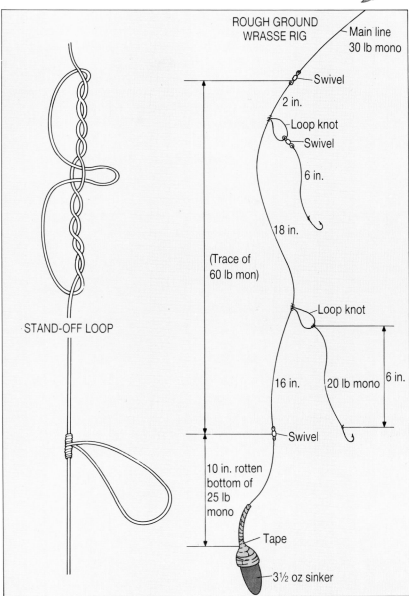

clear of the bottom. Fish the Lead-Lift with a flat lead and you'll lose much less tackle.

WISHBONE RIG

A long, flowing hook trace offers a bait more naturally in a moderate tidal flow than the relatively rigid paternoster presentations. In deep water cod fishing this often makes all the difference between success and failure. But the problem with long traces is that they severely curtail casting distance. The solution lies in the imaginatively named Wishbone rig.

At the moment I use a variation of the Wishbone called the SeeSaw created by

Portsmouth's Ian Golds. Its chief feature is a 4ft long snood which is held in place on the cast by a bait clip (see page 140). A fixed grip or Breakaway sinker is a must and the Wishbone only truly works in a light to moderate tide. If the current is too strong and the sinker starts to move, the rig is liable to tangle.

Assembling wishbone rig

The basic rig is constructed on a 6ft length of 60lb mono. Thread two small beads and a small swivel, followed by the bait clip, onto the trace. Then tie 2/0 swivels to each end. Fix the two beads and swivel between stop knots near the top of the trace (as shown in fig.12) and then attach 4ft of 25lb mono to the small swivel. Another small swivel is tied to the other end of this loose snood. Thread a 20in length of 25lb line through the swivel on the bottom of the snood length. Then tie swivels to both ends of this line. Finally, tie two 6in hook lengths of 25lb line to both of these swivels followed by 2/0 hooks.

This trace is not as complicated as it sounds but it will take ten minutes to build! Both hooks are trapped against the bait clip during the cast and fall free once the rig hits the water.

A shorter version of the Wishbone rig is most effective for small fish.

CONGER RIGS

Conger are among the strongest and meanest fish found in our waters and there's the real possibility of meeting up with a 50-pounder. To take on this challenge, I normally make up a beefy fixed sinker rig which is similar to the paternoster although I only use one snood attached well down a 2ft trace. It's just the ticket for casting into a rough bottom where the conger mustn't be given an inch of line. Big eels will soon wrap a muscular tail around a rock given half a chance or disappear down a bolt-hole. If that happens you couldn't budge them with a crane. Where the seabed is particularly intimidating a rotten bottom link to the weight is essential.

Constructing conger rig

My snood lengths are normally 2ft lengths of 100lb nylon. A pair of pliers are needed to tie knots in the darn stuff. Attacking it with scissors is useless! The beauty of heavy mono is that it will not twist or kink and is relatively cheap.

I occasionally use plastic coated wire which is widely advocated for conger because of their sharp teeth. But wire's tendency to kink over rough ground in the tide run can be fatal if you bend into a hefty eel. I only use wire with large, stainless steel swivels to minimise kinking at fairly clear marks where the tide is not severe.

Plastic coated wire leader is obtainable by the metre or in handy 25ft lengths on spools. I find 25-30lb breaking strain adequate. A purpose-made crimping tool is

SEE-SAW WISHBONE RIG

- Swivel — 50 lb leader
- Bead — Stop knot — 2 in.
- Swivel
- 4 ft
- 25 lb mono
- 60 lb mono
- Swivel — 5 ft–4 in.
- 10 in. — 6 ft
- Swivel
- Swivel
- 6 in.
- Hook
- Hook
- Bait clip
- Swivel
- Link
- Sinker

FIXED SINKER CONGER RIG

- Leader
- 2 ft
- 60 lb mono
- Beads — Stop knots
- Swivel with McMahon clip
- Sinker
- 100 lb mono — 2 ft.
- size 2 hook
- 7/0 hook

required to attach the wire to swivels and hooks. Never tie it direct without a crimp it's asking for trouble. And unlike 100lb mono, pliers are nonstarters because they're capable of cutting deep into the crimp and damaging the wire underneath.

For a professional looking crimp job, first thread the wire through a crimp, then through the eye of the hook or swivel and back again through the crimp. Double the wire through the crimp once more leaving a small length protruding at one side and a loop at the other. Now it's just a case of squeezing both ends of the crimp tight with the crimping tool. It's a most secure method which will accept a tremendous strain.

Store ready-prepared wire traces separately in envelopes or rig wallets. Coil the wire carefully and tape the loose ends to stop them unfolding.

Running leger

Conger have a habit of playing with the bait and sometimes drop it when they feel the resistance of a fixed sinker. The answer is a running leger which shouldn't startle the fish as it allows the conger to take line unimpeded.

To construct this rig, first run a swivel on the main reel line followed by a bead and then tie the line directly to the trace swivel. The sinker is hung from the free running swivel on the main line with a clip or rotten bottom link. There are numerous links and booms on the market for constructing running legers but they cost a fortune and a solitary swivel does the job just as well at half the price.

Hooks and bait for conger are in the big league. I prefer the Daiwa Superstrike 5/0 or 7/0 stainless steel O'Shaughnessy pattern but also use a second bait-holder hook because of the size of the bait.

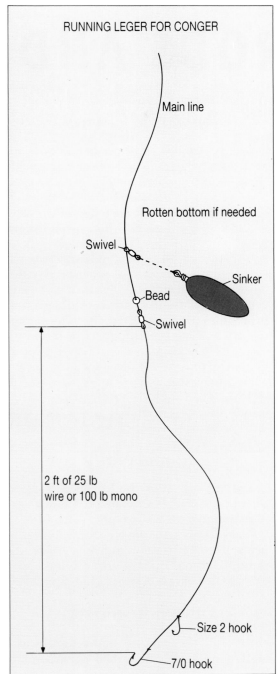

RUNNING LEGER FOR CONGER

Main line

Rotten bottom if needed

Swivel

Sinker

Bead

Swivel

2 ft of 25 lb wire or 100 lb mono

Size 2 hook

7/0 hook

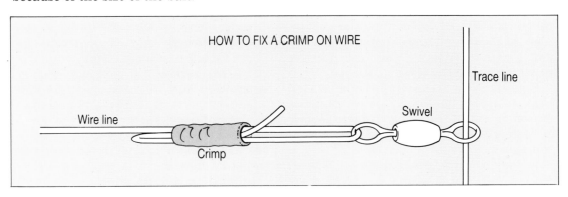

HOW TO FIX A CRIMP ON WIRE

Trace line

Wire line

Swivel

Crimp

RODS AND REELS

THE BASIC ACTIONS

Most mass produced beachcasters have an all-through action and flex throughout their length when under compression. They're only really suitable for simple lay-back styles of casting (see page 136) as they would collapse under a full power pendulum.

But stiff or tip-actioned rods are designed as casting machines and react totally differently from a soft rod. The butt section is usually high quality carbon or aluminium to provide strength and rigidity. The matching top half is also stiff, apart from the tip section. Unlocking the latent power of a stiff blank can only be achieved by a competent pendulum caster.

RECOMMENDED CASTING WEIGHTS

Standard 12ft beachcasters usually accept a range of sinkers from 4oz upwards but they're frequently overloaded by anglers who forget to take the weight of the bait and terminal rig into account as well as the lead. Inevitably, that strips the rod of its true casting capability.

Rods with softer actions normally cast 4-6oz sinkers while stiffer models will take heavier leads up to 8oz. All production rods have the recommended casting weights clearly stamped just above the handle.

CHOICE OF MATERIALS

GLASS-FIBRE

There are still many budget-price rods on the market made of hollow, tubular glass-fibre designed to cast weights from 4oz.

Glass-fibre beachcasters are normally made in two 6ft sections and have a soft, all-through action. But they're a dying breed now that the price of carbon has tumbled.

CARBON COMPOSITES

Nearly all the popular mid-range beachcasters are loosely described as carbon but in many cases the actual material is a composite that includes a high percentage of other materials including glass. The amount of carbon in the blank may be quite small and the actions vary accordingly, depending on the percentage used.

Generally, the butt is appreciably stiffer than a glass rod but the top section might be extremely soft if the carbon content is low. A more rigid top points to a higher percentage of carbon in the blank.

A popular method of construction is to wrap a thin coil of graphite, either in an X-weave or coil, right around the outside of a carbon composite from butt to tip. This strengthens and stiffens the blank significantly.

SEMI-CARBON

A marriage of separate carbon and glass sections in the same rod produces a versatile, high performance blank at a reasonable price that can cope with all styles of casting. The butt and lower part of the top section are carbon with the final 3ft or so of the tip made from glass-fibre.

These top of the range blanks are tailor-made for pendulum casting and the glass-fibre tip shows up bites wonderfully well. The point where the two materials are spliced together is easily visible.

The top section of a semi-carbon is normally 8ft long with a shorter 4-5ft butt. Occasionally, plastic coated aluminium instead of carbon is used for the butt to reduce the cost of the rod. But this is likely to corrode as saltwater inevitably creeps under the plastic sheath.

Semi-carbon rods are widely available in

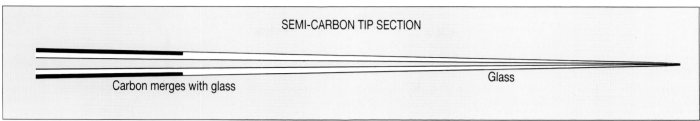

SEMI-CARBON TIP SECTION

Carbon merges with glass

Glass

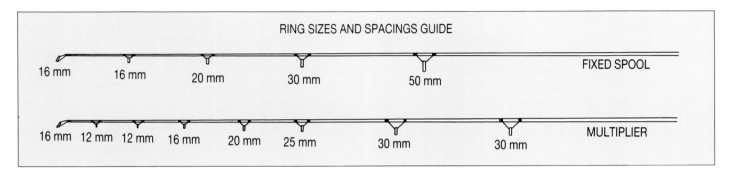

RING SIZES AND SPACINGS GUIDE

| 16 mm | 16 mm | 20 mm | 30 mm | 50 mm | FIXED SPOOL |

| 16 mm | 12 mm | 12 mm | 16 mm | 20 mm | 25 mm | 30 mm | 30 mm | MULTIPLIER |

blank form and many tackle shops offer a fitting-out service with the rings and reel seat of your choice. A limited range of ready-made models is also marketed but in truth there's nothing like having a semi-carbon finished to your own specifications – once you've gained the experience to know precisely what you want.

All-carbon beachcasters are obtainable but at a price. The tips of these rods are rather brittle, in my view, and on balance I would say the semi-carbon is a better investment.

Types of ring

The choice rests between plain wire or hardened steel rings in a cushioned frame and models with aluminium oxide or silicon carbide inserts.

Plain wire rings are out because they're too frail for the beach and are easily crushed. But lined rings like the Fujis, which are justifiably popular in all sectors of fishing, have stood the test of time. Mind you, I'm wary of some cheaper lined models of uncertain origin as there's a tendency for

Spend any time on the shoreline and you will soon realise that bass shine bright in the league of sporting fish.

the hardened inserts to spring clean out of the frame.

Hard chromed steel and stainless rings reduce line friction to a minimum and add yards to the cast but the top eye is liable to become grooved through constant retrieving under pressure.

Ring sizes

Line will only flow unhindered if the right-size rings are spaced out correctly along the blank. The number required depends on whether you use a multiplier reel or fixed spool.

Multipliers: rods fitted out for multipliers need seven rings plus a top eye to funnel the line smoothly. The largest 30mm diameter ring sits approximately 32in above the reel.

Although 12mm is the recommended size for the top eye I prefer one of 16mm. This provides more room for the leader knot to slip through on the retrieve, particularly if it is coated with weed.

Fixed spool reels require a total of four larger intermediate rings plus the top eye to smooth the flow of line which whips on and off the face of the spool in large loops. Recommended diameter for the bottom ring fixed 40in above the reel is 50mm. Again, I like a 16mm top eye.

Plastic coasters.

Ring spacing

Mass produced beachcasters are not always spot-on with their ring spacing but it's generally good enough. The line must follow the natural curve of the rod without touching the blank or creating any sharp angles between the rings that could impose extra wear and destroy its performance.

If you intend having a blank made up then the correct spacing will be found by trial and error. The rings are temporarily

taped in place and the rod flexed with a sinker suspended on the end of the line to check the positioning. Adjustments are made until the rings feed the line as parallel as possible to the curve of the blank.

WHIPPINGS

Apart from being decorative and lashing the ring feet securely to the rod, whipping helps strengthen areas of stress near the spigot joints. Layers of varnish protect the whipping silk from disintegrating but for a totally waterproof seal hard resins are used.

SPIGOTS

The most vulnerable spots on a beachcaster are the spigots which are inserted one inside the other to join the two halves of the rod. Male spigots reinforced with a solid centre rarely pose problems, but some female spigot walls are unbelievably thin and inadequately whipped. These are certain to crack or splinter completely in two when a pendulum caster winds up to a mighty chuck.

Locking Fuji reel seat.

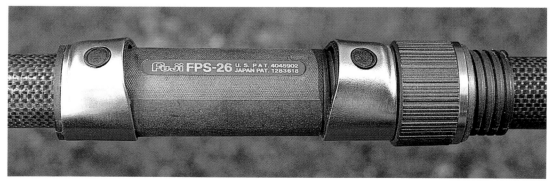

If you've got a rod with a thin female spigot, double up on the amount of whipping but avoid attempting power casting for obvious reasons.

REEL SEATS

The screw-up Fuji FPS reel seat is in a class of its own and holds everything rock steady. Sand occasionally works under the thread and partly jams the screw lock but that's a minor irritation. Stainless steel reel seats with double locking collars seem more prone to gathering grit.

The majority of production rods fix the reel seat 2.5ft up from the butt cap which suits many anglers. But it means that others can't use the rod to its full potential. Pendulum casters often prefer the reel in a much lower position a few inches up from the butt and coasters give them this opportunity.

Coasters

Coasters are sophisticated Jubilee clips with screw-down, knurled knobs which are tightened to clamp the reel feet firmly to the rod. They're chiefly associated with custom-built beachcasters but a select few mass-produced models are also sold without a conventional reel seat so the angler can benefit from the flexibility of coasters.

The great advantage of coasters is that the reel can be positioned to suit your individual casting style. To find the right spot, tuck the rod butt under the arm and adjust the position of the reel until it's possible to rest a thumb or forefinger comfortably on the spool without bending or over-extending the arm.

HAND GRIPS

Many top anglers dispense with bulky hand grips and leave the butt bare or at most cover it with shrink tube. That can make the rod slippery in the wet and uncomfortable to grasp in the cold. On balance, rubber Duplon type grips suit the majority.

Finally, a rubber or plastic bung should be pushed in the bottom of the butt section to protect the base of the blank from chipping on shingle.

FIXED SPOOL REELS VERSUS MULTIPLIERS

The choice in reels boils down to the simplicity of a fixed spool which is heavy and bulky or the more compact but exacting multiplier which transmits a greater feeling of direct contact with a fish.

Fixed spools have always been the first choice for novices because they are more tolerant of casting faults and you can learn to use one in minutes. But much greater control has to be exercised over a multiplier to avoid hideous birdsnests of line. The only certain way to live happily with a multiplier is to develop a smooth casting style . . . and that's asking a lot from a first-timer who is anxious to get fishing immediately.

Although a multiplier and fixed spool might have identical gear ratios, the latter recovers line much faster because of its larger spool. That's obviously helpful where a speedy retrieve saves tackle losses.

FIXED SPOOLS

An efficient bail arm roller is absolutely essential to guard against line wear and this is one department where the fixed spool makers have really got their act together. Smooth, hardened rollers which rotate under heavy loads protect the line at the critical pressure point and all modern fixed spools of quality now possess this important safety feature.

The bail arm itself should lock securely in the open position and not snap back if accidentally knocked. Bail arms which close prematurely are a positive menace. If it happens during casting then a crack-off is inevitable.

Spool size and line length

The average, large beachcasting reel has a spool diameter of at least 2in which will take approximately 400yd of 15lb line. Nobody wants to go to the expense of using up that much main line.

To save costs it's usual to fill out the core of the spool with much heavier backing after attaching it with a timber hitch. Then the main line is loaded as evenly as possible

Top of the range fixed spool with a reliable bail arm.

slight pressure against both ends of the spool. Assuming you have got a helper to wind in, line can then be loaded under slight tension so that it beds down neatly on the reel spool with an even lay from top to bottom. Some fixed spools allow fine adjustments to be made to the line lay and that's a useful feature if the line bunches annoyingly at one point.

Drag systems

The slipping clutch or drag system on a fixed spool allows you to pre-set the spool tension so it releases line with the bail arm closed under pressure from a big fish. In theory, it absorbs any sudden, unexpected lunges that could snap the line.

Front drags: the most dependable system is a front drag which can be fully tightened down for casting and then loosened slightly to give line with the bail arm closed and the anti-reverse switch flicked on. Of course, if the anti-reverse is switched off when retrieving then it's possible to release line direct from the reel handle by back-winding. If you prefer that method then the front drag can be left locked up at all times.

Stern drags are now increasingly popular. They offer a more precise way of tuning in the required amount of tension, using a graduated scale which is clearly marked on the adjusting knob. But it's not always possible to fully tighten down the spool with stern-drag systems and that's potentially hazardous. Any slippage of the spool during casting could cause serious line burns and cuts to your forefinger even if it is protected.

Gear ratios

The gear ratio of a fixed spool reveals its operating speed. Depending on the size of the spool this determines how much line is recovered for every complete turn of the handle. A ratio of 3.8:1 is the average for large beachcasters and that retrieves slightly more than 15in of line for a single revolution of the handle. High-speed rates of retrieve are impractical for most types of beachfishing.

until it is virtually flush with the outer rim of the spool.

This is necessary to ensure the line flows freely from the reel without scraping unduly against the lip of the spool. If the line emerges at an acute angle from deep within the spool, enormous friction is created as it rubs around the rim and casting range is massively reduced.

Around 200yd of main line should be ample on a fixed spool. There are times when an extra 100yd on the spool is a necessity – for example, when fishing for tope which cover 100yd without stopping. But this is an exception and it's a fair bet that your first 50yd on the spool will never see the light of day until it is replaced.

Line loading

To fill up with new line, slide a jumbo spool on a pencil and grip both sides, exerting

Handle

Many fixed spools are ambidextrous which means the handle is detachable and can be

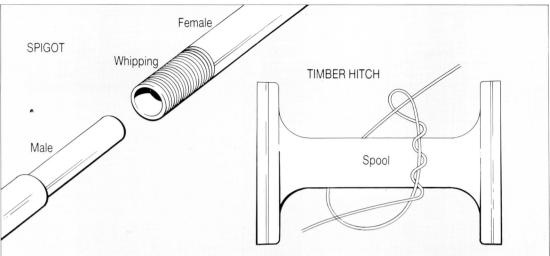

screwed into either side of the reel for left or right-hand wind. Handles must be large for beachcasting to ease the strain of reeling in through heavy seas and it helps if there's a good-sized grip knob.

MULTIPLIERS

These impressively engineered reels feed line directly from a revolving spool which is driven by gears on the retrieve. The spool is slipped into free running mode for casting and that's the moment when so many anglers get into a dreadful flap and find the multiplier such a handful.

Over-runs primarily develop with the free-running multiplier because of unco-ordinated, jerky casting. You'll hear all kinds of theories about the causes but lack of control during casting is by far the most common fault. Line must flow continuously from a multiplier so the sinker speed through the air and spool revs are in syn-chronisation. Once the spool revolves faster than the weight can haul the line, then it's tangle time.

The sinker splashdown also needs watch-ing because it obviously leads to a dramatic reduction in speed while the multiplier is still zipping around. That's the moment to brake the multiplier manually with the thumb and avoid a snarl-up.

Spool speed

Multiplier spools accelerate from station-ary to 40,000 revolutions a minute when a 5oz torpedo is cast 200yd. And that happens within a tenth of a second! Any weaknesses in the bearings or elsewhere soon become apparent . . . not to mention any deficiencies on the part of the caster!

Line loading

Most multiplier reels for beachcasting hold around 300yd of 15lb line. Backing is not normally needed. The mono must be distributed evenly across the width of the spool by the thumb or forefinger on the re-trieve to maintain the reel's balance.

The more compact multiplier gives a smoother performance.

An evenly loaded spool greatly reduces the chance of a backlash by ensuring a free flow of line particularly at night or in windy conditions. The spool's capacity is also increased by an even spread of line.

Level-winds

A level-wind gaurantees perfect lay but at the expense of distance.

A level-wind lays the line automatically between guide bars which feed from side to side across the spool while it is rotating on the retrieve.

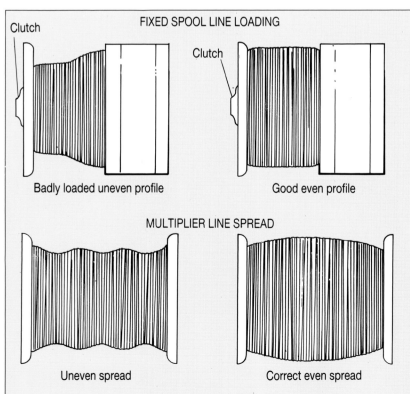

FIXED SPOOL LINE LOADING

Clutch

Clutch

Badly loaded uneven profile

Good even profile

MULTIPLIER LINE SPREAD

Uneven spread

Correct even spread

Level-winds fitted on small reels take up a lot of room, making it difficult to get a good thumb-grip on the spool while casting which, in turn, cuts down on distance. The device also intrudes on line flow and if the leader knot snags between the narrow guides casting is again impaired.

Level-wind conversions

It's feasible to remove the level-wind mechanism from a small multiplier once you've mastered casting with this reel. Conversion kits are obtainable to remove the level-wind bars and internal gears. The top bar is also cut away and a solid crossbar fitted to strengthen the frame. Any screw holes left after the removal of the level-wind are filled with resin.

If you are not mechanically minded, then many tackle shops are prepared to do the work for a small charge. The chief reason for converting a reel is to gain extra casting distance. This can add up to a 20 per cent improvement on a small multiplier. Heavier lines can also be used as there are no guide bars to snag the knots.

Braking systems

At one time, multipliers relied totally on oil viscosity spread over the internal moving parts to slow the speed of the spool and it's still applied as a braking technique today. Thick oil is used in high summer when the normal grade becomes too runny and thin in the depths of winter.

But now there's a choice of more precise braking mechanisms including the latest magnetic models which the manufacturers claim can be adjusted to virtually eliminate over-runs.

Magnetic system: A series of magnets — usually eight — are fitted around the inside of the reel cage to generate a magnetic field which becomes stronger as the speed of the rotating spool increases. The effect of the magnetic forces on the aluminium spool is to progressively slow down its momentum.

An external dial with a graduated scale of click stops is adjusted to push the magnets closer towards the spool, increasing the power of the magnetic field and creating more braking power. Retracting the magnets decreases the field and allows the spool to revolve more freely.

The idea is that you dial in the required amount of magnetic braking to prevent over-runs and then gradually ease off as your casting proficiency with the multiplier improves. Experienced anglers remove the magnets completely so the spool is completely free-running.

Centrifugal system: the popular Daiwa Millionaire series, along with many other smaller multipliers, have a braking system that is governed by centrifugal force pushing a pair of brake blocks on the spool. The two, small hardened plastic blocks are fitted on spindles attached to one end of the spool. As the spool starts to rotate, centrifugal force pushes the blocks up the spindle against the stainless steel rim of the reel cage creating a braking effect. The faster the spool rotates, the more centrifugal force is set up and the greater the braking power.

Millionaire 6HM's form the backbone of my beachcasting. These have two brake blocks although I rarely find it necessary to use more than one. With a single block the line may start to fluff or lift slightly on the spool without actually birdsnesting. If this occurs the block is replaced with a larger one or I revert to the original pair. Multipliers can be controlled by tightening the bearing cap but I wouldn't recommend this method. I always set the cap so the spool is absolutely free running.

Star drag

A star drag or clutch is fitted to most multipliers just below the handle and operates in a similar manner to the fixed spool reel. It is tightened down for casting to prevent slippage.

MAINTENANCE

Corrosion sets in faster than you think. After every trip to the beach make a habit of thoroughly washing your reel under the tap at home and dry off with a towel. Reels benefit from an oiling once a month and multipliers will also need completely stripping and cleaning about four times a year.

ACCESSORIES

RUCKSACK

A large, heavy duty rucksack is much more convenient than a bulky tackle box. Many of the best fishing marks in my neck of the woods involve a considerable walk and a lightweight rucksack stuffed with tackle necessities makes the hike easier.

ROD-STANDS

There are two principal designs: monopods and tripods. The metal or wooden monopod has a curved rest at the top to lean the rod against and a spike at the bottom for forcing into the sand.

On rocks or promenades you'll need the more versatile tripod. My favourite tripod is the Golds stand made from lightweight aluminium in 4ft 4in or 6ft versions. It has single and double rests to prop the rod against – they're interchangeable in seconds – and three separate positions for the cups in which the rod butts sit. Other features include clips for suspending a bait bucket, and spare traces between the tripod legs and a welded foot rest at the bottom of the main shaft for pushing the stand into the sand if you want to use it as a monopod. Versatility indeed!

UMBRELLAS AND BROLLY
SHEETS

The protection of a 50in brolly makes life tolerable on the beach in wind and rain. You will need to wipe it down regularly to prolong its life. Corrosion on the shaft and spokes spreads like wildfire if it is packed away wet. Peg down the brolly firmly with a guy rope at all times on the exposed shoreline otherwise it will sail into orbit.

A brolly sheet shaped to fit round the back of the umbrella and clipped to either side stops rain and wind gusting under the umbrella canopy. Stones or sand are heaped along the back edge of the sheet to hold it down.

GROUNDSHEETS

Over the years I have avoided losing countless small items in the sand or shingle by

Golds tripod is the most flexible rod stand in its class.

best to wrest the gaff from your grasp.

If possible, it's best to gaff a conger under its bottom jaw and a stingray in the edge of the wing to give the fish a better chance of surviving. Never leave a gaff point unprotected; cover it with a cork.

SCISSORS

A pair of sharp, surgical scissors are the most versatile item in the tackle box. They'll cope with all the everyday tasks such as cutting leader line, trimming knots and baits and shelling shellfish. Also essential for removing gills from peeler crabs.

KNIVES

A sharp filleting knife is one of those purchases you take for granted but again it's worth spending that little bit more to obtain a quality product that will serve you well. Jobs for the knife include cutting up fish strips, filleting and gutting. Always use the knife on a flat, non-slip surface and cut away from your body to avoid accidents. When not in use, knives should always be stored in their protective sheath.

RIG WALLETS

A rig wallet contains a number of see-through plastic sleeves in which traces are stored in their own individual compartments. It's a tangle-free system that has been adopted by a good many anglers who previously kept their traces in envelopes.

spreading out a large, heavy duty nylon groundsheet under the umbrella. Mine paid for itself in only a few months.

GAFF

I try to avoid using a gaff, apart from when fishing for conger and stingray, as it damages fish which might well warrant being returned. The gaff is simply a long pole with a large barbless hook lashed to one end. A small strap should be attached to the top of the handle for looping around your arm. This will give extra security when a large or active fish is doing its level

CANTILEVER BOXES

There are some really elaborate cantilever boxes on the market and the biggest of them will swallow an enormous amount of tackle. But one- or two-tray models are quite adequate to take essential items, such as swivels, beads, hook packets and spare spools of snood nylon, as well as all the other bits and pieces that you'll acquire.

CASTING STYLES

Long distance casting looks impressive but in reality it's no guarantee of results. Regardless of whether a fish is feeding at 50 or 150yd, the key skill is a fluent casting technique which lands the bait on the seabed virtually intact. Poor, snatchy casts cause the bait to disintegrate in mid-air leaving very little for the fish to chew on.

SAFETY

A 5oz torpedo reaches speeds of more than 100mph in the first 50yd of a 200yd cast. The potential consequences of a snap-off during this initial surge of acceleration are frightening to contemplate. A 50lb-class shock leader, strong stainless steel swivels and 60lb main trace are a must in the casting arena.

GRIP FOR A FIXED-SPOOL

If your grip on the reel slips at the very moment when full power is applied to a cast, the distance will be much reduced and the sinker is liable to fly in any direction.

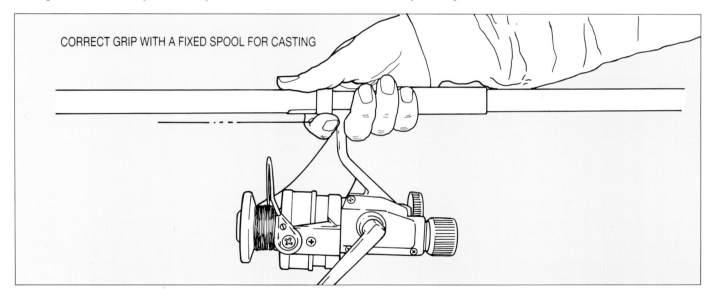

CORRECT GRIP WITH A FIXED SPOOL FOR CASTING

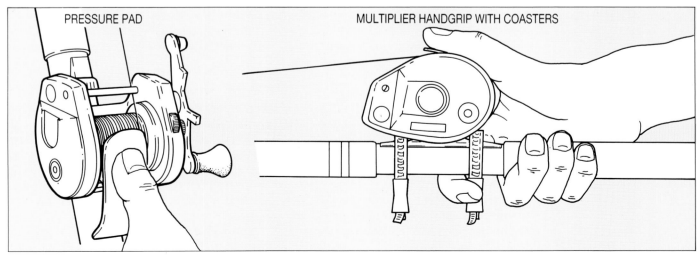

PRESSURE PAD

MULTIPLIER HANDGRIP WITH COASTERS

Before making a cast, tighten down the drag as tightly as possible until it's impossible to rotate the spool. The index finger and thumb are then locked solidly around the rod just above the reel's stem leaving the forefinger free to trap the line. Release the bail arm and run the line over the forefinger which should be directly over or a fraction below the spool. If the finger grips the line above the spool, the mono will be ripped free before the cast is fully executed.

To guard against line burn and cuts, wear a finger-stall or the finger cut from an old rubber glove. There are several makes of line release-clips which trap the line instead of trusting the forefinger but I'm not in favour of them.

Finally, hold the bottom of the butt section with your free hand and you're now ready to cast.

HOW TO GRIP A MULTIPLIER

Multipliers throw up a different set of problems with a rotating spool to control. The rod is grasped by all four fingers with the forefinger directly under the reel. If coasters are fitted then the forefinger is locked around the lower of the two clamps for extra grip. The thumb is placed on top of the spool, covering as much area as possible for a firm grip. Smaller multipliers with level-winds are more tricky to control as there's only a very small area of the spool available for thumbing. Full power should never be applied with these reels – you cannot exert enough downward pressure on the spool to hold it tight.

It's difficult to hold a multiplier spool rigid with the bare thumb when pendulum casting but a small rubber pressure pad helps. This is normally a strip of rubber taped to the rod just below the reel. During casting it is forced down on the spool by the thumb until the moment of release. A rubber finger-stall can also be worn on the thumb to provide extra purchase. Once you have a firm grip on the spool, release the free spool push-button and grasp the bottom of the butt section with your free hand.

CASTING TECHNIQUES

There's nothing like man-to-man coaching to help build your confidence and competence. There are many qualified sea angling instructors throughout the country who are willing to run through the various techniques and iron out any faults.

The three styles – which meet the basic needs of most beach anglers when they are performed properly with mass production or soft-actioned rods – are the overhead thump, layback and off-the-ground casts. But remember that a 175yd cast with a 5oz sinker is about the limit with a soft rod. For the fourth style, the pendulum, a stiff rod is essential.

OVERHEAD THUMP

The overhead thump is the most basic form of casting and is much favoured by novices and youngsters. There are limitations on distance and bait presentation because of its snatchy action.

To start the cast, stand with the feet pointing at an angle to the sea as shown. With the butt in your left hand, raise your elbow to nose level pointing seawards.

Lower the rod tip behind until the sinker, attached to a 5ft trace, just touches ground.

Once in position, turn and face seawards raising and punching the rod with your right arm while the left hand pulls the butt down and in towards the rib cage. At the same time the left knee should slightly bend, the right leg is stretched and the body twisted to face seawards.

Follow the cast through with the rod tip pointing towards the sinker to cut down line friction. The exact timing of line release from the spool on the cast will soon become apparent after a couple of practice casts.

LAYBACK

The layback is a progression of the overhead thump with one significant difference – the sinker is moving before the actual cast is made, creating more compression in the rod and producing improved distances. The drop from rod tip to sinker is again around 5ft and a distance of 175yd would be considered a very good layback cast.

The feet are virtually at right angles to the sea at the start. Twist and lean the body

backwards as you go into the layback. The bottom of the butt is held just out from the groin while your other arm is partly outstretched and pointing the rod at a 40 degree angle from the beach.

The lead is swung up and backwards slightly out to the right of the rod tip. Once the sinker reaches the end of its swing you begin to pivot the body and feet to start pulling through the cast and putting the rod under compression. The weight of the sinker bends the rod into a curve as the

Lower rod tip until sinker touches ground raising left elbow to nose level.

Follow through with rod tip pointing towards sinker.

OVERHEAD THUMP

Bottom of butt is held just out from groin and lead swing out to right of rod tip.

Weight of sinker bends rod into curve as power builds.

Rod held high after release with feet facing out to sea.

LAYBACK

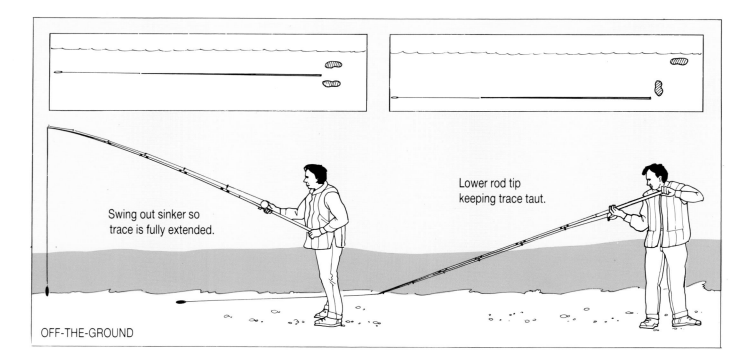

Swing out sinker so trace is fully extended.

Lower rod tip keeping trace taut.

OFF-THE-GROUND

power builds up. As power still builds with the punching and lifting motion of the right arm and the pulling of the left, the rod's maximum height is achieved at which point the sinker is released.

The rod should again be held high after release to follow the lead's trajectory. This will slightly increase the casting distance. Your body and feet should now be facing out to sea with the right foot in front of the left.

OFF-THE-GROUND CAST

The initial stance for this cast is completely different to the previous styles. The sinker is placed on the ground anywhere within an arc of between 180 and 270 degrees. The latter angle produces longer casts and is the one I will be describing here. The drop from the tip of the rod needs to be far longer, around 7ft being the norm.

Turning and facing 270 degrees to the sea, swing the sinker out so the trace is fully extended. This process is known as laying the line out. Leaving the trace on the ground, place your feet so that the right foot is pointing inland while the left is facing 90 degrees to the sea. At the same time your body should be pivoted and the rod tip lowered to within a few inches of the ground while keeping the trace line taut. The butt should now be just in front of your nose.

During this cast the sinker travels in an arc of 270 degrees, slowly getting higher. The main lifting and punching action should start when the sinker is at 180 degrees to the sea. At this stage of the cast the power is considerably increased, putting the rod under full compression. Your body and feet also pivot as the cast progresses and you finish facing out to sea.

Follow through in the same manner as with the layback. This casting action is capable of achieving 200yd.

PENDULUM

The pendulum is the ultimate casting style and will zoom a 5oz sinker on its own well over 250yd. But only stiff, purpose-built pendulum rods are suitable. Many softer rods will snap under the tremendous amount of power that is generated with a full-blooded pendulum.

At the start, the left foot should be at a 45 degree angle to the sea while the right is at about 135 degrees but slightly forward of the left foot. The body is now turned inland with the left hand grasping the butt around groin height while the right hand holds the reel slightly forward of the body at chest level. At this stage the sinker on the end of a 9ft drop should be at nose height.

The next phase is the outswing. This involves swinging the sinker inland at approximately 220 degrees. Once it has

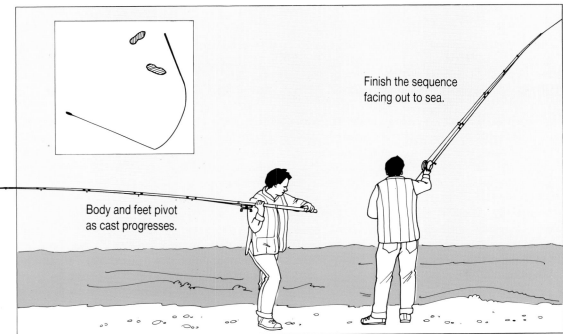

Finish the sequence
facing out to sea.

Body and feet pivot
as cast progresses.

BAIT CLIPS

Stop knot
Bead

completed the outswing the weight automatically starts the inswing. The sinker flows back behind your head so that it is facing seawards. At the peak of this inswing the sinker stops momentarily. This is the critical stage of the cast. The moment you feel that sinker pause, the head is immediately turned seawards, the body starts to pivot and the blank begins to compress. As your body completely unwinds, most of your weight is transferred to the left foot. The left hand, which is now at nose height, starts to pull the butt of the rod down towards the rib cage.

While the left hand is pulling the rod down, the right arm is punching it forward generating maximum power. This has the effect of launching the sinker on an upwards flight path. At this stage your feet and body are facing directly out to sea. Follow the sinker's flight path with the rod.

CASTING FAULTS

Poor timing and body movement and unbalanced foot placings all contribute to inefficient casting styles. Here are some other major faults which need special attention.

Loose clutch

An inadequately tightened clutch on a fixed-spool is certainly a cause for concern.

The problem occurs when you start to build up the power of the cast. If the clutch is not completely locked and starts slipping, line will be released before you are ready, considerably reducing power and compression.

Weak bail arm

The spring activated bail arm on fixed spools can occasionally snap shut prematurely during casting resulting in a crack-off. There's a simple remedy – discard the bail arm. It's an easy operation with most models. Unscrew and remove the arm from one side and cut it at the other end with a hacksaw. Leave the line roller in place for retrieving in the usual manner. Clearly, you will have to hook line on and off the roller manually.

Rather than resorting to using a hacksaw to remove the bailarm, some anglers fix a small elasticated clip to the reel which connects to the bail arm in the open position and prevents it closing.

Wrong drops

The drop is the distance between the rod tip and sinker. If it's too short the rod will not be fully compressed during the cast. Alternatively, if the drop is too long compression will again be lost and the cast is likely to be wayward.

Turn-over period

The turn-over period only lasts for a split-second. As full power is applied on a pendulum cast, the sinker flips 180 degrees from facing nose-down at the back of the arc to nose-first as it is launched seawards.

Because the turn-over is so short it is important that the lead enters it smoothly, the final point of the inswing being the crucial phase. At the peak of this inswing the sinker momentarily comes to a stop and can sometimes wobble. If this happens it will completely destroy the cast's momentum and turn-over period. A long-tailed lead performs more smoothly at this critical stage and often turns a bad cast into a more acceptable effort.

BAIT CLIPS

The basic idea of bait clips is to streamline the tackle cutting down wind resistance and bait whiplash. As the rig hits the water, the line slackens releasing the baited hooks to tumble free on the seabed.

Never cram too much bait on the bend of a hook when using clips. I always try to leave the bend virtually bare where it rests on the clip. It's worth bearing in mind, incidentally, that a clip which is positioned close to the sinker rides in the slipstream of the weight and improves casting performance.

Making your own clips

There are many commercially-made clips but they're easy to make for yourself. Take a long-shanked Aberdeen hook with a gape of around 5mm and snip off the point just above the barb with pliers. Thread the trace line through the eye of the hook and slide it up the line until it is in the approximate position where the hook will just reach. Then twist the trace around the hook shank several times to hold it in place.

Clipping up

Bait clips can be used for holding baited hooks up or down the line but care should be taken when clipping up. The pressure from a pendulum cast is likely to force the bait down the line well away from the hook, resulting in line bites. The solution is to tie a stop knot just above the bait to prevent it sliding. A small bead can also be pushed up to the stop knot for extra security.

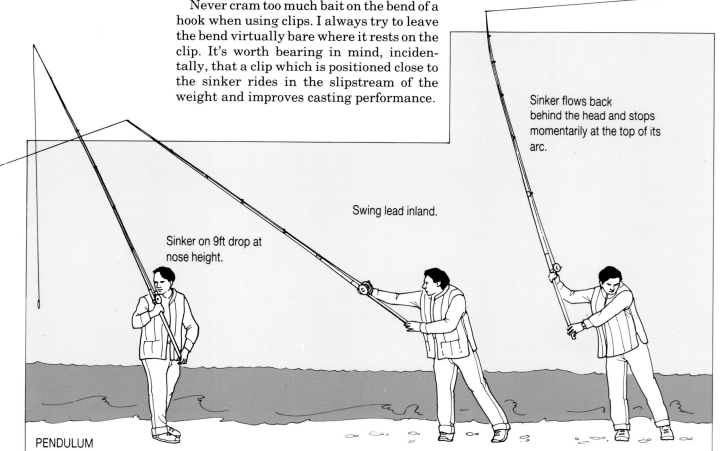

Sinker flows back behind the head and stops momentarily at the top of its arc.

Swing lead inland.

Sinker on 9ft drop at nose height.

PENDULUM

The bait clips themselves also tend to slide on the main trace during casting and their position needs checking before each cast. Adjust them until the hook just reaches the clip again.

REDUCERS

Some top casters prefer the multiplier fixed right at the bottom of the butt. This allows them to flex the full length of the rod during the pendulum and gain valuable extra yards. But it's an awkward position for the reel and a short 16in length of carbon known as a reducer is slipped into the butt to give the angler more control when retrieving. For the average angler these retrievers are not really practicable.

Flat calm on a summer's evening and the mullet are starting to move within casting range in the shallows.

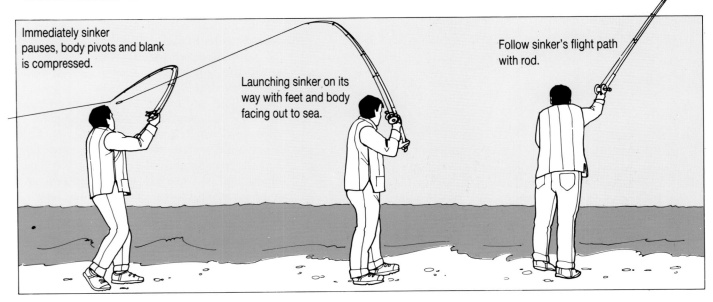

Immediately sinker pauses, body pivots and blank is compressed.

Launching sinker on its way with feet and body facing out to sea.

Follow sinker's flight path with rod.

SPECIAL TECHNIQUES

NIGHT FISHING

Fluorescent tips glow after midnight as Chris watches intently for signs that the cod are about.

The popularity of nightfishing stems from the simple fact that it produces more fish than daytime sessions. The bigger specimens also tend to fall under the cover of darkness.

Nocturnal fish

As the smaller species head for the richer feeding grounds in the shallows at night they are followed by predators like rays, cod and conger. It is generally accepted that large conger in particular lie dormant by day, only leaving their rocky lairs in darkness. By contrast, small strap conger feed by day or' night. Among the flatfish, soles are active nocturnal feeders.

But the most eagerly hunted species at night is cod. They're chiefly nocturnal feeders at inshore marks although when the water is highly coloured they feed just as avidly in the day.

NIGHT LIGHTS

Inevitably, nightfishing calls for specialised equipment including a reliable source of light to show up bites on the rod tip.

PARAFFIN LAMPS

Paraffin or petrol pressure lamps are the most widely used source of illumination on the beach at night. The amount of light generated is measured in candle power and output of different models varies from 200 to 500cp.

The principle behind these lamps is that a heated central tube vaporises the fuel. As the gas escapes out through the fabric mantle at the top it ignites emitting an extremely bright light. The gauze mantle is very brittle and easily breaks if the lamp gets knocked about but it is surrounded by a glass bowl which keeps out the elements.

The big drawback with pressure lamps is that they are static and most times you'll be forced to play fish in the pitch black. Paraffin also contaminates the hands and bait.

As a rule, these lamps should run for approximately eight hours on a single fill of fuel. The most popular makes on the market include the Tilley which has stood the test of time, the ever popular Anchor and the Petromex.

A lamp placed on the beach spreads light over a relatively limited area and is really only adequate for baiting up. A more effective pool of light is created by suspending the lamp from a stand. But it must not be allowed to swing in the wind – buy a stand with clamps that hold the lamp rock steady.

Headlights

Cheap plastic headlights fitted to headbands and powered by batteries are fine if used with a pressure lamp. But they are uneconomical as the sole source of light. The best system is the rechargeable miner's headlight. It's the most versatile, sturdy and dependable of all the night lights and ultimately the cheapest to run.

The light itself clips on the front of a toughened plastic safety helmet and the heavy battery pack is carried on a belt around the waist. It provides a powerful, narrow beam of light which is trained precisely where you want it at all times.

Isotopes

Isotopes are taped to the rod tip and glow brightly against the night sky showing up the slightest knock. The Betalight Tritium Isotope is again classified in candle power ratings and is supplied inside a protective, silicone-type tube. It is claimed the light source lasts up to six years if the isotope is not broken.

Reflective tape

A cheaper way of making the rod tip more visible is to bind the top 8in with reflective tape. Few production rods are supplied with this tape which is a pity because without it the rod tip just won't show up clearly enough against the night sky under the glow from a Tilley. The best source for this tape in a range of colours is a cycle shop.

FLOAT FISHING

The potential effectiveness of a float rig is absurdly under-rated by most sea anglers who seem slaves to legering. In summer, many species move within casting distance of a float including sporting fighters like mackerel, garfish and mullet to say nothing of wrasse, coalfish and bass. Flounders can also be taken on float tackle in winter.

It goes without saying that the set-up needs to be rather heavier than rigs used in coarse fishing to cope with the swell and rough ground. A 1.75lb test curve carp rod and medium-sized fixed spool filled with 5lb to 8lb line achieves the right sort of balance. Cigar-shaped floats like the Drennan Piker No.4 ride the waves well in search of wrasse, pollack and mackerel while the lighter Avons with bulbous bodies are more suitable for flounders and shy mullet.

FLOUNDER RIG

First slide on a 4AAA Avon float before tying a small swivel to the end of the reel line. This prevents the flatties from spinning in the tide and twisting the line. Attach a hook link of 5lb line to the swivel and tie on a size 2 or 4 fine wire Aberdeen.

The float is set at just the right depth so the hook nudges bottom. That way it will stir up the mud as it drifts down on the tide and hopefully prove even more attractive to the inquisitive flounders.

My preferred shotting pattern to achieve this effect is shown in the diagram – note the pair of shot fixed just above the hook which help disturb the bottom mud.

Where to fish

A deep-water channel in a river estuary which runs near the shoreline is the sort of flattie mark which responds to a float if there's a fair run of tide. Just flick the float out a few yards and let it trundle along in the flow. A bite is often signalled by the float stopping dead but you should also strike at any sidewards movement. Flounders are not known for their fighting qualities but on light float tackle they're fair scrappers.

MULLET RIG

The scaled down end rig for mullet reflects the shy biting reputation of this species. There's no need for a swivel and a size 8 or 10 hook is tied directly to the main line. The bottom shot should be at least 12in above the hook as indicated with the rest of the shot spaced out at 6in intervals. Sometimes mullet feed very deep alongside breakwaters and harbour walls and that's a job for the slider. The smaller Drennan Pikers are handy for this task. A stop knot is tied at the correct depth and adjusted until you find the correct level.

Attracting mullet

Top baits are probably bread and maggots. To really attract mullet in numbers, hang a small mesh sack filled with bread that has been soaked in pilchard oil a couple of feet below the surface. Particles will filter out with the tide and maintain the mullets' interest.

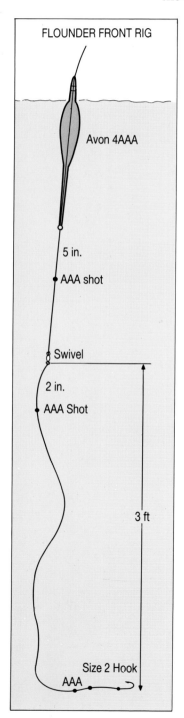

FLOUNDER FRONT RIG

Avon 4AAA

5 in.

AAA shot

Swivel

2 in.

AAA Shot

3 ft

Size 2 Hook

AAA

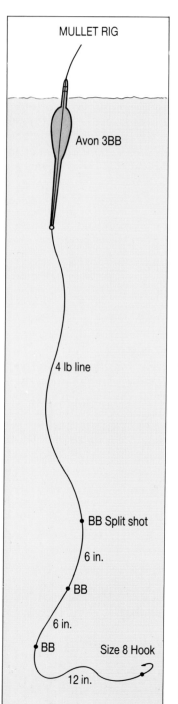

MULLET RIG

Avon 3BB

4 lb line

BB Split shot

6 in.

BB

6 in.

BB

12 in.

Size 8 Hook

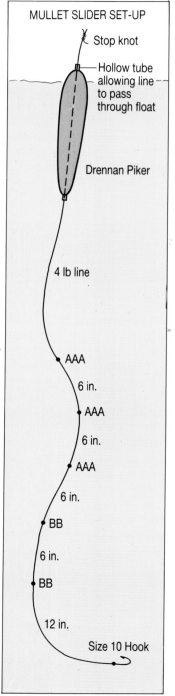

MULLET SLIDER SET-UP

Stop knot

Hollow tube allowing line to pass through float

Drennan Piker

4 lb line

AAA

6 in.

AAA

6 in.

AAA

6 in.

BB

6 in.

BB

12 in.

Size 10 Hook

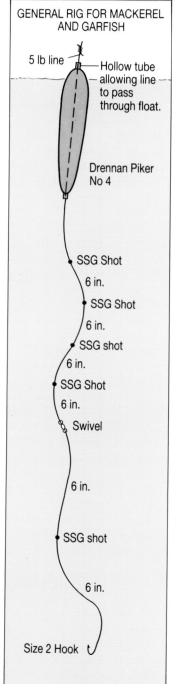

GENERAL RIG FOR MACKEREL AND GARFISH

5 lb line

Hollow tube allowing line to pass through float.

Drennan Piker No 4

SSG Shot

6 in.

SSG Shot

6 in.

SSG shot

6 in.

SSG Shot

6 in.

Swivel

6 in.

SSG shot

6 in.

Size 2 Hook

PIER FISHING

The rusting support structures of piers with their covering of mussels, barnacles and seaweed present rich pickings for fish in what otherwise might be a relatively barren area of seabed.

The bottom below piers is strewn with debris attracting colonies of crabs, winkles, cockles, shrimps and other crustaceans. It all adds up to the perfect refuge for many larger predators along with multitudes of smaller fodder fish.

PIER TACKLE

Tackling up for pier fishing really demands a shorter beachcaster of 11ft. This gives more control over a fish that's some way below your feet. Terminal tackle is similar to that in beachfishing but obviously there's no bait clips on the trace.

If you are casting out about 30yd and letting the rig settle on the seabed then the snood lengths are identical to those used on the beach. But if you intend to simply drop the baited trace down the side of the pier, use a longer bottom snood so it rests on the seabed. The other snoods further up the trace should be fairly short – about 4in.

USING A DROPNET

Obviously, it is risky hauling up a decent fish on the deck of a pier without the help of a dropnet. These are simple to construct using an old bicycle wheel with the spokes removed as the frame. Lash netting over the frame so that there is at least a 2ft belly in the mesh to take the weight of a fish. Three short lengths of rope spaced equally apart are tied to the rim with a steel ring link.

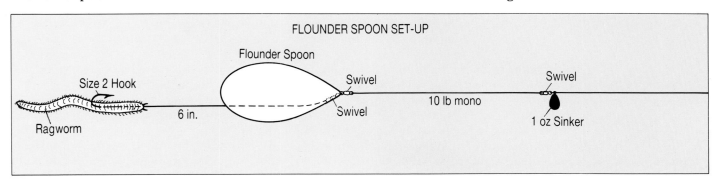

FLOUNDER SPOON SET-UP

Flounder Spoon

Size 2 Hook

Swivel

Swivel

Swivel

Ragworm

6 in.

Swivel

10 lb mono

1 oz Sinker

ROCK FISHING

Fishing from rocks is exhilarating, challenging – and highly dangerous. It's easy to loose your foothold and topple into deep gullies and no fish on this planet is worth serious injury or death. Rogue waves which sweep up the rock face are probably the greatest hazard and many anglers have been swept out to sea from vantage points they considered completely safe.

SAFETY PRECAUTIONS

A hard safety helmet gives some protection against falling rocks and it's also wise to tackle rock fishing in pairs just in case of an emergency. Make sure you tell somebody where you are going and the time by which you expect to return.

BOAT FISHING

Booking a trip on a charter boat does not guarantee huge catches, but it can put you at the heart of the shoals of fish rather than scratching at the edges from the shore. Few anglers find it practical to buy their own boat. The majority charter professional angling boats rather than private craft or commercial fishing boats which supplement their income by taking out anglers.

BASIC COSTS OF
CHARTER TRIPS

It is still possible to book holiday specials which offer two- or three-hour trips around the bay for a couple of pounds a head, often with tackle and bait thrown in. But these serve only as an introduction to the sport.

For an eight-hour day inshore, the cost of chartering a boat is between £100 and £150. You can usually fish with the full complement of 12 anglers, so the charge averages out at around £10 per head. A fast wrecking boat operating up to 40 miles offshore will cost perhaps 250 per day, though it may not be large enough for 12 to fish; and if you want a skipper to go even further out, then expect to pay a great deal more.

Many boats now offer wrecking holidays involving trips to marks many miles offshore, with overnight sleeping on the boat or at a convenient hotel. On the south coast, Channel Island trips are very popular.

There are hundreds of angling charter boats operating out of British ports. Sundance II *of Lymington is typical of many licensed to operate all the way to France.*

THERE ARE ALL TYPES OF
SKIPPER

A charter skipper needs to be many things, but above all he must be an accomplished seaman to run the boat efficiently and safely. Some anglers prefer a sociable skipper to a better one who is perhaps a trifle taciturn. Do you want chat and a helpful skipper – or do you just want to fish?

A good skipper ensures that the anglers on his boat know how they should be tackling the conditions. He may supply and cut baits, provide odds and ends of tackle, check knots, and advise on tackle changes. Some will stand at your shoulder and explain how to play out your specimens, with the gaff at the ready. Others put you over the fish – then stand back and smile at your disasters. A few will stay in the cabin and emerge only if disaster threatens – or not even then!

You must confirm in advance that the skipper caters for your kind of angling. Some do not like beginners or women anglers; others fish only inshore or refuse to allow uptiding or wire line on their boat. Go for a walk along the quay when the charter boats return in the evening and ask the anglers what they thought about their skippers. Check out the reports in the angling press, both nationally and in your local paper.

RULES OF THE GAME

Make sure you take along the right tackle, bait, food and clothing. Keep out of the way when the skipper is working on the boat or landing fish – and don't bang him on the head with your lead while he's unhooking your fish! Treat the boat as if it was yours.
- Don't let your lead bump on the hull if you can avoid it.
- Don't invite yourself into the cabin without acknowledgement from the skipper – and don't smoke inside unless invited.
- Don't cut line or bait on the woodwork or paintwork: ask for a baitboard.

- Don't gut fish on the deck without asking the skipper.

DEPOSITS AND CANCELLATIONS

You pay a deposit when you book a trip. If the skipper cancels you should be offered your deposit back immediately. If you cancel, you must be prepared to compensate the skipper.

When reasonable notice is given – perhaps a month – the skipper may be able to find a substitute crew, and he may return your deposit. But if you fail to give reasonable notice of cancellation the deposit will not be returned and you will probably find yourself liable for most or all of the cost of the trip and any bait you may have ordered. If you want to make your own rules, get them in writing, so both you and the skipper know where you stand.

BUYING A BOAT OF YOUR OWN

In the small ads you may find a second-hand boat offered for under £1,000, but it will be too small to use more than a mile out; and there will be perhaps only 50 days in the year when weather conditions will allow you to launch a craft of this size.

Up the stakes to £5,000 and you could buy a boat capable of getting out 100 days a year, possibly as far as 20 miles on occasions. But how many of these days can you get off work – and how will you find the fish?

Don't let me put you off buying a boat – it can provide you with some of the happiest angling days of your life. But you pay for the privilege with blank days while you learn how to find the fish – and quite possibly with your life if you misjudge the sea conditions.

WHEN THE WEATHER BLOWS UP ROUGH

The crucial decision whether or not it is safe to put to sea provokes many disputes between skippers and crews. A wise skipper will not risk his boat or force you out in weather so unpleasant that you never want to go with him again.

He is likely to cancel if the wind exceeds Force 5. But, in addition to the weather out-

Sundance *skipper Roger Bayzand settles behind the controls for a trip out to the Needles in search of cod. He has been fishing since he was a lad and knows exactly what his anglers expect from him.*

Above: *Electronic navigators, colour sounders and a VHF radio are among the instruments which make the chartering game a great deal safer – and more productive.*

Above left: *A hard, rocky bottom gives the strongest signal and shows as a broad red band on the colour echo sounder. Then, as the sea bed changes from rock to sand, the band reduces in width and there is less red and orange. Bigger fish also show as red and orange splashes on the screen while the fainter blue smudges are probably smaller species like sprats.*

look, he will take into account the sea state, proximity of the fishing mark, what he thinks of your ability, and the kind of angling you have booked. If you really don't like the look of the forecast but the skipper says 'Yes', then pay your money and stay at home.

SAFETY EQUIPMENT

All licensed charter boats are inspected to ensure they carry the required minimum of safety equipment: life preservers for everyone on board, flares, compass, first-aid kit and VHF radio. All boats, commercial and private, must display specific lights at night and in bad weather; they should be fitted, working, and used when necessary. There should also be suitable decklights available for illuminating tackle if necessary and landing fish at the boatside. Radar is desirable in any conditions and a necessity for safe travel at night, in fog or heavy rain, especially in busy shipping lanes.

NAVIGATION

The days when a fishing boat depended on taking sightings from the shore to determine its position are long gone. Accurate and affordable electronic navigators are now available to determine position to within 100ft or so, using the signal from Decca land stations.

DEPTH AND FISH LOCATION

Recorders which trace the detail of the seabed on to a paper chart are giving way to the electronic screen. Some use waterproof liquid crystal screens, while the hi-tech end of the market features colour video sounders to show objects of differing density in different colours. Experienced users can even determine the sizes and species of fish from the signals on screen.

TIDAL INFLUENCES

Few fish feed vigorously at dead slack water, most preferring some movement. But the full force of a big tide may deter all but the most active. Smaller or neap tides make for the easiest fishing, especially if you want to anchor; but mid-sized tides often produce the best sport.

A boat offers the choice of fishing under power, on the drift, or at anchor. In the UK, fishing under power (trolling) is a very specialised activity. Serious conger fishing is carried out at anchor while other species like pollack are usually taken on the drift. Most fish can be caught on either a stationary bait or one that is moving at a reasonable rate.

In strong tidal flows the usual option is to fish on the drift, but if the wind is with the tide it may produce too fast a drift. Conversely, when the wind is against the tide the drift may be too slow. At anchor, too slack a tide can cause problems, especially with a light variable breeze, as the boat will continually swing about on the anchor rope. The shape and size of the mark can also play a part as you may drift across it with too little time to fish, and be forced to anchor.

FISHING POSITIONS

Tradition dictates that the stern of the boat provides the best sport, and there is usually an unseemly scramble to get a place there. It's certainly easier to fish over the stern, as you can place the bait on the seabed with much greater control; but you may suffer from other anglers dropping back onto your tackle. Sometimes the safest place may be at the front – where at least you can choose who you tangle up with!

On the drift, a side position may be better because it allows you to stream your tackle away from the boat. If the skipper turns the boat on alternate drifts you will get one good drift then one bad one when you are fishing under the boat. It is often wiser to persuade everyone on the boat to fish alternate drifts only, to save a lot of wasted time undoing tangles under the boat.

When organised clubs charter a boat, they usually hold a draw for places. I do not believe in reserved places for the organiser or for the pushiest angler on the boat: it can cause bad feeling in a boat full of individuals.

TACKLE REQUIREMENTS

Choose items of tackle that complement, rather than work against, each other. Some anglers prefer light tackle that is only just up to the job, so that they have to work at landing every fish. Others prefer a powerful outfit which will cope with anything. It is unsporting to be smashed by a fish, leaving it trailing hooks, lines and leads. It is not always possible to eliminate this risk but it should be minimised.

The International Game Fish Association, based in the United States, has formulated categories of tackle based primarily on the breaking strain of the line, with rods and reels chosen accordingly.

REEL LINES

Nylon monofilament is the almost universal choice for UK angling. Braided Dacron is rarely used because its resistance to water flow needs too much lead for comfortable bottom fishing, and tangles have to be resolved with a knife.

Wire can be extremely useful in deep water and fast currents. It naturally sinks, and its small diameter for a given strength reduces the amount of lead needed to hold bottom. The lack of stretch increases sensitivity and feel for the fish. Single strand wire is robust, but it kinks and is unpleasant to handle. Multi-strand wire is generally easier to handle, but is inclined to fray and unravel.

BREAKING STRAINS

In the open sea it is unusual to use a line below 8lb, and many consider 15lb to be a reasonable minimum. Lines above this strength should cope with fish of several times their breaking strain.

With lighter line you can use more sporting outfits and less lead is needed to hold bottom – but they also pose problems. When you get tangled up, the line is much more severely kinked and you may need to cut out the affected length. Damage to a light line will have a more serious effect on the breaking strain than it would to a heavier line.

The amount of stretch in a nylon line is related to its breaking strain. If you have 200ft of line out, a fish might stretch 30lb line by 10ft, while the same pull would stretch 15lb line by 20ft.

LINE STRENGTHS

Lines of 20lb, 30lb and 50lb cover most needs in boat angling. Specialists who fish harbours for mullet, bass and flatfish may use 4lb to 8lb tackle, but the majority will rarely risk going below 12lb. In the open sea, sportsmen use 12lb to 15lb for plaice and pollack, though many start at 20lb. Heavy bottom fishing on reefs and wrecks sees 30lb to 50lb line coming into play. Pirking, especially with multiple hook rigs, often demands 50lb to 80lb line. Conger and shark usually get the heaviest tackle, but there is rarely any need to go beyond 50lb.

BOAT RODS

Short rods between 6ft and 7ft in length are used for most forms of boat fishing. They are available in solid and hollow fibreglass, car-

bon fibre, composites of glass and carbon, and carbon blanks reinforced with materials like Kevlar. Some blanks change in structure along their length, typically with carbon lower down for power and hollow fibreglass at the tip for sensitivity.

Hollow fibreglass or glass-carbon composites are favoured. It is wise to look for rods with small-diameter, thick-walled blanks because thin-walled models are easily crushed on a boat.

The traditional design of boat rods is in two pieces with the joint incorporated into a reel seat made of heavy chromed brass for strength. Nowadays there is little need for this design. Up to about 30lb class, perfectly adequate spigots can be constructed. Fuji also make an excellent lightweight seat and ferrule combination. Rods heavier than this are probably better as a one-piece design anyway, using a standard Fuji reel seat.

Dave Cooling with a series of boat rods from his own tackle room that will deal with virtually anything in British waters. From left: 20lb Conoflex glass blank; 30lb Ugly Stik with rollers and modified butt; 30-50lb wire lining blank fitted with Fuji big game rings; and the Stand-Up Ugly Stik rated at 30-80lb.

Below left: A shorter butt and long foregrip gives better balance – and helps you exert greater leverage on a fish.

Below: Chromed, screw-up reel seat and the lightweight Fuji type on two rods demonstrate that butt and foregrip lengths can vary considerably.

Check that the cross bar on your butt pad is a neat fit with the gimbal on the rod butt.

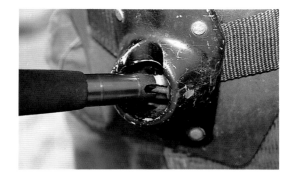

WEIGHT LOADINGS

The rod is a lever working against the angler. The longer the rod, the less force you can exert on a fish. A shorter rod allows you to use more of your strength for heavy lifting. But a longer rod may give a bit of extra control over the direction the fish swims, and make it easier to fish with long traces and steer clear of boatside tangles.

The rod should match the weight being used. A 12lb-class rod cannot cope comfortably with more than about 6oz, 20lb with 12oz, and 30lb with about 20oz. A tip-action rod will always bend to the line more than the relatively stiffer tip of a through-action model of the same power, and it is less capable of coping with heavier leads.

You may need to combine the stiffness of a 30lb rod with the thinness of 20lb line to get round the problem of heavy weights. There is usually sufficient versatility in their design to allow this, but it is as well to slacken off the reel drag slightly.

AFTCO tip and intermediate rollers: superb quality, but at a price.

SEATS AND RINGS

Convention places the reel seat between 16 and 18in from the bottom of the rod. Modern rod designers now realise that, for the heavier rod of 30lb and upwards, a shorter butt of about 10in can give a better balance. This puts the reel in a more convenient position when a butt pad is being used. A longer foregrip is needed so that the upper hand can be positioned as far up the rod as before to maintain the leverage ratio.

Rod rings need sufficient strength to stand up to everyday abuse with a relatively friction-free surface for the line. Top quality steel rings like Diamite and lined rings from companies such as Fuji and Seymo achieve this at a reasonable weight.

For extreme loads, or with wire line, quality AFTCO roller rings are recommended, although a set of these rings may cost more than the rod blank. A good roller tip ring is a sound investment on any rod of 20lb class and upwards.

BOAT REELS

Multipliers with robust metal spools rule supreme in boat fishing. Gears and other mechanical parts should be strong and smooth, and the whole thing corrosion free.

DRAG SYSTEMS

The choice in slipping-clutch mechanisms lies between lever and star drags. The lever mechanism consists of a single large drag washer next to the spool of the reel, while the star drag consists of a number of small washers with the gears between the spool and the drag reducing the sensitivity. Sadly, the choice is usually available only in larger reels; small multipliers are offered only with star drags.

GEAR RATIOS

All multipliers have gears which increase the spool revolutions and decrease the lifting power. If relatively light end tackle is being used, a high ratio of 4:1 or more is often chosen. Where there are greater lifting demands on the reel – from the likes of big conger – a much lower ratio is favoured, perhaps 2:1. If the ratio is too high for the task in hand, the fish can still be pumped up by raising the rod tip without winding, then dropping the rod tip and retrieving the slack line onto the reel. Then you raise the rod tip to gain more line and repeat the operation. The rod takes all the strain off the gears of the reel.

Manufacturers indicate the range of lines for which a reel is suitable, and the capacity at each strength. Obviously a model with a large line capacity will be bulkier and heavier than a similar reel with a smaller line capacity, and it may also be more sturdily built.

A capacity of about 350yd of your chosen line is about right for general fishing, but on wrecks I tend to favour the larger multiplier loaded with about 500yd. For light inshore work, I sometimes sacrifice capacity in favour of the joys of using lightweight

Far left: Multipliers for all occasions. Top: Policansky 4/0, suitable for 30-50lb class fishing, and a mid-priced Shakespeare Fulmar built for outfits up to 30lb. Bottom: Ambassadeur 5000, suitable for light line fishing up to 12lb, and a Policansky 2/0 that Dave matches with 20lb tackle.

Left: The Fulmar 365 offers a lever drag at a price that will suit most pockets, and there's even a level wind fitted.

tackle, and will go down to a capacity of perhaps 200yd.

I like to control the rod with my strongest hand, the right one, so I use what most manufacturers call a left-handed multiplier. Despite the fact that about 15 per cent of the population are left-handed, such multipliers are rare to say the least. I will give an honourable mention to Policansky and Penn, who make convertible or left-handed models.

CARE AND MAINTENANCE

Saltwater is one of the more corrosive of natural substances, and even the highest quality tackle will be defeated by it eventually. Reels and rods should be washed in warm freshwater after every trip and allowed to dry in the air.

Bags should also be washed, as any salt left on them will attract damp. A smear of light oil on any exposed metal parts, and a drop occasionally in the lubrication ports will increase the life of reels without overtaxing your mechanical skills.

WEIGHTS

Bomb designs fulfil most requirements. Wired grip leads are normally used only for uptiding, and watch leads are sometimes favoured for drifting over sandy bottoms. Ball and barrel leads in the smaller sizes can work inshore, and bell leads may be satisfactory when you need a very large lead – perhaps over 2lb – for fishing at anchor.

For fishing on the drop with a flying collar trace, a round-section bomb is favoured as it doesn't twist on the way down. If a square or diamond section bomb is used, you should include a swivel in the attachment. The square- and, especially, the diamond-

section bombs are preferred for a static bait on the bottom because they are less inclined to roll.

HOW TO SELECT THE RIGHT SIZE

The amount of weight needed depends on the resistance of the tackle (mainly the line) to the tide. Thin line – monofilament or, more extremely, wire – reduces the need for lead. If 25lb line needs 12oz of lead, then 15lb line may well hold bottom with 8oz. Carry a range of sizes, and make sure you have enough: on a wrecking trip you may need to take 20lb of lead to be sure.

Anglers at the front of the boat should try to prevent their tackle tangling with those

If you need a lot of weight to hold bottom at anchor, then bell leads are the answer. Bomb shapes are the best profile for most boat fishing, although watch leads are sometimes favoured for drifting over sandy marks.

Zip slider: simple but highly effective.

The search for a perfectly tangle-free system has inspired designs of booms in all shapes and sizes. Dave rates the L-shaped French wire boom as best for flying collar rigs.

behind them by increasing the weight slightly above the absolute minimum. Those fortunate enough to be at the back should play their part by lightening off slightly and paying out a bit more line, so the tackle settles further behind the boat.

The same idea works on a drifting boat. Depending on the balance between wind and tide, anglers on one side of the boat will find themselves fishing underneath the boat while the others have the luxury of their tackle streaming away from the side. Those fishing under the boat should increase the size of their weights, and those streaming away reduce theirs.

BOOMS AND ROTTEN BOTTOMS

A boom permits the lead to slide on the line without damaging it, prevents tangles forming as the tackle is lowered by spreading the hook trace away from the reel line, or allows the attachment of hook traces along the reel line.

I prefer to keep the tackle as simple as possible, so my box does not hold a wide variety of booms. If I think there is any prospect of fouling the lead I attach it to the boom with a rotten bottom (a short loop of lighter line) rather than a link swivel.

The Zip slider is my general purpose leger boom. It is simple and tidy, slides freely, does not cause tangles, and is cheap and convenient. For very light fishing I favour the coarse angler's Roberts beads with a small swivel snap to hold the lead.

Using a very long flying collar trace to present sandeel imitations requires good tackle control on the part of the angler, and a tangle-free boom to eliminate hang-ups while it is being raised and lowered perhaps 150ft through the water. The traditional 8in or 10in wire boom is still the best, though I prefer an L-shaped design to the older triangular one. Ensure that the wire is straight, and that both sections of line are attached with small swivels.

WIRE AND NYLON TRACES

Wire traces are essential for shark and tope fishing but for little else in UK waters. A 12in biting trace of wire with a 6ft rubbing trace of heavy nylon will defeat tope, but for larger shark up to 18ft of wire may be needed to stop them twisting up the trace and fraying the line with their rough skin.

Big skate, halibut and giant conger may merit wire, but the average conger, ling and the like will be defeated by 100lb monofilament, which is much easier to handle. Cod and rays rarely need more than 60lb monofilament, and 30lb mono will handle just about everything else. Check the trace after each fish, and be prepared to change it regularly.

GRINNER KNOT

Almost all requirements are met by a properly tied Uniknot or Grinner (Fig.1). The two ends of the line point in the same

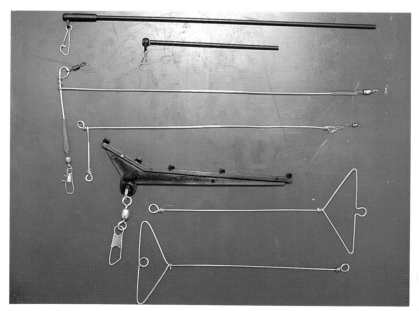

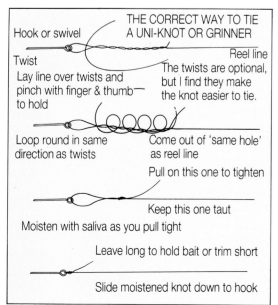

THE CORRECT WAY TO TIE A UNI-KNOT OR GRINNER

Hook or swivel

Twist

Reel line

The twists are optional, but I find they make the knot easier to tie.

Lay line over twists and pinch with finger & thumb to hold

Loop round in same direction as twists

Come out of 'same hole' as reel line

Pull on this one to tighten

Keep this one taut

Moisten with saliva as you pull tight

Leave long to hold bait or trim short

Slide moistened knot down to hook

direction, so it is easy to thread a bait over the knot; it is held in place and does not slip back.

With fine lines – perhaps 8lb – use five turns; use four turns for 15-30lb, and three turns with lines over 50lb. If a lead-carrying boom is stopped by the knot, I put a plastic bead on the line to act as a buffer. The bore of the bead should be sufficient to fit over the knot.

SWIVELS

Swivels must be stronger than the line, and should turn reasonably freely. Companies like Berkley, Mustad and Sampo indicate the strength of their swivels, though they should be checked individually, like any item of tackle. Too large a swivel offers no advantage in efficiency and is a considerable weight on the line. Performance is less easy to guarantee: few are really effective, and they all work least efficiently when under a load.

Links on a swivel are undesirable; if you must have them, use only quality ones that you have tested individually. Their only use, in my view, is to hang leads on. I always tie the line to a swivel.

HOOKS

Never use a stainless hook unless it is built into flies, feathers or some similar lure. Bronze hooks take a better point and will rust out of a fish if it is necessary to leave them in place – which is better than killing the fish to get the hook back.

The hook needs to be the right size for both the fish and the bait, the right strength for the fish, and always very sharp. Smaller sizes can be chosen from the range of fine-wire hooks available to the shore angler: Aberdeen, Spearpoint, or the lightly-forged Limerick or Viking designs. Bigger prey demand heavier hooks, and always forged. The O'Shaughnessy pattern covers the needs of most British anglers, up to size 8/0, for skate, cod, ling, pollack and conger.

I rarely use treble hooks in boat fishing, and I replace those on pirks with a single 8/0 O'Shaughnessy. To my mind the treble foul-hooks far too many fish.

TECHNIQUES AND TACTICS

FEATHERING FOR MACKEREL

Fresh mackerel is the nearest thing to a universal bait for sea angling, and it must be gathered on the day by a feathering session on the way out to the fishing mark.

Use a trace of four to six feathers, but no more than about five feet in length, with a weight large enough to keep it out of everyone else's way. Work them vigorously up and down with the rod, while paying out or recovering line in an attempt to find the depth the fish are shoaling at. The feathers themselves may be actual feathers, bits of cloth or tinsel, or even fluorescent beads slid down the trace above the hooks. Handle your feathers with care as the string of hooks can be very hazardous.

INSHORE FISHING

In shallow estuaries or when drifting along the shoreline in a dinghy, you can use a freshwater carp or spinning rod with a fixed spool reel or a small baitcasting multiplier. The fixed spool is usually favoured for leads below about ½oz. Team this outfit with line between 4lb and 8lb and a light leger rig baited with worm, or worm and squid – then flounders and plaice will really show their mettle.

A few beads or an attractor spoon above the hook may sometimes be an advantage. Replacing the worm with live sandeel on a longer trace will improve your chances with bass and pollack, and plaice are still a possibility.

As the water deepens and the ground gets rougher, your tackle must match not only

Pick of the hook patterns and sizes. Top (left to right): 496B Limerick Mustad 4/0s; Viking 4/0; and 6/0 and 7/0 O'Shaughnessy patterns for big Redgills. Bottom: O'Shaughnessy 8/0 and 6/0; and Mustad pirking trebles.

the fish but the conditions. A boat rod suited to lines between 15 and 20lb with a beach-casting-sized multiplier will be the most likely choice. A much wider range of fish may be expected and fish baits like mackerel strip will attract various dogfishes, skate, conger and whiting. Large worm or squid baits will probably be better for cod and pouting.

The terminal tackle is usually a simple leger, though whiting, especially, often prefer a bait held off the bottom by a simple paternoster. For species with teeth, use a hook length of at least 20lb and step up to 40lb if there are skate around. If conger are a possibility, I would suggest at least 60lb nylon.

UPTIDING

In fairly shallow water – possibly up to 70ft or so – the fish may avoid the area directly below the hull of an anchored boat because of vibrations. One solution is to cast the tackle away from the boat. Uptiding, or boatcasting, is one form of boat angling that demands a specialised rod and reel: there is no way you can cast with conventional boat gear.

The rod is not unlike a shortish beach-caster, 9ft or 10ft in length, with a stiff lower half and long handle for powerful casting. A softish tip is needed for bite detection and to avoid the lead being dragged out with each movement of the boat. The casting weight determines the power of the rod, with various models handling from 3oz to 10oz.

A medium to large beachcasting multiplier is used, loaded with 15-18lb line and a shock leader for safe casting. As in beach-casting, the usual terminal rig is a paternoster with a grip lead, although for tope fishing the trace needs to be at least 6ft long with a foot of wire next to the hook.

SANDBANKS

Drifting over sandbanks, whether inshore or offshore, can produce excellent sport. The favoured tackle is a long trace, up to 20ft, with a small swivel in the middle. The lead should be chosen so as just to hold bottom. Tackle should reflect the target species, and may range from 8lb to 12lb for bass and plaice, to 20lb or 30lb for turbot and blonde rays. Bait is a live sandeel or a long, thin

mackerel strip cut to imitate one. If plaice are the target it is also worth trying peeler crab, lugworm or slivers of squid – or a cocktail – on the same rig.

DEEP WATER

At more than about 100ft the conditions of depth and tide dictate the tackle as much as the fish. There are many deep-water rough ground marks holding worthwhile numbers of a variety of species, typically cod. Fish like pollack, coalfish and ling favour reef areas, where rock stacks rise up from the seabed. But the favourite offshore target is usually wrecks, often of ships sunk by torpedo in the two World Wars.

Fish are rarely evenly distributed and many areas of the open sea are almost totally devoid of them. Structural features on the seabed, whether natural rock or wrecks, act like magnets to fish. The vertical hard faces support weed growth which gives cover to the crustacea and small fish that form the food for the specimens anglers want to catch. Around the structure there are usually small sandbanks which may support yet more species like plaice, turbot and angler fish.

TRACE LENGTHS

For fish which feed on the bottom, a conventional leger is the usual tactic (Fig.2). A Zip slider stopped by a bead and swivel, a trace of 100lb nylon and an 8/0 O'Shaugh-

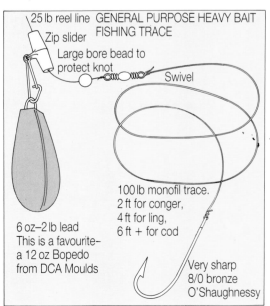

25 lb reel line GENERAL PURPOSE HEAVY BAIT FISHING TRACE

Zip slider

Large bore bead to protect knot

Swivel

6 oz–2 lb lead
This is a favourite – a 12 oz Bopedo from DCA Moulds

100 lb monofil trace.
2 ft for conger,
4 ft for ling,
6 ft + for cod

Very sharp
8/0 bronze
O'Shaughnessy

nessy hook make up the usual rig. For cod, the trace may be up to 8ft long, about 4ft for ling, and perhaps only 2ft for conger. The shorter trace is more sensitive, and allows you to respond to a conger before it takes the bait back to its lair. Cod and ling prefer more time with the bait, but are less likely to reject it.

While a long, soft-tipped rod may give the best bite indication, a shorter rod is more effective for playing the fish. The line may be between 25lb and 50lb – anything less will make it very difficult to turn the fish from the snags. There is little point using line above 50lb since the average angler couldn't break it even if he tried. There is so much stretch in nylon line that striking is a futile exercise, and you then just wind into the bite.

A large, smelly whole bait like cuttlefish, squid or fish is used. Mackerel is the usual choice, though pouting, scad and others also work. Large fillets are hooked through the small end, making them flutter in the water. The frame, which is the head, backbone and guts with the tail trimmed off so it doesn't spin, makes a bait that many anglers unwisely discard.

A flapper is the head and fillets, with the spine and tail removed. These baits are usually hooked through the lower lip and out through the top of the head which closes the mouth and helps stop the bait spinning.

The whole fish, again without the tail, makes an excellent bait for conger, particularly when ling are present. It doesn't leave such a trail of blood and scent, so the ling are slower to locate it, giving the conger more of a chance.

WIRE LINE

Wire is popular with some anglers in these conditions, as its low stretch makes it extremely sensitive, and its small diameter reduces the amount of lead needed. A slightly longer rod of 7-8ft with roller rings is often favoured, and a narrow spool multiplier will reduce the need to guide the line on to the reel by hand.

A tip-action rod is often used as it reduces flexing when the line passes over the tip roller, gives better bite indication, and damps the movement as the boat goes up and down. Wire requires a certain degree of expertise or the tangles can be horrifying,

and some skippers will not allow its use on their boats.

FLYING COLLARS

Predatory fish, including cod, coalfish, pollack and bass, spend much of their time hunting in midwater. A favourite for these fish on reefs or wrecks is called the flying collar rig (Fig. 3), or just Redgilling. Reasonably light line can be used as there are no snags in midwater, and 12-20lb is usual, depending on the size of fish expected from the area.

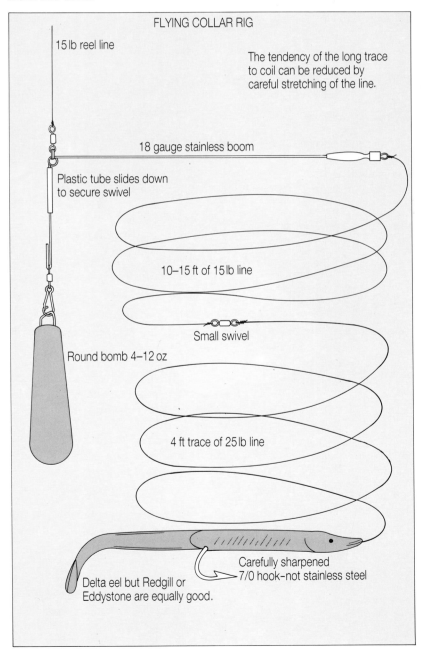

FLYING COLLAR RIG

15 lb reel line

The tendency of the long trace to coil can be reduced by careful stretching of the line.

18 gauge stainless boom

Plastic tube slides down to secure swivel

10–15 ft of 15lb line

Small swivel

Round bomb 4–12 oz

4 ft trace of 25lb line

Delta eel but Redgill or Eddystone are equally good.

Carefully sharpened 7/0 hook-not stainless steel

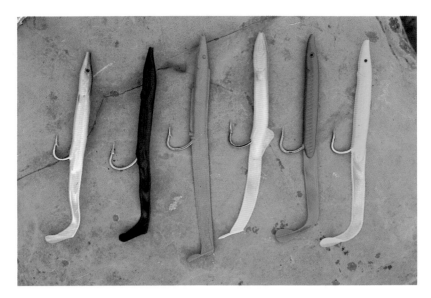

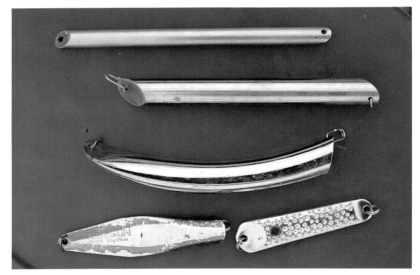

just keep on winding at the same steady rate until the rod tip is dragged over the side of the boat – then pray that your clutch is correctly set.

PIRKING

Pirking involves working artificial metal lures near the seabed for predatory fish, mostly cod and ling. The pirk is a bar of shiny or painted metal between one and two pounds in weight, usually accompanied by a number of rubber muppets or feathers.

The rig is lowered to the seabed and then vigorously raised and lowered to imitate the actions of a baitfish. The rod and line are often 50lb class or more to reduce stretch when whipping the gear clear of the wreck, to pull it out of the inevitable snags, and to cope with multiple hook-ups of fish. I prefer not to use multiple muppets (though I know they can be successful) and use a pirk on the end of four feet of 100lb nylon, blood knotted to a large swivel, with about one foot of stub projecting from the knot. A muppet or a rubber eel is attached to this, and the reel line is tied to the other end of the swivel, giving the fish a choice of two baits.

Top: *Carry rubber sandeels in a range of colours: these are some of the most killing shades.*

Above: *Flashy pirk bodies from Dave's huge collection, including home-made and commercially produced models.*

Right: *The beauty of this bright pirk is that you can add or subtract weight from the hollow body chamber as conditions dictate.*

A long wire boom ensures the trace stands off from the reel line. Both the main line and the trace should be attached to the boom with small swivels, and a small swivel is used in the middle of the trace, which may be up to 20ft in length. A rubber sandeel is the most common lure and a range should be carried, including at least black, red, orange and white. A live sandeel or long, thin fish strips may also be used. To hook a live sandeel, put the hook right through the lower lip, and then nick it lightly in the flesh of the belly. Lower the tackle to the bottom as steadily as possible to avoid tangling the long trace, and then retrieve it steadily to make it flutter in midwater. The retrieve speed and the depth at which the fish will bite vary from day to day. Don't try to strike at a fish or it will reject the bait:

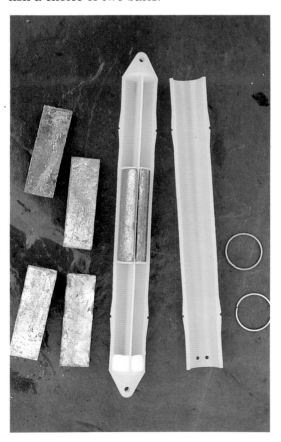

ACCESSORIES

BUTT PAD

Use a butt pad where big fish are expected. I prefer one with a cross bar that fits the gimbal on the rod butt and stops the rod twisting when I am winding in. Shoulder and kidney harnesses are normally used with 50lb tackle and upwards.

GAFFS AND NETS

Every skipper worth his hire carries all the gaffs and nets he will ever need. If he asks for a volunteer to help landing fish, make sure you are up to the job: nobody likes to lose a fish at the boatside.

Nets should be large and strong enough to cope with lifting fish, with open, tangle-free mesh. The most likely candidates for netting are prime eating fish, ranging from plaice and bass through turbot to pollack and cod, and anything to be returned alive.

T-BARS AND ARTERY FORCEPS

Small and medium-sized seafish can be unhooked with artery forceps. But you'll face problems with a big fish firmly hooked far down the throat. An 8/0 hook can take a lot of shifting. If you intend to return the fish, the hook must be removed with care or left to rust out. But if the fish is to be eaten, leave the hook in the fish until you cut it up.

When the hook is accessible, pliers can be used, but the current favourite for wreck fishing seems to be a steel T-bar, with the end bent into a small hook. Put the line into the bend of this hook, raise the T-bar and lower the trace. The hook on the T-bar should slide up the trace until it engages in the bend of your hook. At this point, your hook should be point down, with the fish hanging on the barb. A sharp jerk and the weight of the fish should dislodge even the most solid hookhold.

FILLETING KNIFE

For preparing baits and cleaning small fish, I carry a 6in thin-bladed filleting knife in a sheath on my belt. Scissors can be useful for preparing some baits, and are much safer

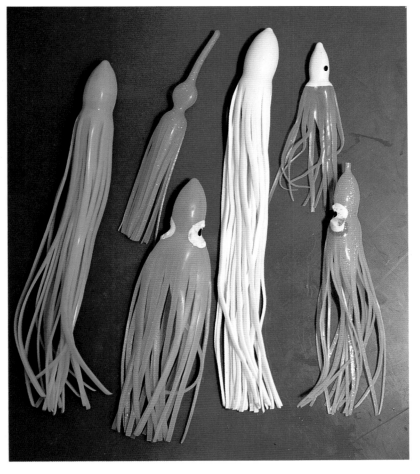

to use than a knife. I also keep a rigid professional boning knife in my box for filleting large fish.

Both knives should be extremely sharp, and I carry a sharpening stone with me; a blunt knife is the most dangerous. Do not cut bait or anything else on any part of the boat other than a proper cutting board, and never use a knife on line if you can avoid it: nail clippers are safer. With wire, always use proper sidecutters, which can be obtained with a holster for hanging on the belt. Suitable screwdrivers, spanners and pliers should be carried for emergency repairs on reels and other tackle.

TACKLE BOXES

Cantilever trays and bags of any sort are never satisfactory on a boat. The cheap solution is to get hold of a five-gallon plastic cooking-oil drum or a brewing barrel. It is the right size, absolutely waterproof – and if you reinforce the lid with a circle of plywood, it makes an excellent seat. If you

Rubber muppets give a pirk even more appeal when jigged over the seabed.

don't mind spending money, get a coarse angler's reinforced plastic seat box. You'll find inexpensive waterproof plastic food boxes in many shapes and sizes at your local supermarket. Half a dozen of these will keep all your kit tidy and dry inside the box.

COOL BOXES

Cool boxes are a much neglected item. Whenever the air temperature is above cool, I take one with me. Frozen bait, my lunch, and a cold drink go out in it. Prime fish – whether for food or for freezing down as bait – come back in it.

FOOD AND DRINK

Make sure you take enough, and always include a drink – but never alcohol. A day afloat, apart from the fishing, is a strenuous one, and plenty of cake, biscuits and chocolate suit me best.

CLOTHING

Most boats have wet decks, so I always wear boots – lightweight wellies in the summer, thermals in the winter. For fine weather I favour moleskin trousers, sleeveless shirt and denim smock. In winter it is thermal underwear, thermal one-piece suit, and gloves. I always wear a Heron buoyancy waistcoat, and take a pair of Polaroid glasses and a cap with a generous peak. Survival suits are excellent value if you can find one you are comfortable in, but good waterproof bib-and-brace trousers and a quality waterproof jacket with hood will cope with most eventualities.

SAFETY

Remember that you are responsible for your own safety and that of the people around you, so think before you take any risks. I carry a small first-aid kit for my own use, containing a few plasters, sunscreen and aspirins. If a problem goes beyond these meagre resources, I would want a second opinion anyway.

SEASICKNESS

Make sure you get a good night's sleep beforehand and choose your meals for the day before the trip with care, avoiding excesses of anything – especially alcohol. Take sensible food and drink with you and stay in the fresh air if you feel unwell. If you are prone to seasickness, test the various treatments available; you will probably find one that works. I have heard good reports of acupressure pads.

CONSERVATION

I return any unwanted fish if it has a chance of survival. Sadly, this is often not possible. Conger, flatfish, skate and bass will usually survive, but many species from deep water, including cod, coalfish, pollack and ling, will have suffered fatal decompression by the time they reach the surface.

Personally, I find it difficult to reconcile the sport of angling with the selling of the catch by the angler or skipper. It smacks of commercial fishing.

GAME FISHING

Most anglers live within easy reach of
quality trout fishing at an affordable price. The most
satisfying way of chasing rainbows is to use
light tackle with a delicately presented fly. All the
gear and patterns you will need are covered in
this final section.

TROUT FISHING

Below: The featureless expanses of Queen Mother Reservoir might appear uninviting but the deep waters pose a fascinating challenge for big brownie and rainbow hunters.

Below right: The intimate atmosphere at leafy Lakedown fishery in Sussex contrasts sharply with the concrete bowls.

Fly fishing for trout probably has a longer tradition than almost any other branch of angling, but it is only in recent years that it has become widely popular. More development has taken place since the early 1960s than in the entire evolution of the sport up to that time. Almost every major water-supply reservoir is now open for business and there is an increasing number of smaller, specialised fisheries.

Good quality and affordable trout fishing is within reach of almost everybody. But as pressure has grown on the fisheries to provide more fish for more anglers, variations have emerged in the quality of the sport, surroundings, facilities and even in the fish themselves. This has produced healthy competition between fisheries, as anglers who consider they haven't received value for their money are unlikely to return. It is a fact that the most successful fisheries are those that are well managed.

TYPES OF WATER

There are relatively few natural lakes, and most of them are found in Ireland and Scotland with a sprinkling in Wales. Before the days of reservoir trouting, which forms the bulk of the fishing in England, these natural lochs were the home of the pioneers in the stillwater fly methods and were relatively under-fished.

Water-supply reservoirs vary enormously in size and depth, from the mighty Rutland, at over 3,500 acres, to relative ponds at five acres or less. Small stillwater fishing has developed into virtually a sport in its own right due to the specialised tactics it demands.

Trout fishing in running water is more widely available than many imagine and is equally accessible. Again, it offers almost infinite variety, with small peaty streams in Dartmoor contrasting with the richness of the classic Hampshire chalkstreams or the great rivers of Scotland and Wales.

NATURAL LAKES

Fishing in a truly natural stillwater is sheer delight. Often the water quality will be very acid, and this dictates the size of the fish. In regions where there is a shortage of food the trout can be quite small.

In a remote Highland loch a fish of 1lb is a real achievement and may well be four years old or more. What these wild fish lack in size is more than made up in quality. Their strength and fighting ability is amazing. Light tackle and considerable watercraft is required to really enjoy them. To survive in these lean places they live on their wits and tend to be extremely shy.

But there is a bonus factor here. Because of the scarcity of food the fish are less selec-

tive than their reservoir cousins and can be easier to tempt with the fly. They will snatch at the most unlikely offerings, and success is often more a matter of presentation than choosing the right fly pattern.

Another plus point that will be appreciated by many who have taken holidays in Ireland and Scotland is that this kind of fishing is usually very cheap. A permit for a whole week's fishing will often cost only a few pounds. This ticket might include more than a dozen small hill lochs or lochans. As ever, the best place to inquire will be the local tackle shop or estate office if the location is far from habitation.

RESERVOIRS

Man-made lakes and water-supply reservoirs are the backbone of British still-water fly fishing. Over the past 20 years so many of these waters have been opened up that virtually every angler has fishing on his doorstep. It is a happy coincidence that clean water for drinking goes hand-in-hand with an ideal environment for trout.

The range of reservoirs varies from austere concrete bowls to the most delightful moorland waters that look for all the world like natural lakes. This is not meant to denigrate the concrete bowls: they frequently provide fishing close to major towns or cities that would otherwise be out of reach to youngsters and others without transport. Boats are often available, allowing both bank and loch-style fishing.

Concrete bowls usually rely on water pumped from local rivers, while more conventional reservoirs have a natural catchment depending on rain-fed streams and run-off water for their supply. This tends to give a more stable environment for the fish and their food items. Pumped water can be at a vastly different temperature to the main body of the lake and may disrupt feeding patterns and affect water clarity.

WHAT IT COSTS

A day's bank fishing will cost from around £5 to £8 for a typical six-fish limit – potentially great value. Make sure you also purchase the relevant water authority rod licence, as this is rarely covered by the reservoir ticket. These licences cost about £2 for a week or £10 for the year.

Boat fishing is inevitably more expensive, usually working out between £15 and £18 daily per rod. But when you consider that at the height of summer it buys you 12 hours of sport with six fish at the end of it, the figure looks more than reasonable. Add to that a well-maintained boat and engine and the freedom to explore thousands of acres of water and you can see it represents exceptional value for money.

TICKET OPTIONS

Many fisheries offer a flexible range of tickets. For instance, half-day rods are usually available and sometimes an evening ticket. In Scotland, where summer days are longer, places like Loch Leven operate a shift system, allowing the angler to purchase as many shifts in a day as he pleases.

The best value of all has to be the season permit, as long as you live close enough to the fishery to take full advantage. Most big waters give you free rein to fish at any time throughout the season with a daily limit bag applying. Other season permits offer a ticket that allows you to take a total of, say, 100 trout. You then keep as many fish as you like on each visit until your quota is filled. For those who prefer to restrict themselves to a brace per visit, this can be a very economical way of managing their season.

SEASON TIMES

Until the rainbow trout was introduced to Britain the fishing season was clearly defined. It usually extended from 1 April to 1 October, with some rivers not opening until 1 May. More recently, there has been a shift towards earlier opening dates, with many reservoirs starting in mid-March and continuing until mid-October.

For my money, the weather is the most important factor. I prefer to wait until spring before venturing out. On Chew and Blagdon, in the lovely Mendip Hills, this coincides with the arrival of the swifts and swallows, which is early enough for most. Similarly, at season's end, October winds take the colourful leaves from the trees, so I am happy to hang up the rods at the end of September.

Another growing trend is towards year-round fisheries which rarely close their doors. They stock with rainbow trout, which remain in good condition even in the depths of winter. But all too often it is a case of blue fingers and frozen ears for little reward. Winter trouting is very much for the hardy.

In my experience, fishery staff are the salt of the earth. They are always willing to share local knowledge or pass on tips about the latest fly or the best holding area. Bailiffs and fishery managers are well worth cultivating as friends.

SMALL STILLWATERS

The increase in the number of small stillwaters has been astonishing. From a mere handful in the late 1970s, there are now so many that it would be virtually impossible to name them all. Avington lakes in Hampshire, where the concept of growing-on huge rainbows first caught the imagination, is still the first of these fisheries that comes to mind, closely followed by Damerham, Rooksbury and Rockbourne.

During the 1980s the idea of fishing in a small confined lake, often for specimen-sized fish, came into vogue. Most of these waters are spring-fed and very clear, offering an extra visual element to what is already an exciting prospect. Latterly, fish in the 15-20lb class have become almost commonplace.

Tactics are fundamentally different. Small stillwater experts tend to use shorter casts, often with a single weighted fly, and prefer to stalk individual fish using Polaroid glasses. They induce the take, giving added life to the fly in the way it is moved.

Small stillwaters can be no larger than half-an-acre, which means the fish have nowhere to escape. But they can quickly become very educated, requiring stealth, patience and a steady nerve. Many of these fisheries remain open right through the winter; Steeple Langford and Dever

Springs are among the best when the weather is kind.

Some small waters require more conventional bank fishing methods, with a longer cast and more mobile fly. The larger weighted lures, with marabou feathers in the tying to give added movement, are very effective. But there is rarely a need to depart from the general principle of imitating items in the trout's diet. Favourite flies for small waters include Damsel nymphs, Stick Fly, Pheasant Tail and the eternally popular Corixa.

RIVERS AND STREAMS

For some reason, anglers are convinced you need a second mortgage to gain access to river fishing, and that mystical skills are required. Certainly there are some chalk-streams – notably the Hampshire Test and Itchen – where the price of sport is prohibitive for most of us. But there are club and association waters available for less than £5 a day which offer superb fishing. Many of these waters are open to visitors; the best policy, as always, is to seek the advice of your local tackle shop.

Obviously, river tactics are quite different from stillwater, but there is no reason why a tackle change should be needed. A standard-length rod, matched to a 5- or 6-weight line, is more than adequate. On most rivers a floating line and dry fly offer the most fun, but there will also be days when sinking lines and wet fly are needed, so your standard reservoir outfit will be fine.

THE BASIC OUTFIT

The basic outfit consists of rod, reel and line – which have all benefited hugely from modern technology. We have progressed from cane rods, through glass, and now to carbon fibre or graphite. Similarly, lines that used to be made of silk are now of hi-tech plastic. The purchase of any piece of equipment represents a serious decision. In the case of a rod or reel, you are also making an investment in pleasure for many years to come: with top companies offering a lifetime guarantee on their products, it is an important choice. Let's start with what I regard as the most important single factor in trout tackle: line weight.

A hefty rainbow hooked under the rod tip at Avington Lakes in Hampshire makes a determined dash for the weed beds.

*Chris Ogborne (**far left**) plays out a spirited winter trout at Steeple Langford near Salisbury. His silvery rainbow (**left**) demonstrates that there's nothing wrong with the condition of the fish at this time of year.*

FLY LINES

The AFTMA ratings are a simple numerical scale for assessing the physical weight of a fly line; they enable you to match it to a rod designed to cast that weight correctly. Heavy lines cast greater distances, but sometimes at the expense of accuracy and presentation. The real value of the AFTMA scale is that it allows you to balance the outfit, making rod, reel and line compatible.

For many seasons I have been advocating a return to the first principles of fly fishing. The basis of my philosophy involves deriving as much pleasure as possible from the act of catching fish. To my mind, these pleasures are increased many times over by the use of lighter and finer tackle.

For today's angling – bearing in mind the range and quality of rods on the market – there is absolutely no need to use a line weight heavier than AFTMA 6. There need be no pre-occupation with fishing at distance. Presentation is everything, and the accent is placed firmly on accuracy coupled with a lack of surface disturbance. An AFTMA weight of 5 or 6 makes much less disturbance when it lands on the water than one with a rating of 8 or 9. The line is lighter, slimmer and easier to control.

Even in a heavy wind, there is no real problem in using a lighter line weight, although of course in rough conditions the advantages of presentation are somewhat negated by a heavy wave. Better-quality lines are generally the most expensive. I prefer either Cortland or Orvis for floaters and Scientific Anglers for the intermediate and sinkers.

All my lines are in the weight-forward (WF) format as I find that these give far greater control over presentation. All serious trout anglers carry floating, intermediate and fast sinking lines in their tackle bags. Most competition anglers, for instance, need at least three different densities of sinker to cover all eventualities and conditions.

SHOOTING HEADS

The one specialty line that needs particular mention is the shooting head. This is usually a short (10m) length of line – the equivalent of the front 10m of a forward taper – that is attached to very fine running line. This is aerialised by the caster, who then shoots it forward, with its own weight and momentum carrying it for a good

Trout men travel lighter than any other type of angler. Chris Ogborne lays out his basic kit on the banks of Steeple Langford lake.

Braided leaders have caught on fast in trout fishing but tapered nylon remains a favourite of many.

Above: *Double-figure trout are commonplace these days and Stafford Moor in Devon produces many admirable full-tailed specimens like this early season heavyweight.*

distance. The light running line slips easily through the rings, allowing long casts.

This has great relevance to bank fishing, where distance can sometimes be essential. But there is inevitably a sacrifice in subtlety and presentation, as it is much more difficult to control than a full line. For this reason it has little or no relevance to the boat fisherman.

Most anglers use a loop or a nail knot to attach the shooting head to the backing, which is either 25lb monofilament or fine braided nylon.

BRAIDED LEADERS

In my opinion, braided leaders are among the most significant developments of recent years, as they definitely improve casting and presentation. The basic principle is that a braided-section leader offers a smoother turnover between the fly line and tippet. It does this by ensuring a progressive transmission of energy from the unfurling fly line, thereby controlling the leader's loop.

In practice, it works even better. In the case of the floating line, it gives greatly improved presentation, which in turn means more accuracy. Much longer leaders can be fished than with a conventional format.

Different manufacturers offer different systems, but the principle is common to all. The best undoubtedly come from Bob Church, Orvis and Sue Burgess.

REELS

Using a quality fly reel is a pleasure in itself, and having the confidence that it will not jam at a critical moment must surely justify any extra cost.

There is a huge variation in the price of reels. At the inexpensive end of the market, it is hard to beat the Speedex models from Shakespeare. With their new green surface finish, they are serviceable and reliable fly reels offering every facility the angler requires.

At the other end of the scale, it is possible to part with over £100 for a precision-engineered reel that is either handmade or at least hand-finished. Anyone who has seen the designer reels of Ari Hart from Holland will know that they are things of beauty: they are genuinely a lifetime investment as they will outlive the angler and in time may become a family heirloom.

The middle ground is, as ever, inhabited by the greatest numbers. The long pedigree of tradition that Hardy have established in fly-reel design is still evident in their

Right: *Top of the range reels constructed from lightweight metals and marketed by Orvis and Shakespeare are a worthwhile investment. The Dragonfly is more modestly priced but is a proven performer.*

current models. As always, you pay your money, and take your choice.

For those who do not wish to invest in large numbers of reels to hold their varying lines, most makers offer the spare spool as a viable alternative. If you opt for one, make sure it is of the quick change variety.

ROD CHOICE

The range and variety of rods currently available can be bewildering, especially for the novice. Without expert advice, the latter may find himself with entirely the wrong tool for the job.

The function of the rod during casting is to extend the fly line and to present the fly to the fish without disturbance. Every part of the casting action should be smooth and progressive – hence the value of a balanced outfit.

The development of the carbon-fibre or graphite fishing rod has undoubtedly changed freshwater fly fishing, probably for ever. There has probably been more innovation in fly rod design in the last 20 years than in the previous 200. There are still devotees of cane rods; but they are few, and they pay a high premium for their preference. Most built-cane rods now are either made to order or available from specialists at upwards of £300.

Glass fibre has its place in a beginner's outfit, but few experienced people would recommend using glass when the obvious benefits of lightness, versatility and convenience of graphite are available.

I believe that the development of graphite has probably gone as far as it reasonably can, and that the latest variations are really just that: Kevlar and other graphite mixes could be said to be change for change's sake. There are graphite rods on the market from £30 to £300, with some extremely good products in the lower price range.

A rod length of 9ft 6in to 10ft is ideal for most forms of trout fishing. Anything longer and the rod becomes cumbersome, while a shorter model limits flexibility of approach. Several highly successful international anglers use 12ft rods with consummate ease, but even they would admit they are in the minority. I dread to think of the state of their wrists after a full day's fishing!

Follow the light line philosophy to its logical conclusion and look for a rod capable

of handling a 5- or 6-weight line. This outfit will cover virtually every angling situation, and will be flexible enough for almost any trout-fishing venue in the British Isles.

PUTTING IT ALL TOGETHER

Assembly of the basic outfit is a fairly simple task, but again I come back to the best advice: consult your tackle dealer. Most retailers are quite happy to put backing and the line on the reel for you and some will even give you the backing free. If you do it yourself, use the Arbor knot (Fig.1) and wind the line on the reel without kinks.

Attaching the leader or braided-butt leader to the fly line is also a job best done by the retailer. If he can't do it, you need to choose from two alternatives. The first is a 30in length of 10lb nylon joined to the end of the fly line by a nail knot (Fig.2); this becomes your permanent butt to which the leader is attached. The second alternative is the braided butt, which is joined to the line by superglue. Strip a little plastic off the core – about ½in – and push this into the

Above left: Most reservoir rods in the heavier ratings are sold with extension butts to give extra support under the forearm.

Above: Bridge, snake and single leg rings are found on rods through all the price bands. The simple snake still has a big following.

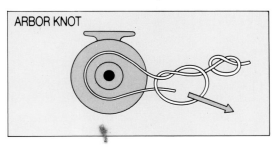

ARBOR KNOT

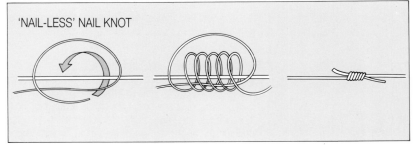

'NAIL-LESS' NAIL KNOT

open end of the braid; then roll some super-glue over the finished join. It should never let you down.

In the final analysis, choosing tackle comes down to two simple factors – personal preference and available cash. No rod or outfit will directly improve an angler's casting ability. What it can do is to hugely increase his enjoyment of his sport.

TERMINAL TACKLE

There are various alternatives in leader construction. It is the the most important item of tackle because the leader is the last thing the trout sees – or rather, doesn't see! – before it is hooked.

You can either buy pre-tied leaders of a

If you're wary about tying up your own droppers then Masterline produce a special dispenser. It contains 20 leader lengths with two 4in droppers on each.

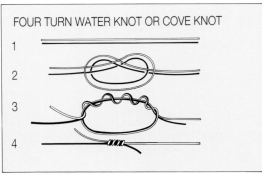

prescribed strength and length or construct your own from nylon monofilament. I find the pre-tied leaders too fussy, and I also distrust other people's knots, which is why I always tie my own. Using a permanent butt of braided leader, it is very simple to attach the monofilament either by a double over-hand knot or by a four-turn Water knot. The simplest leader is a straight-through length of nylon to a single fly; the length will vary according to wind, general conditions, depth of water and the fly being used.

If droppers are used, always tie them with a Grinner or four-turn Water knot (Fig. 3). This also enables you to step down the breaking strain. For instance, you may have 6lb to the top dropper, 5lb in the middle and 4lb for the point fly (Fig.4). The length of each section is infinitely variable: the best advice is to use the longest leader with which you feel comfortable and are able to cast without tangles.

Knots for attaching fly to leader are probably the most important ones you will ever tie and must be totally reliable. They are the final link between you and your fish. A tucked half-blood is my own first choice, although many of my colleagues prefer either Clinch (Fig.5) or Turle knots. The choice of nylon monofilament brand is crucial as some on the market are far better than others. But it's also a question of personal preference, so I suggest you get a consensus of opinion from other anglers and your tackle dealer.

ACCESSORIES

A good fishing bag with a shoulder strap for ease of carrying is essential. Not only will

LEADER CONSTRUCTION
The following leaders should be attached to your permanent butt consisting of 30 in braided section, or 30 in of 10 lb nylon. All lengths quoted are exclusive of this permanent section.

1. STANDARD LEADER (Two Fly) (All sections same breaking strain)
Butt ⊢——— 36 in ——— Dropper ——— 60 in ——— Tail Fly

2. Standard Wet Fly Leader (Three Fly) (All sections same breaking strain)
Butt ⊢——— 36 in ——— Top Dropper ——— 45 in ——— Middle Dropper ——— 72 in ——— Tail Fly

3. Stepped down Leader construction
Butt ⊢——— 36 in of 6 lb ——— Dropper ——— 45 in of 5 lb ——— Dropper ——— 72 in of 4 lb ——— Tail Fly

In all cases, dropper lengths should be around 6–8 in maximum. Do not join lengths of say 10 lb and 5 lb together, as the diameters are not compatible and this produces too much strain on the knot. Step down leaders in smooth, progressive drops.

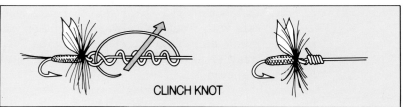

CLINCH KNOT

this store all your tackle in one place, but it will keep out dirt that might clog or damage your reels. Rubber-lined canvas bags are the best bet: good looks are not nearly as important as waterproof qualities. Incidentally, I have assumed that you appreciate the importance of waterproof clothing and footwear. If you are not comfortable when fishing, you will not fish well, and we all know what English fishing weather is usually like. Similarly, fly boxes, scissors or clippers for trimming nylon – all essentials – don't need to be described here.

Next on the list is a reliable net. For stillwater bank fishing this has a dual purpose as it doubles as a wading staff, essential for safe wading. Triangular frames with a minimum gape of 20in are ideal. For those who require greater mobility, or for boat or river anglers, a folding net is preferable; it can be clipped to your belt when necessary.

A good priest is essential, as it is imperative that as little suffering as possible is caused to the fish. It should be a matter of conscience for all of us to kill our trout cleanly and quickly. It is unacceptably cruel to leave a fish gasping on the bank while you search for a stone or log. The best priests come combined with a marrow scoop, enabling you to examine stomach contents easily. This can provide useful pointers as to the right fly to use, as you will be able to choose a pattern that closely represents the type of food on which the trout are feeding.

Good-quality floatant is a must. The very best is Gink, used by all the top stillwater specialists. Often overlooked but just as essential is a sinking compound like Orvis Mud, both to help sink the leader and to remove the shine on the monofilament left by the manufacturing process. On bright and calm days, this can make the difference between a brace and a blank.

It should be obvious that, as well as good quality monofilament, you should also carry nylon of varying breaking strains. If you decide to concentrate most of your fishing on, say, 5lb line, you should also have spare spools of 4lb and 6lb to cover varying water and weather conditions. There will be times when you can increase the strength of your leader without adverse effect, but also times when fishing fine is compulsory.

OTHER LUXURIES

The following additional accessories are not absolutely essential but will make life easier for you.

Line cleaner Useful if the line becomes discoloured or dirty; improves floating qualities and casting.

Bass bag Keeps fish fresher (a polythene bag is OK – but it will cook the fish on a hot day).

Boat seat Keeps you well up in the boat, improving vision; also helps prevent your back aching in badly designed boats.

Rod tube Usually aluminium or hard plastic; helps protect rod in the car boot, etc.

Waistcoat Almost an essential: keeps all your gadgets – particularly clippers, floatant, and fly boxes – to hand and improves your overall comfort.

WHY TROUT TAKE A FLY

Part of the joy of trout fishing is that there are so many variations of techniques and

Far left: There's a whole range of products to dry off flies and make them float. Leader sink and fly line conditioner are also worthwhile investments.

Left: A marrow spoon to scrape out the trout's stomach and identify its last meal.

tactics that you never stop learning. Success with trout will always depend on unpredictable factors, such as wind and weather, as well as your ability – which is as it should be.

We can, however, take some of the guesswork out of the game by a brief study of the fish, together with its environment and general behaviour. If I can watch and identify items on the trout's menu and then copy them reasonably well in terms of a fly, I am well on the way to catching him.

This apparently simplistic view is actually well-founded. True, fish will often take large gaudy lures and streamers, but they do so out of aggression or territorial instinct. Very rarely do they see such flies as food items. Most of the time they prefer flies that mimic existing or potential items in their diet. These flies will be taken more readily, with more confidence, and much more often. Many fly fishermen learn to become fly tyers as well, adding a further sense of achievement to the process of deception.

In recent years I have spent many enjoyable hours researching the history of fly fishing. While a good deal of the research has been to do with tackle and tactics, an equally large portion has centred on the evolution of artificial fly patterns. To me, one of the most remarkable things is the inventiveness of our angling predecessors. It is worth remembering that they had to do without much that we now take for granted. For instance, we have today many magazines to keep all anglers aware of new techniques. We also have modern fly dressing aids of every conceivable type and from all corners of the world.

BUZZER REIGNS SUPREME

One of the first flies tied by any newcomer to the tying bench will probably be something very simple like the Black and Peacock Spider; equally, it might be a basic Buzzer pattern.

The humble Buzzer, or Midge Pupa to give it the correct title, is the most vital item in the food chain. It accounts for more fish during the season than any other fly and is available in great profusion from April to October. The Buzzer reigns as the supreme reservoir pattern, and has done so in varying forms for many generations.

WHY LURES ARE REJECTED

Apart from the first week or so of any season, when the rainbows, in particular, will snap at almost anything, fish soon become educated. This is hardly surprising as their peaceful banksides suddenly erupt with the pounding of hundreds of wader-clad feet, and the water around them is full of thrashing lines. They quickly get used to seeing the gaudy lures in the shallows, and learn to shun anything that does not look or move like a natural food item.

I most certainly do not subscribe to the view that says all fish are stupid – after all, I always seem to get landed with intelligent ones that steadfastly refuse every offering! Trout do learn what an artificial looks like, and it follows that if everyone is using exactly the same pattern, the trout will quickly recognise it.

THE INSECTS TROUT PREFER

Studying food items is not the complicated affair that some experts would have you believe. There are relatively few items that you need to identify. It may be that trout do feed avidly on daphnia, water beetles and the like; but they are so small that they cannot be imitated by an artificial fly, so they have little or no relevance to us.

In order of importance, trout feed on midge, sedge, damselflies, and Corixa. Imitating these insects, in their various stages of development, is generally termed imitative fly fishing, or, more often, just nymph fishing.

The midge and sedge are generally the two most important, and the pupal stage of their development is the one that matters. Much of my own tying either *imitates* or *suggests* the pupae, or hatching pupae, of these two insects.

The damsel nymph, prolific in the summer months on all waters, is represented by a fairly close copy fly pattern and should be fished with a good deal of movement. Its preferred habitat is around rush or weed beds, where the trout will take them as they climb the reed stems to hatch. They are also free swimming, which is why you can be

fairly liberal with your speed of retrieve. In contrast the sedge pupa, in caddis form, lumbers around very slowly and must be fished accordingly.

This brings us conveniently to two vitally important aspects of nymph fishing: movement and variation. Staying with conventionally patterned flies for the moment, the critical factor in fishing them is the way the flies are moved or not moved, as the case may be.

The natural midge pupae are available to the fish for only a short period in their life cycle. Their ideal habitat is around areas of soft mud or silt, where they can make their burrows more easily. When the time comes to hatch, they work their way up to the water surface with that familiar thrashing, tail-waggling movement. Here, their breather filaments penetrate the film of surface tension and they hang rigid for varying periods of time before the actual process of eclosion (emergence from the pupal case), which is fairly rapid. The sedge pupae follow much the same pattern, the only major difference being that they prefer rocky or reedy areas.

PLAY THE WAITING GAME

In anything but a heavy wave, then, it follows that the best way for an angler to imitate a pupa on the top is without any sort of retrieve, no matter how slow.

The natural spends most if its time in the hatching process, absolutely still, sometimes hanging by the head, at others by the tail. The only way to imitate him is with a static retrieve. To do this with fish moving all around you requires considerable willpower, but there is no doubt in my mind that it is the most effective method. The best way is to cast fairly well in front of a moving fish, retrieve a little line to straighten the leader, lift the pupa to the top . . . and wait.

Figure-of-eight or even faster retrieving, which many anglers seem to favour, cannot possibly represent the natural's movements with any accuracy. The only way this can truly be done is with a long, slow, sink-and-draw technique which might suggest the ascent from the lake bed. But this can be found wanting in that the best Buzzer fishing takes place right on the top; and certainly I have rarely had great success with sunk pupae in the evening.

It's a different story during the day, when trout are likely to be foraging for pupae near the bottom. At times like these, I often use a weighted imitation, allowing it to sink and then lifting it gently from the lake bed. This is a much underrated method of nymph fishing. It does, however, require good eyesight because you need to watch the leader for any indication of movement, as the trout take the fly gently in these circumstances.

Pupa copies should not be restricted solely to the Buzzers and Amber Nymphs, even though they are by far the best known. In fact, they can include patterns like Hare's Ear Nymph, Diawl Bach (a West Country favourite) and even the ubiquitous Pheasant Tail.

THE ENIGMA OF WET FLIES

Traditional wet flies have always been something of an enigma, as no one has yet come up with a satisfactory explanation for their effectiveness.

True, there is the general shape and silhouette theory for flies like the Invicta, which is often said to represent the confused outline of a sedge pupa on the point of hatching. In fact, a small sedge and a large midge look remarkably similar, at least in silhouette, and there is reason to suppose that there was some cross-over in the design principles of many favourite traditionals; after all, most of them share many elements in construction, not the least of which is their general wing-back shape.

For this reason most of my own fly-tying is oriented towards the midge and sedge families, especially the midges in view of their greater availability. I would certainly

The best way of imitating a pupa on the top is to play a waiting game. Artist Tony Whieldon bided his time at Stafford Moor to good effect.

Right: Dry flies. These are specials tied by Chris Ogborne and used by his Bristol flyfishing team in major competitions like the Benson and Hedges. Left (top to bottom): Orange Emerger, Standard Hopper and Claret Hopper. Right: Black Emerger and Shipman style Buzzer.

Far right:
Wet flies. More proven tyings from the Ogborne vice, all of which are variations of traditional patterns. Left (top to bottom): The Clifton and Hot Orange. Right: White Squirrel, Claret and Black and the Teal and Green.

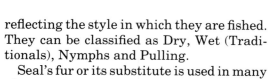

never ignore either general representative flies or traditionals, but as the bulk of my fishing follows a natural-food philosophy, these two insect orders are prominent.

IT'S BETTER TO DECEIVE

The range of gaudy and complicated lures that trickle incessantly into the tackle shops is little more than the result of experimental fly tying, given credibility by a temporary degree of success. Such creations will not stand the test of time to which the traditionals have been subjected. Nor will they catch fish as consistently as the suggestive or representative patterns. It is better to deceive a fish by tying something that he genuinely thinks is food, rather than by provoking an aggressive reaction to some nameless lure.

THE FLIES

My flies fall into four distinct categories reflecting the style in which they are fished. They can be classified as Dry, Wet (Traditionals), Nymphs and Pulling.

Seal's fur or its substitute is used in many of my tyings, as it has a natural quality that adds life to the fly. There is no substitute for top quality materials, and because the overall cost of tying your own flies is so low, it is folly to economise. Various feathers are used to give shape, outline or movement to a fly as well as colour. The best hooks to use are chemically sharpened, high carbon patterns. Most flies are available in a whole range of sizes and you will need to match this to the water you are fishing.

DRY FLIES

There has been a tremendous upsurge in the use of the dry fly, largely due to competition anglers. It is through them that the effectiveness of the method has become known and the level of interest created.

Dry-fly tactics can be employed on still-

water at any time and in any water conditions. Their use is not restricted to calm conditions, nor are they evening-only tactics. Indeed, dry flies left on the surface in a big mid-day heatwave can pull fish from nowhere, when there is no sign on the surface of any activity. This is probably because on most stillwaters, and particularly those with sparse sub-surface fly life, fish will often be cruising at depths of several feet, depending on water clarity, looking for food but without advertising their presence.

There are three basic styles of dry fly that we use: Emergers, Hoppers and Shipman-style Buzzers. Emergers are used to best effect at the beginning of a rise, and Shipman's Buzzers will perform during an established rise or, at least, when there are plenty of visible moving fish. The Hopper is more of a fly for all occasions. It has a more general appeal and in this respect it could be termed as more of a suggestive than an imitative fly. Indeed, it is so effective that on any day that appears to be right for dry fly we would think very hard before removing the Hopper from the cast.

When it comes to using these flies, there is a good deal of latitude in the technique. The static retrieve is the most common, which from a drifting boat really means casting out and retrieving only enough line to ensure there is no slack, with the fly essentially motionless.

In most conditions this is a good method, and in flat calm it is absolutely essential. It is probably most effective when casting at a specific fish. If you spot a moving fish and can predict his direction of travel from the rise-form, give him plenty of 'forward lead' by dropping the fly a couple of yards ahead of his last known position.

WET FLIES

This group of traditional flies, usually categorised in the broadest of generalisations as wet-fly patterns, have been around the fishing scene as long as any. In many ways they are impossible to categorise, in that they do not fall into any obvious group.

There are undoubtedly some points in their general shape and in their overall outline that could be said to represent insect forms, but in general terms they are a series of flies that have evolved over many generations to cover a wide variety of fishing circumstances and for use in widely varying conditions.

We are talking here about a series of wet flies, tied in a generic style, and usually including a tail, wing and throat hackle. In broad terms, they conform to a general shape and outline and are typified by the well-known patterns of Peter Ross, Mallard and Claret, and the like. The origins of many are lost in the mists of time, although it is fairly certain that loch style fishing in Ireland and Scotland influenced the evolution of most of them. More recently some patterns have come our way from North America, perhaps due largely to the spate of innovative fly-tying over there some 12-15 years ago.

Wet flies can be fished at any time of year, all through the day, and from both boat and bank. They are usually used as part of a team of flies, using two of them as droppers with perhaps a nymph on the point. Equally, a full team of three traditionals is frequently seen, and this is at the very heart of the famed loch-style fishing.

The speed of retrieve is variable, and they can be used on both floating and sinking lines to good effect. A reasonable yardstick is sometimes quoted as 'bright day, bright fly'; but like all the other traditional rules of fishing, it should not be taken too literally.

I am very much a close-copy fisherman in that I like to use patterns that directly, or at least fairly closely, represent natural items in the food chain. But I have many of the traditional patterns in my fly box and more often than not, they are the first line of attack in a day of boat fishing.

For those who like shortlists, my own would comprise Mallard and Claret, Peter Ross, Connemara Black, Wickham's, Invicta, Butcher, Teal and Green, and the Coachman. This short selection covers most of the possibilities in terms of colour, shape, and outline that we have already discussed, and each fly is a worthwhile addition to the armoury.

PULLING FLIES

This group has some similarities to the standard wet flies but serves a very different purpose. It gets its name from the way it is used. The retrieve is usually fairly fast, pulling the flies quickly through the water. The flies are intended to pull fish to

Pulling flies. Bristol's best attractor patterns which are usually pulled through the water very quickly. Left (top to bottom): Mallard and Green, Green Grenadier and White Sedge. Right: Wet Hare's Ear and The Fancy.

the cast by virtue of their many attractor properties.

Many pulling flies are bright, even gaudy, creations that grossly exaggerate the colour or shape of a more conventional fly. This has the effect of provoking reactions from the fish, as they will come to investigate anything this unusual.

Even if they don't actually take the pulling fly, they may still be tempted by one of the other flies in the cast. For this reason, the pulling fly is best suited to the middle dropper position, or top dropper in very clear water.

Pulling flies are useful in all water conditions, but they have an obvious benefit in murky water with low visibility. They may have a negative effect in clear water, and if there is no reaction from the fish after half an hour, the fly should be removed from the cast.

NYMPHS

We have already discussed many aspects of nymph fishing. They are certainly the most important group of flies and should always be among your first choices on the cast.

Nymphs can be artificially weighted to take them to the required depth more quickly. Care should be taken not to add too much bulk to the overall shape as this can ruin the main effect of the pattern.

These flies can also be fished on all line densities from floaters through to very fast sinkers. Longer leaders are sometimes called for to get the fly to swim correctly and to reach deeper areas; 12-15 feet is by no means unusual.

STORING THE FLIES

Choosing the right box to store your collection of flies is vital. My choice is the Wheatley foam-lined aluminium box with centre leaf. Foam is better for holding the hooks and, unlike some of the metal-clip versions, it doesn't rust. This box has the added advantage of four distinct sections, conveniently holding all four categories of fly, so that they can be easily seen at a glance.

BOAT OR BANK?

This is the eternal dilemma facing the angler. Should he fish from the bank, with the freedom to wander miles of shoreline exploring all the interesting features? Or should he opt for a boat, and spend the day drifting in the classic loch style, always covering new fish?

In reality, the decision can rarely be a last-minute one as boats normally have to be booked well in advance. For most of us, it seems, a fishing outing has to be planned way ahead, and we must look to seasonal trends and weather patterns to give us pointers to the best option.

LOCH STYLE

I have a personal preference for the boat. To me, loch style is the very cream of the sport. Free drifting downwind, casting at the occasional moving trout, and always covering new water – this is the very essence of fly fishing. Sometimes a drogue can be used to slow the drift, but mostly we tend to leave

Nymphs.
The most important group of flies. Top row (left to right): Peacock and Green, Green Tag Stick and Pheasant Tail. Bottom: Green Nymph and Diawl Bach.

the boat drifting free. You can quickly use the oars to adjust the drift, or to cover a fish that you have seen moving towards you.

Some people contend that a longer rod is necessary for boat fishing, but just as many anglers disagree. My own outfit is based on the standard 9ft 6in rod, for the 5- or 6-weight line. With this you can use either long or short casts without any sacrifice in accuracy or presentation. Very long rods are tiring to use for a whole day, and their benefits are far outweighed by their drawbacks.

Flies are also pretty much the same, although the superb dibbling method – holding the flies in the surface before lifting off – requires some bushy palmered patterns to be truly effective. Because the fish are generally far from the bank in open water, they tend to move more freely and consequently the floating line is preferable. Even when they are not easily visible, a team of traditionals with a bright pulling fly will provoke a reaction.

It is also perfectly feasible to fish from an anchored boat, although you must take care not to anchor in other people's drifts or near enough to disturb others. In this way, you can explore underwater features like a sunken hedgerow, ditch, or old river bed.

Many anglers use the technique of 'counting down' their sinking lines, in such a way as to build up a mental picture of the lake bed. This method has some benefits in early season, when few fish are on the top, but it is not needed for high summer. There is simply too much pleasure to be had from drifting!

Bank fishing also has its charms, and there are those who prefer this to the exclusion of all else. One of the great joys is that it is possible to be quite alone on the bank, wandering the shore with just a rod and net and casting where you please. Again, it pays to look for sub-surface features like weed beds, areas of stones, submerged hedges and the obvious deep holes. All will be fish-holding spots and offer a better chance than just blind prospecting.

In all forms of fishing, trout will take in various different ways. Some will snatch savagely at the fly, as if to pull the rod from your hand. Others will take with the merest sip – if you are not alert, you will never even know that it has looked at your offering! The best tip is always to watch your line or your leader. Any unnatural movement, particularly sideways movement of the leader, is an indication of the take. With floating lines this is mostly visual, and occasionally you will see the flash of a fish as he turns underwater to take the fly. On sinkers, it is largely a matter of touch, and you will feel everything through the line.

It is always preferable to trap the line with the forefinger of your rod hand, leaving the other hand free to control either the retrieve or the line itself when playing a fish.

Such are the pleasures of trout fishing. Whatever branch of the sport you choose, the pure elements are still the same . . . the one-to-one contest of man with fish, using rod and line. That at least has not changed for many generations.

INDEX

Page numbers in italic refer to the illustrations